'THE SPECIAL RELATIONSHIP'

A POLITICAL HISTORY OF
ANGLO-AMERICAN RELATIONS
SINCE 1945

WITHDRAWN

The Postwar World
General Editors: A.J. Nicholls and Martin S. Alexander

As distance puts events into perspective, and as evidence accumulates, it begins to be possible to form an objective historical view of our recent past. *The Postwar World* is an ambitious new series providing a scholarly but readable account of the way our world has been shaped in the crowded years since the Second World War. Some volumes will deal with regions, or even single nations, others with important themes; all will be written by expert historians drawing on the latest scholarship as well as their own research and judgements. The series should be particularly welcome to students, but it is designed also for the general reader with an interest in contemporary history.

Decolonization in Africa
J. D. Hargreaves

The Community of Europe:
A History of European Integration since 1945
Derek W. Urwin

Northern Ireland since 1945
Sabine Wichert

A History of Social Democracy in Postwar Europe
Stephen Padgett and William E. Paterson

'The Special Relationship':
A Political History of Anglo–American Relations since 1945
C. J. Bartlett

'The Special Relationship':
A Political History of Anglo-American Relations since 1945

C. J. Bartlett

Longman
London and New York

LONGMAN GROUP UK LIMITED
Longman House, Burnt Mill, Harlow,
Essex CM20 2JE, England
and Associated Companies throughout the world.

*Published in the United States of America
by Longman Inc., New York*

© Longman Group UK Limited 1992

First published 1992

British Library Cataloguing in Publication Data
A catalogue record for this book is available from the British
Library

Library of Congress Cataloging in Publication Data

Bartlett, C.J. (Christopher John), 1931–
  'The special relationship': a political history of Anglo-American
  relations since 1945 / C.J. Bartlett.
    p.   cm. -- (Postwar world)
  Includes bibliographical references and index.
  ISBN 0-582-02396-3 – ISBN 0-582-02395-5 (pbk.)
  1. United States--Foreign relations--Great Britain. 2. Great
  Britain--Foreign relations--United States. 3. World politics--1945-
  I. Title. II. Series.
  E183.8.G7B22 1992
  327.41073'09'045–dc20   91-34721
                                                                  CIP

Set by 7B in Bembo

Produced by Longman Singapore Publishers (Pte) Ltd.
Printed in Singapore

Contents

Editorial Foreword

The aim of this series is to describe and analyse the history of the World since 1945. History, like time, does not stand still. What seemed to many of us only recently to be 'current affairs', or the stuff of political speculation, has now become material for historians. The editors feel that it is time for a series of books which will offer the public judicious and scholarly, but at the same time readable, accounts of the way in which our present-day world was shaped by the years after the end of the Second World War. The period since 1945 has seen political events and socio-economic developments of enormous significance for the human race, as important as anything which happened before Hitler's death or the bombing of Hiroshima. Ideologies have waxed and waned, the industrialized economies have boomed and bust, empires have collapsed, new nations have emerged and sometimes themselves fallen into decline. While we can be thankful that no major armed conflict has occurred between the so-called superpowers, there have been many other wars, and terrorism has become an international plague. Although the position of ethnic minorities has dramatically improved in some countries, it has worsened in others. Nearly everywhere the status of women has become an issue which politicians have been unable to avoid. These are only some of the developments we hope will be illuminated by this series as it unfolds.

The books in the series will not follow any set pattern; they will vary in length according to the needs of the subject. Some will deal with regions, or even single nations, and others with themes. Not all of them will begin in 1945, and the terminal date may similarly vary;

once again, the time-span chosen will be appropriate to the question under discussion. All the books, however, will be written by expert historians drawing on the latest fruits of scholarship, as well as their own expertise and judgement. The series should be particularly welcome to students, but it is designed also for the general reader with an interest in contemporary history. We hope that the books will stimulate scholarly discussion and encourage specialists to look beyond their own particular interests to engage in wider controversies. History, and particularly the history of the recent past, is neither 'bunk' nor an intellectual form of stamp-collecting, but an indispensable part of an educated person's approach to life. If it is not written by historians it will be written by others of a less discriminating and more polemical disposition. The editors are confident that this series will help to ensure the victory of the historical approach, with consequential benefits for its readers.

A.J. Nicholls
Martin S. Alexander

Preface

Circumstances have required Britain and the United States to act in close partnership with each other for much of the twentieth century. But the relationship, however 'special' when in existence, was not automatic or even – save in the case of a few individuals – instinctive. It was at its strongest, as with all alliances, in the face of powerful common enemies, and when each country saw the other as her most useful and reliable ally. In contrast, in the 1930s, before the start of the Sino-Japanese War in 1937 and the growing threat posed by Nazi Germany, there was no hint of anything 'special' in the official relations between London and Washington. Indeed, without the actions of the aggressor states, relations might well have been dominated by disputes over economic questions.

The present work attempts to see the alliance through the eyes of contemporary British and American policy-makers, and to illustrate how the two countries could simultaneously agree and differ over a variety of issues. It attempts to reconstruct official British and American perceptions of the relationship as they developed and varied through the period under review; to explain in what ways each government considered the partnership to be important; and to set out how each hoped to benefit from it. Overall, while a 'special' relationship often existed, it was never constant nor could there be any guarantee of its permanence.

I am greatly in the debt of family, friends, academic colleagues, librarians and archivists. My special thanks are extended to the editors of this series and to Longman. The footnotes are an attempt to acknowledge my obligations to the work of others in the field of Anglo-American relations. I am particularly grateful to Mrs Jessie Young who instructed me in the mysteries of the word processor and rescued me on many an occasion from imminent or actual disaster.

Broughty Ferry, July 1991

CHAPTER ONE
Before the Cold War

ANGLO-AMERICAN RELATIONS BEFORE 1941

From the last years of the nineteenth century a number of notable British figures began to advocate or at least speculate on the possibility of a close relationship with the United States. Across the Atlantic, where only a tiny minority took a serious interest in global politics, there was little obvious response. Nevertheless a handful of American politicians, writers and others were coming to believe that situations could arise wherein close, if not formal, co-operation with Britain might be appropriate. Indeed Theodore Roosevelt was suggesting before 1914 that, if the British Empire faltered and was unable to preserve a global balance of power which was compatible with American interests, the United States might have to take an equal or even the leading role in world affairs.

Profound disappointment and frustration, however, awaited those – especially in Britain – who hoped that American involvement in the First World War might prove to be the first step towards an on-going partnership. Thus President Woodrow Wilson not only insisted that the United States fight as an 'associated' power – not an ally – but also later failed to persuade the US Senate to agree to his vision of a League of Nations. Worse, Anglo-American relations after 1919 were frequently soured by differences over such issues as war debts and naval parity. The effects of the Great Depression and a renewed possibility of war in Europe in the 1930s made most Americans all the more determined to isolate and insulate themselves from the quarrels and atavism of the nations of Europe.

On the British side of the Atlantic there were many who tended to dismiss the Americans as moralizers who would be generous with advice and opinions but who could not be trusted to back up their words with actions. Some went further. Neville Chamberlain, for instance, expressed fears that British and imperial interests might suffer if the United States became a major player in world affairs. In so far as the assistance of the Americans was seen to be desirable or even imperative against Nazi Germany, he feared that they would exact a heavy price at the expense of Britain's trade and her links with the Empire.

It was the dramatic and unexpected fall of France in the early summer of 1940 which persuaded the British leadership as a whole that, whatever the cost, it was now imperative to secure American assistance. It had to recognize, too, that while the German threat was the most immediate and damaging, any further setbacks would almost certainly be followed by a Japanese assault on Britain's increasingly vulnerable possessions in the Far East. By this time, fortunately for the British, the alarm over the advance of the aggressors was spreading to the United States. More and more of the American leaders were coming to the view that the United States herself would become dangerously exposed unless Germany and Japan were at least contained and preferably defeated. The survival of Britain and her empire was clearly essential to American security. Further Axis successes might compel the United States to become a 'garrison state'. The militarization of her society and economy could erode individual liberties at home, while abroad the United States might have of necessity to become an imperialist power.

As it happened American efforts to restrict Japanese expansion precipitated the attack on Pearl Harbor in December 1941. War with Germany soon followed. Britain and the United States became full-scale allies, and if the relationship seemed to falter with the defeat of the common enemies in 1945, the Cold War soon revived it. But hard-headed calculations in both Washington and London in response to the grim realities of power politics do not wholly explain the remarkable Anglo-American relationship which developed from 1941. Scholars, however, differ over the degree to which a common language, cultural and family ties, and shared values explain its strength and intimacy. The British historian, H.C. Allen, for instance, accorded them great weight. But these positive ties have to be examined in relation to continuing Anglo-American tensions and contradictions. These persisted even at the height of the war. Thus David Reynolds and Christopher Thorne have resorted to such phrases as 'competitive co-operation' or 'allies of a kind' in their attempts to sum up the famous wartime partnership. Others again, such as Christopher Hitchens, have been yet more cynical and critical when analysing the post-1945 era of co-operation.[1]

Anglo-American relations in the 1930s are particularly instructive. Opinion polls late in the decade suggested that at least one-third in each country entertained positive feelings towards the other. Indeed at times between December 1936 and November 1938 pro-British feeling in the United States ran higher than this.[2] On the other hand there is much reason to suppose that, had there been no major threat to the Eurasian balance of power, trade and other economic differences would have been the most prominent issue, particularly if those in the United States who favoured multilateral and freer trade had gained sufficient backing for their policies at home. As it was Britain's shift to protectionism and Imperial Preference provoked much criticism from Washington.

Furthermore there existed a very real, if often nebulous, American distrust of the British Empire. The argument was heard that even if, in the 1930s, there were other and perhaps more dangerous aggressors in the world, the latest imperialists had been inspired and encouraged by the deplorable yet seductive empire-building example set by the British. The latter were continuing to draw prestige as well as profit from their ill-gotten gains. In addition, since 1919, the British had largely failed – so it was argued – to promote alternatives to imperialism and traditional power politics. They were thus readily perceived as drags on the movement of the world towards greater political and economic freedom. President Franklin D. Roosevelt himself commented bitterly in July 1937, when faced by British obstructionism to American proposals on trade liberalization, that the 'British Tories were Tories still'.[3]

Fortunately for the British, Roosevelt was even more interested in grand strategy. He was one of the first, in response to developments in Europe and the Far East, to conclude that German and Japanese expansion might in time threaten the interests and even the security of the United States. There had to be a balance of power in Eurasia, and Britain (above all others) was the state which could help to preserve that balance by realistic diplomacy, deterrence or war.[4] Despite his experimental and evasive approach to foreign policy from 1937–38 – a product of his own character and temperament, divisions within his administration, and especially his fear of isolationists at home – it is still possible to detect an underlying strategy among his cryptic statements and devious tactical moves. Although Roosevelt might have hoped to escape direct American involvement in any war, there is no reason to question his belief that somehow or other Germany or Japan had to be constrained, contained or defeated. Earlier than most Americans he saw that this might not be possible without some American involvement.

The germ of several measures whereby Britain (and other states) might receive assistance can be traced back to at least the autumn of 1938. These (and more) were implemented between September 1939 and American entry into the war in December 1941. It was in these conditions that such amicable and intimate connections as existed between the two societies could begin to make a positive contribution, notably by facilitating and deepening the interchanges between policy-makers. Friction, jealousy and suspicion of all kinds, of course, persisted, but without any doubt, even before American entry into the war, the intimacy and exchanges between the two nations were beginning to exceed the norms to be found within the ordinary run of international partnerships. Co-operation reached into the more secret realms of intelligence and science. The first contacts were being made in nuclear research – even if the British were asking themselves whether nuclear co-operation would prove a step towards a postwar international police force led by Britain and the United States, or whether it would simply result in American domination of the whole project.[5]

TENSIONS IN THE WARTIME ALLIANCE

The Atlantic Charter of August 1941, a much publicized product of the first meeting of Roosevelt and Churchill, similarly gave rise to mixed feelings. It was undoubtedly a valuable public demonstration of convergence by the two powers against common enemies. But the meetings and discussions also indicated that the British, after the defeat of the Axis, could find themselves exposed to American pressure over the future of the Empire, Imperial Preference and the Sterling Area. Britain's growing dependence on American economic aid in the form of Lend-Lease was also leading to a disturbing degree of American control over British gold and dollar reserves. Most ominous of all was the widening gap between the economic power of each country.

Indeed as early as April 1944 the US secretary of war, Henry Stimson, argued that it was now up to the 'virile' Americans to defeat the Axis. The British, he asserted, were 'really showing their decadence – a magnificent people, but they have lost their initiative'.[6] Henry Morgenthau as US secretary of the treasury was equally confident. 'We recognize the fact that the United States is going to have to take the relief over in [postwar] Europe, and in return for that ... we will set up once and for all the kind of Europe that we expect.' Though not without some sympathy for the British, he included their imperialism among the malign forces which had distorted the 1919 peace settlement. Without firm American direction there could be another war within a generation. 'Prosperity, like peace, is indivisible', he affirmed. As part of his strategy he intended that the US Treasury and not the City of London – or for that matter Wall Street – should dominate world finances after the war. Stimson and US secretary of state Cordell Hull were convinced that world peace and prosperity were two sides of the same coin, with 'unhampered trade' as a major means to those ends.[7]

Some of this exuberance was tempered in time by a greater appreciation of just how much of the world economy would have to be rebuilt after the war, and of the range of obstacles which stood in the way of the realization of the dream of 'unhampered trade'. By the end of 1944 Morgenthau seemed persuaded that the task would be eased if Britain were to serve as a junior partner in pursuit of these objectives. The British were 'a good credit risk, a good moral risk', and were needed to help keep the peace. A little more tentatively Cordell Hull, on 8 September, had suggested to Roosevelt that 'the most important' postwar international economic problems would be the revival of the British economy, the relationship between the dollar and sterling, and whether the British would – in the long run – choose to follow a liberal foreign economic policy.[8]

But such views were not universal. Many believed that the United States did not need to intervene on this scale in the international economy. Others simply recoiled at the thought of handing out yet more American largesse. Bernard Baruch spoke for many business people when he complained that the British were quick to moan but not to help themselves by making their economy more productive and competitive. William Dexter White, the US Treasury official entrusted with the management of that department's foreign interests, had his own vision of a future international economic order. In his experience the British – and especially the noted economist, Lord Keynes – seemed too addicted to unorthodox and inflationary experiments. At the same time he was rightly sceptical of the readiness of the American taxpayer to foot the bill once the war was over.[9] Indeed the enthusiasts in the administration for the creation of a liberal, multilateral international economic order were increasingly impeded by all sorts of objections from protectionist and tax-conscious Congressmen and business interests. Further opposition came from isolationists and the inveterate critics of Britain and her empire.

All this had major practical implications for the British. In July 1944 Bretton Woods was the venue for a major effort to devise plans and instruments to promote postwar world trade and to avoid a return to the inter-war economic policies of beggar-my-neighbour. Remedies were sought for the lack of international liquidity and for the other causes of the decline in international trade – especially during the 1930s. In these talks the British were inevitably overshadowed by the Americans, and Keynes's more radical (and expensive) schemes to re-build and expand world trade were either frustrated or severely pruned. Indeed, it was not long before some of the concessions which the British had secured – after considerable persuasive effort on their part – to assist in the postwar reconstruction and conversion of their own economy to peacetime purposes were found to be at risk. Even before the defeat of Japan, the fears of Dexter White were being confirmed as the most ardent American multilateralists lost ground, both to their more cautious and nationalistic supporters and still more so to those who were determined to protect home markets and reduce taxes. To such people the world abroad too often resembled a sewer down which credulous Americans were persuaded to pour money only to be surprised when it disappeared without trace. Too many smooth-talking foreigners, it was said, were able to exercise an hypnotic and manipulative influence over callow Americans.

This was all very frustrating for Keynes. As he sadly remarked to an American official in the spring of 1945, Britain's gloomy economic prospects meant that she was in need of another 'brain-wave by your President Roosevelt'.[10] But Roosevelt was close to death, and the British had to wait another two years until the 'brain-wave' at last arrived in the form of discreet signals from the US State Department – signals which led in due course to the European Recovery Programme and Marshall Aid.

Meantime the British were trying to evaluate the seriousness of American proposals for decolonization or for international trusteeships as staging posts on the road from colony to self-government and independence. Direct American wartime experience of British colonial rule often strengthened the belief that imperialism was incompatible with freedom and rapid material advance. There was the barbed American joke that the acronym, SEAC (the South-East Asian Command) really stood for 'Save England's Asiatic Colonies.' Americans were not willing to die simply to restore the British Empire.[11] Nevertheless the

Foreign Office in London and British diplomats in Washington, unlike those directly involved in the running of the empire, were increasingly persuaded that the Americans might prove less impatient and dogmatic than their rhetoric suggested. In any case, as the permanent under-secretary in the Foreign Office philosophically remarked, if the Americans were asked to 'underwrite the Empire, they would expect some say in its running'.

In general the news from Washington by the first half of 1945 was moderately reassuring. Roosevelt towards the end of his life seemed content to make haste slowly. He was mainly intent upon establishing the principles of 'independence' for colonial peoples, of worldwide economic development, and of equality of opportunity for all business people in the world's markets. He looked to the United Nations to devise a system of trusteeship which (so it was very carefully phrased) 'would make effective the right of colonial peoples to choose the form of government under which they will live as soon as in the opinion of the UN they are qualified for independence'.[12] Roosevelt can best be understood as a rare blend of the realist and the visionary. He was also, as D.C. Watt has observed, 'maddening yet admirable', and blessed with an unusual ability to rise above the prejudices of his generation.[13]

But even if American anti-imperialism were diluted in practice, the British knew they still faced an uphill struggle after the war to regain the degree of international power and influence which they believed was rightly theirs. The emergence of the United States and the USSR as permanent superstars on the world stage had to be accepted. Even the unique wartime relationship with the United States could not conceal the continuing decline of Britain within the 'Big Three'. This was forcibly brought home to Churchill at the first of the conferences attended by Stalin as well as Roosevelt. At Tehran, in November 1943, Roosevelt did his best (often at Churchill's expense) to forge a lasting bond with Stalin, a course which he continued to pursue (with some reservations) until his death in April 1945. Though often condemned as naive, his efforts to conciliate Stalin probably owed much to his estimates of American public opinion and of the likely postwar balance of power in Europe, and his desire to win the war as quickly (and cheaply in terms of Americans lives) as possible.

It seems reasonable to assume, for instance, that he was – at least in part – influenced by the calculations of his own defence establishment from 1943 (calculations which could not easily be challenged until the United States acquired nuclear weapons) to the effect that the defeat of Germany must make the USSR the dominant military power in Europe. Even Britain and the United States in combination could not hope to defeat the USSR.[14] Furthermore, neither Roosevelt nor the State Department was persuaded that the British would necessarily or at least wholeheartedly support the United States over the whole range of its postwar interests and aspirations. Despite the importance of the positive aspects in Roosevelt's relationship with Churchill, he regarded the latter as a political anachronism once thoughts turned from the defeat of the Axis to the world of the future.

There were also obvious international reasons to try to defuse crises before they developed. For instance, British and Soviet interests might collide in Europe and parts of Asia. If a major crisis occurred the United States might find itself sorely embarrassed and perhaps ulti- mately drawn into the affray. Better therefore to try to anticipate such a calamity by assuming the role of an active and vigilant peace-maker. With this end in view the United States could not afford to be seen by the USSR as firmly aligned with Great Britain.

The US State Department, in its advice to a new president (Harry S. Truman) from April 1945, took up this theme in some detail in its preparations for the Potsdam Conference (July–August). Both Soviet and British spheres of influence should be discouraged as far as possible, though it was accepted that such spheres would be among the inescapable facts of contemporary life. The United States itself would not be guiltless. The State Department was also eager to test the potential and effectiveness of the United Nations. Indeed, as a matter of political necessity at home, it had to assume (and this had also weighed heavily with Roosevelt) that a return to the 'old power politics system' would be abhorrent to the great mass of Americans.

The State Department noted that a weakened Britain, with no im- mediate restoration of the balance of power in Europe in prospect, might feel compelled to look initially to the United Nations (UN) for help in the defence of her interests. It accepted that in due course the British would probably try to use the United States as a counterweight to the USSR. Even at this early date those drafting memoranda in the State Department were sufficiently troubled by Soviet actions in East- ern Europe to add the observation:

> Specifically it is not in our interest to deny to the United Kingdom protection against possible dangers from the Soviet Union.

For the moment, however, the United States should not prejudge the future. Options should be kept open until Soviet intentions were fully revealed.[15]

Meanwhile detailed research in the British archives has revealed that the policy-makers in London down to 1945 (and later) were neither united in their interpretation of postwar Soviet intentions, nor single-mindedly intent upon the cultivation of the closest possible ties with the United States. There had even been, as early as 1942, 'a long and frank discussion' in the Foreign Office as to whether Britain could remain a world power. It was anticipated that this would be seen by 'many people' as undesirable or beyond Britain's powers. They would argue for a handover of 'the torch' to the two new giants. But the officials agreed 'on the whole' that without her world role Britain would be doomed to second-class status. She would become a dependant of the USSR or the United States.[16]

Over time, however, detailed analysis of the nation's prospects led to increasing appreciation of the width of the gap between ends and means. As early as 1944 one Foreign Office memorandum (entitled 'The Essentials of an American Policy') frankly recommended that Britain should 'make use of American powers for purposes which we regard as good'.[17] But many remained sceptical of American reliability as an ally once the Axis had been defeated. In any case there were those who preferred to discover what links could usefully be cultivated between some western and northern European states and the Commonwealth under British leadership. Such thinking was influential in the Foreign Office until at least 1948, and was strongly encouraged by Ernest Bevin as foreign secretary.[18] This fact must be continually borne in mind in the following pages which are concerned first with the decline and then with the tentative, uneven, but ultimately decisive revival of the relationship with the United States. The triumph of Atlanticism, however, became clear only towards the end of the 1940s, driven by necessity and the absence of more appealing alternatives.

At the end of the war Churchill was the most famous of those who wished to give the highest priority to close and continuing ties with the United States. Not even American hostility to the British Empire as then constituted – and so resolutely defended by him – seriously disturbed his belief that Britain would find her main security in a transatlantic relationship.[19] He spoke of the inevitability of another war without such an alliance. Admittedly even he was sometimes touched by doubt, but in contrast to many other leading political figures his faith in the American connection was remarkably strong and consistent. Eden and still more Ernest Bevin (when he became foreign secretary in July 1945) were sceptical when they were not hostile. In October 1945 Sir Orme Sargent, soon to serve as permanent under-secretary in the Foreign Office, wrote of the awful threat posed by the 'almighty dollar' and of Britain's duty, in company with France, to build herself up against both the superpowers. Earlier he had envisaged a British revival on a scale which would ensure that Britain was treated as an equal by her wartime partners.

Meanwhile Germany's defeat found British diplomats earnestly discussing Soviet intentions and the appropriate Western response. For many it seemed expedient and not seriously damaging to British interests to give the Soviets the benefit of many doubts – at least for the time being. There was a school of thought which argued that the USSR was rapidly ceasing to be a messianic and revolutionary power. Any differences with Britain were more likely to arise from Soviet conduct as a conventional state. They were impressed by the security needs of the USSR and its awesome task of reconstruction. Though Churchill frequently spoke (from 1944) in alarming terms of Soviet ambition and conduct, neither his government nor its Labour successor despaired immediately of finding some way to co-exist with the USSR – even when they were confronted by its increasingly heavy-handed and ruthless behaviour in Eastern Europe.

Thus at the end of the war, both in the United States and in Britain, there was a definite loosening of the relationship. It was understandable that the government of each should have tried to reappraise its policies and priorities, and been anxious to explore its range of options. Nevertheless what was being demonstrated in the course of 1945 was that – whatever the feelings of affinity that might exist between Britain and the United States – a substantial relationship could not endure without a strong sense of common interests and above all a sense of exposure to common dangers. Indeed, without such unifying pressures, the two peoples could be just as conscious of their differences – cultural and otherwise – no matter how happily individuals might mingle in Washington, London, Harvard or Oxford, and despite the multitude of personal ties and experiences.

POSTWAR OPTIONS UNDER REVIEW

It is very evident that in the early months of the Truman administration the new US president was far from settled in his views on foreign policy, not least because of the divided counsels of those around him. There were enormous popular pressures for the demobilization of the armed forces and for a speedy return to normal life. In so far as attention was given to foreign affairs, there was a powerful inclination to test out the potential of the United Nations. At the same time, however strong the desire to cut defence costs and to give priority to home affairs, too much had happened since the mid-1930s for the United States to return to its prewar foreign and defence policies. The occupation forces in the territory of defeated enemies might be seen as temporary inconveniences, but there was at the same time a natural tendency to acquire overseas bases from which to extend the reach of America's armed forces. Top service brass, diplomats and the intelligence community all tended to look at the world in more interventionist terms than a decade earlier. This was particularly true of the thinking of the US navy and air force. A slow – admittedly a very slow start – was being made to the build-up of a long-range nuclear bomber force. At the same time habit, and the realization that funding for the services would be tightly controlled (if on a more generous scale than in the early 1930s), meant that the eastern Atlantic, the Mediterranean and the Indian Ocean were still seen as regions which might primarily and appropriately be left to the British. As early as 2 April 1945 the US Office of Strategic Studies noted the value of the British and other European empires in any competition with the USSR.[20]

The British defence planners were similarly trying to divine the future. Admittedly war with the USSR was seen as only a distant possibility. But planners are paid to be pessimistic, and for the time being they felt it prudent to assume that American assistance in a crisis – imperative though it would be – was likely to be forthcoming only after an unpredictable interval.[21] The British Foreign Office had still more immediate and tangible experience of American aloofness. Truman's new secretary of state, James F. Byrnes, was at first serenely confident that he could carry on the Roosevelt approach to Stalin with the American nuclear monopoly in reserve in his 'hip pocket', and with no automatic supporting role for the British. But Byrnes failed to appreciate the importance of Roosevelt's personal standing in the Kremlin (even Stalin professed to be moved by his death), while his own successful experience as a horse-trading domestic politician led him to underestimate the difficulty of dealing with foreigners – and especially the Russians who shared few if any of his values and assumptions. It took time before Byrnes began to make full use of the American foreign service, let alone to give much thought to working with the British Foreign Office.

In any case the election of a Labour government in Britain in 1945 had disturbed mainstream American opinion, especially the conservative groups. Admittedly some American liberals hoped that a moderate socialist government might turn out to be more progressive than British 'Toryism' as understood across the Atlantic. But these were a minority, and when the question of a postwar American loan to Britain arose later in 1945 US Congressmen were quick to ask why the United States should subsidize 'too much Socialism at home and too much damned imperialism abroad'.[22] The British embassy in August 1945 did its best to summarize the mixed feelings with which Washington viewed Britain. They noted that the latter was now seen as a 'junior partner in an orbit of power predominantly under American aegis'. At the same time the belief persisted that the British possessed a 'well-nigh inexhaustible store of superior cunning' by comparison with Americans. Some years later the influential Republican senator, Robert Taft, was still exploiting the American belief that the British were 'the best propagandists and the most unprincipled people' in the world when he accused Acheson, the then US secretary of state, of doing whatever the British asked him to do.[23]

Nevertheless the British embassy did not believe that Britain was being written off as a 'negligible' force, nor had the common Anglo-Saxon heritage been totally forgotten. Already increasing suspicion of the USSR was encouraging Washington to pursue rather more policies in parallel with Britain. For their own good, however, the British should learn to adopt a less patronizing tone than in the past. Americans were an idealistic, emotional, and impatient people whose suspicion of British reliance on traditional power politics should be respected. It would be expedient to speak in a language which appealed to progressive Americans, not least when the delicate question of the British Empire arose.[24] British responsiveness to this advice was to be, at best, irregular.

Even when Bevin as British foreign secretary speedily found himself entangled in tough disputes with the USSR, this did not lead him to follow Churchill's line that Britain had of necessity to work as closely as possible with the United States. He responded cautiously in November 1945 to the exuberant proposals from the ex-prime minister for joint Anglo-American occupation of certain strategic bases as a step towards a 'fraternal association' in defence of world peace. Bevin's reply hinted at his fear that such arrangements might reduce Britain to the position of a humble deputy to the American sheriff. Nor did he want to do anything prematurely which put a question mark against the potential of the United Nations or which unnecessarily provoked the USSR.[25]

The British foreign secretary late in 1945 was also a somewhat re-luctant supporter of the proposed American loan to Britain. With others he was dismayed by its stringent terms. Indeed the British cabinet thought of suspending the negotiations altogether – the de-mand for speedy and general convertibility of sterling being the most disturbing of the terms. The British embassy in Washington, however, predicted serious damage to Anglo–American relations if the British were too critical or tried to go their own way.[26] In the long term ministers were persuaded that the advantages would outweigh the ob-vious and possible drawbacks. Nevertheless Bevin joined with the economic ministers, Hugh Dalton and Sir Stafford Cripps, in recom-mending a continuing search for alternative sources of food and raw materials outside North America.[27] The loan, it must be emphasized, was seen as a step on the road to Britain's restoration as a power of the first rank.

An assessment of the likely consequences for Britain if Congress rejected the loan makes interesting reading.[28] The conclusions were not totally negative, though they were swayed by some rather bold assumptions as to the degree of help and co-operation to be expected from the Dominions and the Sterling Area. The possibility of action in company with leading European states was also raised. Britain would still require foreign loans, especially to meet the nation's overseas ex-penditure, although a multilateral system based on sterling and exclud-ing the United States was considered feasible. Keynes agreed on 13 February 1946 that overseas commitments would be the main casualty without the American loan. While he described any retreat from a world role as a virtual impossibility, he admitted that even with American aid the position abroad would be 'all but intractable'.

The British Treasury finally came down firmly against the idea of trying to 'wriggle through' without the loan. As a precaution it drew up contingency plans in May 1946 in case the loan was rejected by the US Congress, plans which included a list of significant import cuts. Hugh Dalton, the chancellor of the exchequer, was already worried by such a prospect, not least because of the damaging electoral implica-tions of even greater austerity over a period of time.

Nevertheless the loan was not well received either in Britain or in the United States. Dalton privately described his own reaction as 'tepid'. He drew some comfort from the expectation that revision would be necessary inside a year or two. Pressnell suggests that only a brilliant speech by Keynes prevented its rejection in the Lords.[29] The loan was damaging to British pride, while among its terms the insist-ence on sterling convertibility within a year of payment of the first instalment was particularly ominous. Indeed A.P. Dobson suggests that it is 'an irony' of the so-called Anglo-American 'Special Relationship' that probably only its existence made 'such draconian terms' possible.[30] But no such relationship was necessarily apparent in 1945, with *The Economist* in London indignantly protesting on 8 December 1945 that the communists seemed to be correct in their claim that the American object was to ruin Britain.[31] It expressed the feelings of many with its claim: 'In moral terms we are creditors; and for that we shall pay $140 million a year for the rest of the twentieth century.' In fact, amid the contemporary indignation the generously low rate of interest on the loan tended to be overlooked. Even the 2 per cent figure obscured the reality: Britain was in effect being charged 1.62 per cent since repayment would not begin until December 1951.

Doubtless the British would have muddled through somehow without the loan. But at the time the government decided that it was perhaps the lesser of two evils, especially when all the anticipated damaging domestic and foreign implications of refusal were taken into account. Ministers also noted that more generous terms were simply not attainable at that time. They could not forget that the American government had already backed away from some of its more liberal inclinations on postwar world economic development in the face of various domestic pressure groups.[32] There was fierce US Congressional criticism of the loan as it stood, and this did not begin to lessen until concern at worsening relations with the USSR brought a change of agenda and priorities. Indeed in the absence of the Cold War the loan – assuming its final approval by Congress – might well have had further damaging effects upon Anglo-American relations. Without the Soviet threat American domestic constraints could have weakened further the drive for a new American-led international economic order. The importance of the Cold War was strikingly underlined at the time by a comment of the future American director of the International Monetary Fund. If American–Soviet differences were settled, he observed, American relations with Britain (like American interests in the Balkans) would be of little consequence.[33]

Not surprisingly British ministers continued to deal warily with the United States, concerned both for their own freedom of action and over the reliability of the Americans as friends. Thus unease over Soviet conduct in Eastern Europe and further afield did not immediately end Bevin's search for ways to co-exist with the USSR despite a warning to Attlee on 10 April 1946 that, while he believed the Soviets preferred to expand without the risk of war, their policy might acquire a dynamic of its own, and result in an unintended conflict.[34] Certainly neither Attlee nor Bevin took account of those in the Labour party who suggested that Britain could or should pursue a 'socialist' foreign policy, nor did they accept the claims of the Labour left that the United States was more aggressive than the USSR. Yet they did not simply follow the views of the Foreign Office where disillusionment with the USSR was rapidly increasing. A Foreign Office memorandum of 2 April 1946, for instance, bluntly asserted that Soviet aggression was 'based upon militant Communism and Russian chauvinism'.[35]

Significant changes in British policy did not begin to occur until the full extent of the weaknesses of the nation and of Western Europe began to be appreciated. Some interest persisted in a 'third force'. Bevin hoped, by mobilizing European, African and other imperial resources, to end British economic dependence on the United States, and 'to re-establish a position of global power and influence equal to that of the Americans and Russians'. Britain would be able to exploit America's need for African raw materials. In time he hoped to see Britain and France as the 'joint standard bearers' and moral leaders of a 'middle of the planet' third force.[36] He also liked to portray British social democracy as an alternative to the 'red tooth and claw' of American capitalism and Soviet communism.[37]

Such ideas were abandoned only when advocates of a third force were squarely confronted in 1948 with a precise timetable – namely that Britain's needs were so great that (to be of value) such a 'force' would need to be created within five years. That was clearly impossible. Similarly by 1948 detailed study was seemingly demonstrating the unattractiveness of closer economic co-operation with European neighbours. A Treasury official concluded on 27 September 1948, Britain and the Commonwealth would have to make so many sacrifices to European states that a 'third force' would damage, not promote the nation's interests. In contrast, so his argument confidently ran, 'Union' between the United States and the British Commonwealth (or an 'Atlantic Union') seemed 'wholly possible'. It would be facilitated by a common language and historic ties. The gains would far outweigh the losses, provided Britain made full use of all her bargaining strength, and offered herself as an equal partner and not as a beggar. Britain would be 'a profound stabilising influence', so that the Americans would gain 'just what they need to carry out their responsibilities as world leader'.[38] With hindsight such an argument might seem wildly optimistic, but it was the sort of argument which was beginning to find favour in London by 1948.

In the winter of 1945–46, however, all this lay in the future. Churchill was not properly representative of influential opinion in Britain on the subject of close Anglo-American relations. In London, as in Washington, the ending of the war in 1945 gave rise to the feeling that, if each state was not about to go its separate way, the wartime intimacy had definitely weakened. Britain and the United States pursued separate policies in their respective occupation zones in Germany. Supreme Headquarters Allied Expeditionary Force (SHAEF) was abolished. Even where links were still in place, their future remained uncertain. This can be seen in Truman's decision on the future of the joint body, the Combined Chiefs of Staff, which had been set up in 1942 to co-ordinate Anglo-American strategy against Germany and Japan. It could remain quietly in being at least until the peace treaties had been formally concluded.

The British, for their part, did not want the United States to return to isolationism. Americans still had an important role to play in war-ravaged Europe in ensuring that Germany did not again threaten the security of Europe, and in being on hand to help counterbalance if necessary the enigmatic and possibly dangerous USSR. As already noted the British service chiefs were emphatic that American aid was imperative in the event of war with the USSR. But all this did not yet add up to a widespread expectation in London that Anglo-American relations would or should retain their wartime intimacy.

NOTES AND REFERENCES

1. H.C. Allen, *Great Britain and the United States*, Odhams Press, 1954; D. Reynolds, *The Creation of the Anglo-American Alliance, 1937–41: a study in competitive co-operation*, London: Europa Publications, 1981; C. Thorne, *Allies of a Kind: the United States, Britain, and the war against Japan, 1941–1945*, Hamish Hamilton, 1978; C. Hitchens, *Blood, Class and Nostalgia: Anglo-American Ironies*, Chatto and Windus, 1990.

2. Bruce M. Russett, *Community and Contention: Britain and America in the Twentieth Century*, Cambridge, Mass.: MIT Press, 1963, pp. 136–7.

3. Donald B. Schewe, ed., *Franklin D. Roosevelt and Foreign Affairs, 1937–39*, 10 vols, New York: Garland Publishing Inclusive, 1979, ii. 355.

4. Schewe, vol. v. 904, viii. 1481

5. See M. Gowing in D. Dilks, ed., *Retreat from Power: studies in Britain's foreign policy of the twentieth century*, Macmillan, 1981, ii. 124–5.

6. G.R. Hess, *The United States' Emergence as a Southeast Asian Power, 1940–50*, New York: Columbia University Press, 1987, p. 83. Felix Frankfurter, a visiting professor at Oxford before the war, warned Cripps in 1942 that many Americans feared a Tory-dominated postwar Britain with class

privilege at home and imperialism abroad. He admitted that there were prejudices on the American side as well, but Britain could win American favour only by giving convincing support to democracy and nationalism. M. Freedman, *Roosevelt and Frankfurter: their correspondence 1928–45*, London: Bodley Head, 1967, pp. 664–7.

7. J.M. Blum, *From the Morgenthau Diaries*, Boston, Mass.: Houghton Mifflin, 1959–67, iii. 123, 143–6, 228 ff. See also *Foreign Relations of the United States*, Washington DC: Government Printing Office (hereafter *FRUS*), Washington and Quebec, 1943, 167n, for Stimson on the need for anticipatory action to prevent another great depression.

8. *FRUS*, 1944, iii. 53–6. Blum, iii. 310–23. L.S. Pressnell, *External Economic Policy since the War*, vol 1, London: HMSO, 1986, pp. 11–12, agrees that Roosevelt and Morgenthau were seemingly looking for ways to help British recovery as far as American politics would permit.

9. Blum, iii. 323. D. Rees, *William Dexter White*, Macmillan, 1974, pp. 139–53.

10. Rees, *White*, 287.

11. See R. Harris Smith, *OSS: the secret history of America's first Central Intelligence Agency*, Berkeley, University of California Press, 1972, pp. 32–5, 123–6, 286–316. The emphasis here on OSS debts to the British secret service is qualified by Rhodri Jeffreys Jones, *The CIA and American Democracy*, Yale University Press, 1989, p. 17.

12. T.E. Hachey, ed., *Confidential Dispatches: analysis of America by the British Ambassador, 1939–45*, Evanston, Ill.: New University Press, 1974, pp. 263–8, 281–5; *FRUS, Conference of Berlin*, 1945, i. 917. Note also H.G. Nicholas, ed., *Washington Dispatches, 1941–45*, Weidenfeld and Nicolson, 1981, pp. 512 ff.

13. D.C. Watt, *Succeeding John Bull: America in Britain's Place, 1900–75*, Cambridge University Press, 1984, p. 83.

14. I have set out my views on Roosevelt in *The Global Conflict, 1880–1970*, Longman, 1984, pp. 245–9. Note *FRUS, Conference of Berlin*, 1945, i. 264–6, for a Joint Chiefs of Staff (JCS) paper 16 May 1944. Roosevelt's close adviser, Harry Hopkins, was aware by September 1943 of the JCS expectation that the USSR would be the dominant military power in Europe after the war – if Hopkins knew, so, surely, did Roosevelt. See Henry A. Adams, *Harry Hopkins*, New York: Putnams, 1977, p. 334.

15. *FRUS, Conference of Berlin*, 1945, i. 257–64. See also pp. 267 ff. for worries over USSR and communism. On 15 April 1945 the British embassy reported opinion poll evidence of the immense popular support for some world organization (81 per cent). Even so 52 per cent favoured a permanent Anglo-American alliance after the war, but with a stong minority (38 per cent) against. T.E. Hachey, p. 544.

16. Lord Gladwyn, *The Memoirs of Lord Gladwyn*, Weidenfeld and Nicolson, 1972, p.117.

17. R. Edmonds, *Setting the Mould: the United States and Britain, 1945–50*, Oxford University Press, 1986, p. 21.

18. See John Kent in M.L. Dockrill and J.W. Young, eds, *British Foreign Policy, 1945–56*, Macmillan, 1989, chapter 3, especially p. 70.

19. This is usefully if somewhat uncritically set out by H.B. Ryan, *The Vision of Anglo-America, 1943–46*, Cambridge University Press, 1987. See also D. Reynolds, 'Eden the Diplomatist, 1931–56', *History*, February 1989, pp. 70–1.

20. M.S. Sherry, *Preparing for the Next War: American plans for postwar defence, 1941–45*, Yale University Press, 1977, p. 235; R. Ovendale, *The English-Speaking Alliance: Britain, the United States, the Dominions and the Cold War, 1945–51*, Allen and Unwin, 1985, p. 11.

21. J. Lewis, *Changing Direction: British military planning for post-war strategic defence, 1942–47*, London: Sherwood Press, 1988, p. 244.

22. A. Bullock, *Ernest Bevin: foreign secretary*, Heinemann, 1983, p. 202. See also A.P. Dobson, *The Politics of the Anglo-American Economic Special Relationship, 1940–87*, Sussex: Wheatsheaf, St Martin's Press, 1988, pp. 80–5 for American reactions to the election of Labour and the consequent place of liberal economic policies in the loan negotiations.

23. J.T. Patterson, *Mr Republican*, Boston, Mass.: Houghton Mifflin, 1972, pp. 602–3.

24. *Documents on British Policy Overseas* (hereafter *DBPO*), edited by R. Bullen and M.E. Pelly, London: HMSO, 1986 ff, series I, iii, especially pp. 14–20. See also iv. 2–11.

25. There is a revealing Bevin memorandum of 8 November 1945 on post-war power realities in *DBPO*, I, iii. 310–13. For the evolution of Bevin's thinking in 1945–6, when he came to appreciate the extent of Britain's postwar problems, see Bullock, pp. 116–18.

26. Pressnell, pp. 323–5.

27. See Kent in Dockrill and Young, p. 51. Also *DBPO*, I. vol 3, pp. xix–xx, 227–32, 354.

28. Pressnell, pp. 360–1; Sir Richard Clarke, *Anglo-American Collaboration in War and Peace, 1942–49*, Oxford: Clarendon Press, 1982, pp. 53, 70.

29. Pressnell, pp. 329–30. Britain raised the matter of a delay to convertibility as early as November 1946. There was a sympathetic State Department response (p. 367), but note also the documentation in *FRUS*, 1947, iii. 9 ff, 271–2. In the end one might surmise that convertibility had to be attempted if only to demonstrate that it could not be sustained – and especially to prove this point to Congress.

30. Dobson, p. 87.

31. Edmonds, pp. 105–6.

32. R.A. Pollard, *Economic Security and the Origins of the Cold War, 1945–50*, New York: Columbia University Press, 1985, pp. 67–71.

33. Rees, *White*, pp. 373–5.

34. Bevin continued to talk of Germany as the main or a major threat for some time, as well as of his developing concern with reference to the USSR. See Bullock, pp. 234–5, 764–5.

35. J. Lewis, pp. 261–2.

36. W.R. Louis, *The British Empire in the Middle East, 1945–51*, Oxford: Clarendon Press, 1984, pp. 4–5. See also Kent in Dockrill and Young, chapter 3; R.B. Manderson–Jones, *The Special Relationship: Anglo-American relations and Western European unity, 1947–56*, Weidenfeld and Nicolson, 1972, especially pp. 22–3; Sean Greenwood, 'Ernest Bevin, France and "Western Union", August 1945–February 1946', *European History Quarterly*, July 1984, pp. 319–38.
37. Edmonds, pp. 28–9.
38. Clarke, pp. 201–8

CHAPTER TWO

A New Enemy and a New Relationship, 1946–50

EARLY FEARS OF THE SOVIET UNION

Some of the first signs that Britain and the United States might draw together against a new common threat appeared in the Middle East, a region ironically where the British had been particularly anxious to uphold their predominant influence, even against the Americans. But as fear of Soviet intentions increased, so some in Britain began to feel that concessions might be necessary in order to secure at least a degree of American backing in the region. Such hints can be detected as early as 1946. Bevin himself spoke of his fears of Soviet expansion in the Near East to two influential American visitors in January 1946.[1] The more the USSR began to probe for influence in Iran and Turkey, and to try to exploit Anglo-American 'capitalist contradictions', the more London began to see possible advantages – for instance – in the spread of American oil interests in the Middle East. These might encourage American resistance to the USSR in the region.

Disillusionment with the USSR was also gathering momentum in the United States. Whereas 54 per cent had professed faith in Soviet postwar co-operativeness in answer to an opinion poll in the middle of 1945, by February 1946 this figure had been almost halved. More and more members of the American foreign service were coming to question the belief, strongly held at the end of the war, that the USSR was more likely to be caught up in rivalry with the British than with the United States. Byrnes began to retreat from his unilateral dealings with the USSR, especially when the limited agreements he had concluded in Moscow in December 1945 were sharply criticized back home as a return to appeasement. Truman commented that it was time to stop 'babying the Soviets'. Some of the first Americans to urge a tougher anti-Soviet stance were also quick to see closer relations with Britain as an obvious corollary. In the USA *Time* magazine, for instance, expressed sympathy for British policies in – of all places – the Mediterranean (the source of numerous American wartime complaints that British strategy was based as much on selfish imperialism as on winning the war).

Truman indicated late in 1945 that the United States would not be a passive bystander in the Middle and Near East as it had been after the First World War. At that time, however, he seemed to discount superpower rivalry in the region.[2] Washington even seemed prepared to go some way towards meeting the desire of the USSR to revise the treaties relating to the rights of passage by warships through the Straits between the Black Sea and the Mediterranean – an issue with a long and complicated history reaching back into tsarist times. Yet distrust of Soviet intentions in those regions soon followed. Both Washington and London began to suspect Soviet motivation with respect to the future of the Straits and relations with Turkey in general. Bevin told the British House of Commons in February 1946 that he did not want Turkey to become 'a satellite state' of the USSR.[3] Neither Britain nor the United States relished the thought of the Straits being controlled essentially by the USSR, and with Russian warships being able to gain easy access to the Mediterranean.

Changes of attitude relating to East–West relations in general were becoming evident in London, Washington and Moscow in the early months of the new year. There was a greater disposition all round to put sinister interpretations on what was said and done by the other side. A major speech by Stalin, for instance, on 9 February 1946 was widely interpreted in the West as proof of his belief that war was unavoidable 'under present capitalist conditions'. A few days later, George Kennan, chief of mission in the American embassy in Moscow and a foremost American expert on the USSR, submitted a very detailed analysis of Soviet aims in his 'Long Telegram'. This sophisticated report was used selectively by hard-liners in Washington to support their argument that the USSR posed a major threat to American interests. At such a time, when attitudes were changing but no effective consensus had emerged, it was not surprising that Truman should see in Churchill's forthcoming speech at Fulton (Missouri) an opportunity to discover how far a sea-change was taking place in American opinion.

Of immediate practical significance were a series of small American moves in the same month such as the tougher notes on the future of Bulgaria and Romania and the despatch of an American battleship with the body of the deceased Turkish ambassador to Istanbul. The US State Department also supported the creation of a permanent American naval presence in the Mediterranean (although this was not formally announced until September 1946). As early as February 1946 the US Joint Chiefs of Staff sent a strong signal to their British counterparts on the need for military conversations. But equally significant was their insistence on total secrecy, such was the fear of an adverse response among the American public if news were to leak out. Co-operation over defence matters and intelligence had to take place 'underground' and be buried in the maximum secrecy.[4] The US secretary of state on 28 February gave the new trend in American thinking an acceptable public face when he underlined American support for the United Nations against acts of 'aggression'.

Such was the American background to Churchill's famous speech at Fulton on 5 March 1946. But while he captured the headlines with his anti-Soviet warnings and his proposals for Anglo-American co-operation, it is important to remember that in the short run his call for 'a fraternal association' between the Anglo-Saxon powers was poorly received by a majority of Americans. In Britain most of the newspapers of the left and centre were critical. On the right only the *Daily Mail* and the *Daily Telegraph* wholeheartedly backed Churchill. The *Daily Express* applauded his performance, but not his argument. In addition to its own suspicion of the United States and its 'dollar imperialism' it published an opinion poll on 11 March 1946 which demonstrated the strong sympathy which the USSR still excited among the British people for its part in the defeat of Germany.[5]

The British cabinet itself wished to avoid any precipitate action. It was conscious of Britain's economic weaknesses and the public's desire to concentrate on domestic problems. Hopes persisted that the USSR might yet prove conciliatory, and there were reservations about close co-operation with the United States. For domestic and international reasons the United Nations was still seen as the most appropriate forum for exchanges with the USSR. Thus, while the British government shared the concern in Washington over Soviet encouragement of a separatist movement in the northern Iranian province of Azerbaijan in the early months of 1946, Bevin wisely chose to act merely in parallel with the United States at the UN. Both governments gave diplomatic support to the Iranian government against communist and Soviet activities in Azerbaijan. Over the ensuing months the Iranian government gained sufficient confidence to reassert itself in the disaffected province whereas the Soviets appeared to lose their nerve and sense of direction. Anglo-American diplomacy, it seemed, had had some effect.

Meanwhile it is important to remember that if the leading officials in the British Foreign Office were becoming increasingly hostile towards the USSR, Attlee was still putting the case for an accommodation as late as January 1947. Bevin himself had earlier remarked that internal problems might moderate Soviet policy. He had not yet adopted a position of unequivocal hostility. It is true that at a meeting of the Council of Foreign Ministers in April–May 1946 Byrnes seemed unusually eager to exchange views and to talk in broad terms of how Soviet influence in the Middle East and elsewhere might be resisted. But there were reservations, too, in Washington, with the emphasis being put on selective, not unlimited co-operation with the British.[6]

The Combined Chiefs of Staff, meanwhile, continued their secret and ad hoc talks. The British chiefs were anxious for American aid at the earliest possible moment in the event of war with the USSR.[7] Although a clash with the USSR was not considered a serious possibility until the late 1950s at the earliest, the British defence chiefs were arguing from April 1946 that the West's ultimate aim should be to make a successful stand against a Soviet offensive as far to the east in Europe as practicable. This implied the reconstitution of part or all of Germany as an ally against communist expansion. As it was, and for the foreseeable future, the continent seemed indefensible against a determined Soviet attack.[8]

Similar conclusions were being reached in Washington. Early in 1946 the US State Department emphasized the crucial importance of Britain in Europe, especially in the absence of any other significant ally. Although the US Joint Chiefs of Staff in March 1946 seemed to regard the Far East as the most likely arena for a Soviet–American collision, they agreed that Soviet expansion from its borders westward or to the south could result in a conflict with Britain into which the United States might finally be drawn. At the same time they warily described military support for threatened states as 'difficult if not impractical' given the massive reductions in the size of America's armed forces. Nevertheless the Joint Chiefs were steadily coming to share many of the assumptions of the British military. In addition doubts were expressed if the United States could hope to fight the USSR successfully without British assistance.[9]

Already in 1946 the highly secret talks between the British and American air chiefs were leading to agreement that bases should be built in East Anglia for the use of American bombers in the event of an emergency. This was the first step towards the creation of one of the most significant and controversial of Anglo-American connections during the Cold War. It immediately distinguished Britain from the rest of Western Europe, especially as nuclear facilities were being created almost from the outset. In the same year the US Navy began to envisage co-operation with the Royal Navy if the Yugoslavs took aggressive action in the Adriatic.[10] By the autumn of 1946 the Chiefs of Staff on both sides of the Atlantic were assuming that the two nations would work together in the event of a global war. Talks, however, remained informal and secret, with Eisenhower, the army Chief of Staff, again emphasizing the danger from anti-British feeling in the United States if anything were made public. The British were equally secretive. Their government did not wish to foreclose other options, provoke the USSR, or antagonize its own left-wing.

In August 1946 there was a striking display of American independence. The McMahon Act publicly put an end to the wartime nuclear co-operation with Britain. While this was bitterly resented by the British, they too were moving towards the acquisition of a national nuclear force. The formal decision was taken in January 1947 by Attlee, Bevin and a handful of other key figures. Any direct link between this and the McMahon Act is unlikely. Ian Clark and Nicholas Wheeler demonstrate the degree to which British thinking had been moving in this direction since 1943. The British Chiefs of Staff were convinced that British possession of nuclear weapons was a strategic necessity. Attlee welcomed the move as a safeguard against American isolationism. With Bevin he also believed that Britain would have much less influence in Washington without some nuclear capability of her own.[11]

It is important, therefore, to note that, in so far as there was movement towards Anglo-American co-operation in 1946, future relations were by no means predetermined. It is necessary to forget what happened later, and to appreciate just how tentative and ambiguous these early contacts were. Essentially they were informal contingency exchanges whose future character would be determined by perceptions of Soviet actions and intentions. It is in this light that one should read the US State Department's assessment of 1 April 1946.

> If Soviet Russia is to be denied the hegemony of Europe, the United Kingdom must continue in existence as the principal power in Western Europe economically and militarily. The US should, therefore, explore its relationship with Great Britain and give all feasible political, economic,

and if necessary military support within the framework of the United Nations, to the United Kingdom and the communications of the British Commonwealth. This does not imply a blank check of American support throughout the world for every interest of the British Empire, but only in respect of areas and interests which are in the opinion of the US vital to the maintenance of the United Kingdom and the British Commonwealth of Nations as a great power.[12]

The British were equally selective. Despite some discussion of possible links with the United States in certain Middle Eastern questions, they were jealously trying to exclude American influence from their African empire.[13]

There was a hesitant start to Anglo–American co-operation in Germany. Bevin's distrust of Germany persisted even when circumstances within that country and growing distrust of the USSR produced moves designed to prevent communist gains outside the Soviet occupation zone, and to begin the recreation of a balance of power in the heart of Europe. Given Britain's limited resources, dialogue with the United States became increasingly necessary. Thus the British Foreign Office, against Treasury objections, came to favour the fusion of the British and American occupation zones in Germany. This was part of a wider search for lasting American involvement in Europe. The pace, however, was very much dictated by changing American attitudes towards the USSR and the creation of some measure of unanimity in Washington. It took time for the Americans to commit themselves to a battle for the stomachs, hearts and minds of the people living in the Western zones of Germany. In September 1946 an assurance was finally given that American troops would stay in Germany for as long as necessary. This was followed by the agreement at the end of 1946 to fuse the American and British occupation zones. Yet, as an American historian has explained, the negotiations leading to bizonia provided the British with 'ample evidence to disabuse them of any misconceptions that American policy in Germany was devised to aid Great Britain'.[14]

The Foreign Office, too, had no intention of departing from its search for a leading role for Britain in Western Europe and elsewhere. This was outlined, for instance, in 'The Strategic Aspect of British Foreign Policy' in September 1946. Any grudging admission of Britain's ultimate dependence upon the United States in the event of war was accompanied by the usual warning that Americans were a 'mercurial' people, governed by so 'archaic' a constitution that the government might be paralysed by its own people in a crisis.[15] At the same time any talk of strong policies in Europe ran up against the belief that the continent was indefensible for the foreseeable future. Thus, once military and Foreign Office discussion of strategy moved beyond the British Isles and the great sea lanes, it was usually to the Middle East that attention turned. Even here such ad hoc Anglo-American co-operation as occurred produced mixed feelings in London. Most of the British leadership still wished to retain the upper hand wherever possible, and there were the usual doubts as to American consistency of purpose. These were not without foundation. As late as September 1946 Truman was complaining, 'There is too much loose talk about the Russian situation. We are not going to have any shooting trouble with them but they are tough bargainers and always ask for the whole earth, expecting maybe to get an acre.'[16]

CONVERGENCE AND DISSENSION IN THE NEAR AND MIDDLE EAST, 1947–49

Some detailed reference to the evolution of Anglo-American relations in the Near and Middle East is necessary at this point. It is all too easy for accounts in this period to be dominated by two issues – the transfer of the British commitment in Greece to the United States in February–March 1947 (followed by the formulation of the Truman Doctrine), and the angry Anglo-American exchanges over Palestine and the creation of Israel. Attention should also be given to Anglo-American discussions over the importance of the Near and Middle East in the context of a Soviet threat which was believed to extend from Western Europe to Asia Minor.

Several scholars have questioned the long-held view that the British Foreign Office's note to Washington of 21 February 1947 announcing the early end of British aid to Greece and Turkey was a classic diplomatic coup – a calculated and timely transfer of an uncomfortably expensive commitment to the United States. It now appears that Bevin was beginning to doubt if the anti-communist regime in Greece could prevail in the civil war with the communists. He was also looking for ways to satisfy the recurrent Treasury demands for economy. Lord Bullock further suggests that he may even have been reluctant to transfer this particular responsibility to the United States.[17] The note of 21 February did, however, ask Washington to help the Greeks.

In Washington the surprise was mostly caused by the shortness of notice. The US State Department was already anxious to prevent any communist gains in the eastern Mediterranean. The British note gave Acheson and other officials the opportunity to force a decision. The politicking which followed in Washington and the actual wording of the Truman Doctrine itself were designed to secure prompt and adequate action from Congress. Especially revealing were the warnings from officials to their masters that as far 'as possible mention of the British should be avoided'. Indeed Robert Hathaway suggests that the universalist wording of the Truman Doctrine was in part designed to disarm those who suspected a British manoeuvre at America's expense.[18] These efforts did not stop protests in Congress and the media at the 'free-handed' way in which the British had passed 'the buck' across the Atlantic.

Meanwhile in 1946–47 a lively debate was in progress in London with respect to British policy in the Middle East. Several times during 1946 Attlee questioned whether Britain could meet the heavy costs of a military presence in the Middle East. But Dalton, who as chancellor of the exchequer naturally welcomed ideas for cuts to overseas commitments, seemed less happy with the prime minister's further comment that the situation might look very different if the Americans acquired a big stake in Middle Eastern oil and consequently took an interest in the defence of the region. The British Chiefs of Staff and the Foreign Office put up an obdurate defence, yet it seems that Attlee did not begin to retreat until January 1947, around the time of the decision to proceed with a British nuclear bomb. The Chiefs of Staff insisted that nuclear weapons alone would enable Britain to offset the almost unlimited manpower of the USSR. Furthermore the increasing vulnerability of the home islands to modern weapons made it imperative to think not in terms of defence but of deterrence. This could best be achieved by the threat of nuclear strikes against the USSR. Even if deterrence failed, such attacks would inflict more injury than anything that the British could hope to achieve with conventional forces. The case for British bases in the Middle East was strengthened by such calculations, but the doubts of Attlee and others were not finally overcome until June 1947.[19] Meanwhile the British began to drop hints to American diplomats to the effect that, while they wished to remain a Middle Eastern power, this could not be considered a certainty without some assurance of American support.[20]

In fact both the US State Department and the Joint Chiefs were already beginning to rank this region immediately after Europe in their list of strategic priorities. About 80 per cent of Russian industry, and also the oil of the Caucasus, lay within reach of B-29 bombers using bases in Egypt, Turkey and Britain. In May 1947 the Joint Chiefs, while acknowledging that planning had to remain flexible, observed that 'it appears at the present time that initial establishment of Allied forces in the Middle East is the most promising course of action'.[21] The advance of American interest in Britain was underlined a little later with a request to the embassy in London for an assessment of that country's likely value in a global struggle against communism.[22]

In the summer of 1947 Britain experienced a major economic crisis. Inevitably this re-opened the question of the nation's ability to remain a Middle East power, and encouraged more serious consultations with the United States.[23] A sufficient convergence of interest took place for the so-called Pentagon talks to be held in the last quarter of 1947. Ideas and information were exchanged, and an attempt was made to map out in very general terms what the two nations had in common in the Middle East. Admittedly the British, despite their economic problems, still tried to retain the leading role. As for the Americans, they were quite content to talk of 'parallel policies'. No formal understanding was reached. Bevin and Marshall agreed on 4 December 1947 that the two governments had done no more than receive broadly similar recommendations from their advisers. Indeed Bevin did not want joint bases in peacetime: these might simply provoke the USSR. It was enough to know that American help might be forthcoming in a war. Meanwhile the Americans could draw up contingency plans on the assumption that there would be air bases in Egypt from which to strike against southern Russia.[24]

In practice, apart from the navy, the United States had no forces it could immediately deploy in the eastern Mediterranean and Middle East. The main priority in the event of war with the USSR was the safe evacuation of American forces (if necessary) from southern Europe. Bases in Britain alone might suffice to service the Strategic Air Command at its current strength. But the potential of the Cairo-Suez-Khartoum area for air strikes against the USSR was still acknowledged.[25] Thus, given that there might come a time when forces were available for deployment in the Middle East, it made sense for American diplomats to encourage what friends and allies they could to hold the line in the interval.[26]

American strategic interest in the Middle East declined sharply with the formation of Nato in 1948–49. It was now possible – and also politically essential – to give serious thought to the defence of continental Europe, and to ways in which a Soviet offensive might be halted no further west than the Rhine. The despatch of American reinforcements to the Middle East thus became an even lower priority. In the Mediterranean the Americans concentrated upon the defence of

Italy and its islands on Nato's southern flank. Spain also began to attract attention, especially in the context of the defence of Allied lines of communication in the Atlantic and into the western Mediterranean. Finally, if the worst happened, Spain was seen as a last line of continental defence.[27]

Nevertheless, until the creation of Nato, Anglo-American contacts relating to the eastern Mediterranean and Egypt were a formative and educative element in the reviving relationship. They need emphasis at a time when Anglo-American relations in the Middle East seemed to be dominated (and hopelessly soured) by the crisis in Palestine.[28] Bevin (as well as many of his countrymen) was infuriated by the lack of consistency – as he saw it – in America's Palestinian policy. The British, he believed, deserved support in their struggle against Jewish efforts to establish their own state in defiance of local Arab opposition.

Yet even on this issue both the US State Department and the Joint Chiefs of Staff tended to sympathize with the British and to object – however ineffectively – to any move which threatened American or Western relations with the Arabs.[29] American interests demanded a friendly and stable Middle East, one which was not exposed to Soviet interference or encroachment, and from which supplies of oil – especially to Western Europe – were assured. But American policy on Palestine was, in the last resort, being made in the White House where Truman, despite the importance of his decisions, paid only sporadic attention to the issue, and, for reasons which are still debated, chose to depart from professional diplomatic and service advice at several critical junctures. Domestic politics and the Jewish vote – with the approach of the 1948 election – were influential. Nevertheless some scholars have argued that his conduct was too inconsistent and too instinctive to be solely attributed to such influences. In anticipation of ultimate Jewish success he made sure that the United States backed the winning side.

But whatever the president's motives, he added to Britain's problems in Palestine. In desperation the British gave up the Palestinian mandate in May 1948, while trying to rescue what they could of their relationship with the Arabs. Thus in the winter of 1948–49 – as fighting resumed between Israel and the Arabs – Britain seemed close to intervention on behalf of Egypt. On this occasion London even seemed prepared to risk a collision with Washington. Warnings were sent that Britain was determined to restrict Israeli territorial gains. This time the US State Department was able to exercise more control over policy-making and so avert a diplomatic crisis. Soon afterwards both governments joined with the French in the Tripartite Declaration of

25 May 1950 in an attempt to stabilize the situation between the Israelis and Arabs.[30]

It is important, therefore, not to exaggerate the long-term effects of Anglo-American differences relating to Palestine, however serious they appeared at the time. Some in Washington held views similar to the British. On a number of other key issues in the Middle East Anglo-American interests and priorities coincided or were not in fundamental conflict. Even in the mid-1950s the differences between the two, however acute in 1956, are better likened to temporary volcanic eruptions than to fundamental alterations to the landscape.[31]

ECONOMIC AND COLD WAR IMPERATIVES

Meanwhile the British, despite these and other differences, retained their undoubted precedence among America's European friends. Britain's physical strength and national confidence (compared, say, with France) and major interests held in common with the Americans were, of course, crucial. Yet Truman for one commented on the utility of the common language. He found that personal exchanges with the French could not flow so freely: interruptions for translation disturbed the train of thought. Forrestal, the key political figure in American defence policy until 1949, had many personal contacts in Britain. His dissatisfaction with aspects of the American political system even led him to explore the workings of the British government. Thus he helped to pass the tedious hours of air travel during a world tour in 1946 by reading Bagehot's *The English Constitution*. Admittedly his diaries also provide revealing insights into his own impatience, as well as that of many other influential Americans, with Britain's postwar experiments in nationalization and the welfare state. The 'dead hand' of socialism and bureacracy was contrasted with the wealth-generating success of American business people and business methods.[32]

The Anglophile American ambassador in London, Lewis W. Douglas (1947–50), a friend of Ernest Bevin and a firm believer in America's interest in the restoration of Britain as a great power, could also complain of Labour's 'incompetence'. He advocated experiments with private enterprise in the coal industry.[33] Some American businessmen wondered if the United States was not doing more harm than good by underwriting the domestic policies of the Labour government. Bernard Baruch asserted that American aid should have been channelled through American businessmen to their European counterparts, so low was his opinion of the economic policies of governments. Much American opinion continued to oscillate between fear of British political 'smartness' (or exploitation of American innocence in the world) and delight in twisting the lion's tail. It was left to a future Democratic presidential candidate (Adlai Stevenson) to argue early in 1947 that Americans had to realize that they were exceptional in their faith in capitalism at that time. Furthermore democratic socialism was feared and detested by doctrinaire Marxists because it offered planning in conjunction with freedom. Such arguments were soon to be developed in the State Department.

Fortunately popular American fears of British 'smartness' were offset by the continuing respect of key American policy-makers for British diplomatic skills and knowledge of the world. More potent still was the dismay which gripped Washington whenever it contemplated the implications of a permanently weakened or uncooperative Britain. Particularly worrying was the thought of British withdrawals from strategically important parts of the world. Regional instability and fundamental damage to Western interests seemed almost certain to follow. Thus Forrestal reflected in July 1946 that the United States might have to tolerate much that it did not like about British conduct and influence in the Far East. The resources and trade of that region were essential to the Sterling Area and to Britain, just as the power of Britain was essential to the United States. This mix of weaknesses, usefulness and potential therefore supplied the British with bargaining power even in the late 1940s, however vulnerable they might appear and despite American dislike of many of their policies and attitudes.

Naturally this bargaining power was not constant. It was usually a more uphill struggle, for instance, when economic differences had to be tackled in isolation from political and strategic issues. Indeed a Foreign Office official in 1947 expected trade and international finance to be the areas most likely to test the relations of the two countries 'over the next few years'. The British believed that Washington was underestimating and failing to grasp the nature of their economic problems. These could be intensified both by American protectionism and by moves for trade liberalization. Furthermore the British, despite the Cold War, were still determined to recover as much as possible of their former independence and influence in the world. On the American side the multilateralists believed that protectionism in the United States might be weakened if they could win a demonstrable success against Imperial Preference. Over the next few years a keen struggle was waged to the entire satisfaction of neither nation.[34]

In the first place the Americans had to accept Britain's inability to persist with the experiment in sterling convertibility in the summer of 1947 – this was attempted in accordance with the terms of the loan agreement. British economic weaknesses also clearly required some discriminatory action against American exports. Indeed global trade liberalization soon had to take second place to the search for regional solutions – notably in Europe. By the spring of 1947 the dollar famine was threatening the economic recovery of Britain and Western Europe. The Americans feared for their own exports. Economic setbacks in Europe might play into the hands of the USSR. Hence priority was given to a recovery programme whereby the Americans hoped to trade massive financial aid for the creation of the sort of Western Europe which would meet America's economic and strategic interests. The outcome was the Marshall Plan.

The British played an important part in triggering off a European response to American signals that large-scale aid would be forthcoming only if the Europeans themselves demonstrated an ability to co-operate and to produce a programme for recovery which satisfied American criteria. On the other hand, despite the deep problems which afflicted the British economy, London still differed from Washington on a number of issues. The Americans believed that priority should be given to the restructuring of the European economies in the long term whereas the British were preoccupied with what they argued was a short-term dollar crisis.[35] They also argued that their place in the world economy entitled them to special and separate treatment from the continental states. Indeed the British hoped at one point that they would be able to act as a partner of the United States in the recovery programme. To their disgust they found themselves required to stand in line with the Europeans.

The Treasury was sufficiently disgruntled to explore the alternative of dispensing with Marshall Aid altogether in the interest of national independence. Its studies quickly revealed the unattractiveness of this option in view of the cuts in food and raw material imports which this would entail. Even so the British were able to dilute the more extreme American demands for their integration into Western Europe, for the introduction of American managerial methods, and for trade liberalization. The Americans found that the deepening Cold War made it impossible for them to give equal priority to all their objectives. The Cold War also relaxed Congress's hold on the purse-strings to Britain's advantage.

Meanwhile efforts were intensified to develop resources in the African colonies to diminish dependence on the dollar.[36] Attachment to the Empire and Commonwealth also persuaded the government to minimize its economic association with Europe – contrary to American intentions. Indeed the British were not alone in their defiance of the United States. The French shared their reluctance at this time to sink their identities in a United States of Europe. A climax of sorts was reached with the British economic crisis of 1949. The devaluation of sterling was accompanied by a grudging American agreement that Britain should be allowed to limit her European responsibilities in order to preserve her role at the centre of the Sterling Area. Although the British offered assurances that they would still work towards freer trade relations as circumstances permitted, the multilateralists in Washington had been compelled to settle for much less than they would have liked.

These setbacks reinforced American impressions of British decline. A new US secretary of defense in 1949 thought Britain was 'finished', and suggested that as her empire began to disintegrate so the United States should concern itself with strengthening the useful parts. There was even speculation that Britain's economic problems might be so entrenched that they could be overcome only by economic union with the United States.[37] But the critics as usual had to bow to America's immediate need of Britain as a Cold War ally. She had to be propped up whatever her defects.

Once again relations were eased by personal contacts. The experiences of Hugh Gaitskell, a rising figure in the British Labour government, provide an interesting example of this. At first, early in 1950, he feared that the two countries were heading for a 'complete showdown' over the world's economic problems. Yet personal encounters, first as Cripps's deputy in the Treasury and later as chancellor of the exchequer, persuaded Gaitskell that there were some people in Washington who appreciated that Britain must be granted some safeguards for her economy. By 1951 he had become one of the strongest champions of the special relationship in the cabinet – despite continuing differences on many economic issues.[38] Unfortunately for Labour the Korean War by 1951 was having an adverse effect on the British economy and precipitated another balance of payments of crisis just after it seemed that Britain could dispense with Marshall Aid.

THE TRIUMPH OF ATLANTICISM

A healthy trend in recent scholarship has been to avoid the old tendency to make excessive claims concerning the role of either the United States or Britain in the creation of Nato. The United States is now less often portrayed as so single-minded or Britain as so uniquely far-sighted in the creation of that alliance. R.A. Best (Jr) captures much of the truth in the title of his study, *'Co-operation with Like-Minded Peoples'*. In his view policy-makers in London and Washington (and in due course in Paris as well) began to react in similar fashion to the problems of Europe and to the conduct of the USSR. They began to journey towards similar conclusions – despite a number of false starts along the way. Bevin, for instance, orginally contemplated three separate associations to deal with Western Europe, the Atlantic, and the Mediterranean (with the last grouping possibly also providing cover for British interests in the Middle East). Nato as finally established also gave the British less influence than Bevin had hoped. The alliance was the work of many minds, was shaped by many compromises, and influenced by the course of events in 1948.[39]

Bevin, impressed by Soviet intransigence during the foreign ministers' conference at the end of 1947, decided that the time had come for a more overt display of Western unity. Hitherto he had felt such a step to be premature, and one that might dangerously provoke the USSR. Bevin was torn between fears of a resurgent Germany in its own right and of a Germany which might somehow be drawn into the Soviet orbit. Such a shift in the balance of power in favour of the USSR would be totally unacceptable. Even now he was careful to suggest nothing more specific to the US secretary of state than the creation of some sort of Atlantic 'democratic system' as a warning to the Soviets that they 'could not advance further'. The US State Department's response was that it needed to see the blueprints on European defence before it could think of pouring concrete. Results were soon forthcoming, with the British providing much of the impulsion behind the establishment of the Brussels Pact (embracing five European states) in March 1948. This was an indispensable demonstration to the Americans of Western Europe's readiness to help itself.

Even then it took time for those in Washington who favoured direct American military involvement as opposed to military aid or some loose Atlantic security system, to gain the ascendancy. In that debate they were powerfully assisted by the shock effects of the communist takeover in Czechoslovakia in February 1948 and by the Soviet blockade of the Western zones in Berlin from the summer of 1948. Britain's role in the Berlin air-lift earned her the accolade of a staunch and like-minded ally. This was the most obvious demonstration to date to the American public of actual co-operation by the two countries. British conduct was also contrasted with the less helpful and less resolute behaviour of the French.[40]

In the debate over Nato itself, the Europeanists in Washington reiterated the arguments of the British (and other Western Europeans) that without a fairly specific American military commitment there would be less chance of a speedy restoration of political stability – and therefore of economic recovery – in continental Europe. A sequel to Marshall Aid was needed to consolidate what the latter had begun. The British vigorously argued this case, and rejected proposals for some looser arrangement, such as a new version of Lend-Lease to help the Europeans rebuild their defences. As late as February 1949 there was a brief panic in London when a US Senate debate suggested that the all-important article 5 (which defined the obligations of members in the event of an act of aggression against one of their number) might be diluted. British (and French) diplomacy encouraged those in Washington who favoured a binding version of article 5 to persevere against their domestic critics. It is for this – and other reasons – that some scholars have argued that both Britain and France exerted influence upon the formation of Nato well in excess of their physical strength – especially when compared with that of the United States.

As it was the American commitment to Europe had its limitations. To satisfy the US Senate article 5 was so phrased as to enable each state to respond to aggression only with 'such action as it deems necessary, including the use of armed force'. Furthermore American military planning for general war in Europe remained equivocal.[41] The Offtackle Plan of November 1949 referred to the need to retard a Soviet advance, but the Americans continued to refine their contingency plans for a fighting retreat to such peripheral positions in or around continental Europe as proved tenable against a Soviet offensive. Meanwhile Anglo-American forces were expected to be fully stretched in air strikes against the USSR and in the maintenance of lines of communication across the Atlantic. Finally, from whatever defence line was established and after a long period of mobilization, Nato's forces (presumably mostly Anglo-American) would launch the great counter-offensive.[42]

The British, for reasons of their own as well as their awareness of American calculations, were slow to commit any extra forces to the continent. They were haunted by the fear of another Dunkirk and were anxious to remain strong in the Middle East. It was not until March 1950 that the British ceased to rank the Middle East equally with Europe, and promised to send two divisions to the continent in the event of war. The British Chiefs of Staff at last committed themselves on paper to the defence of the Rhine as 'the first pillar' of allied strategy.[43] The formation of Nato therefore had only a marginal effect, at first, on the pre-existing Anglo-American defence relationship. The French continued to feel excluded from the topmost 'allied' table of defence planning, and understandably feared that their territory was regarded as expendable by the Anglo-Saxons in the first phase of a war.

The main addition to Western military strength before the outbreak of the Korean War in 1950 was the growing American presence in Britain. In response to the Berlin crisis American B-29s bombers were deployed at bases which had been under development since 1946. The British government initially welcomed this demonstration of American resolve. Furthermore, whatever the unease felt in London when Washington later decided that the bombers should be stationed permanently in Britain, this was accepted as part of the price that had to be paid in order to bind the Americans as tightly as possible to Nato and the defence of Europe. Indeed British reservations began to surface only after the Soviet nuclear test in the late summer of 1949 (this had occurred some years earlier than expected), and when the scale of the American build-up in Britain became apparent. A British Foreign Office paper of 4 January 1950 uneasily acknowledged that the American bases made it doubly certain that Britain was a prime Soviet target. It sought consolation in the belief that this danger was overwhelmingly counterbalanced by the enhanced credibility of the American nuclear deterrent. 'The primary aim of our foreign policy must be to keep the United States firmly committed to Europe.'[44]

The British, however, could not simply leave the matter there. Already in January 1948 they had yielded up the clause in the wartime Quebec Agreement which stated that neither Britain nor the United States would use nuclear weapons without the consent of the other. Talks in the winter of 1949–50 over the possible concentration of all nuclear weapon production in the United States had, in the end, only highlighted the differences between the two parties. Leading British political, diplomatic and military figures were confirmed in their belief that it was not in the national interest for the United States to hold a monopoly of this crucial weapon among the Western allies. As Lord Tedder, the Chief of the Air Staff, had insisted earlier, without nuclear weapons of her own Britain would be no more than a temporary

American advanced base in a major war. Furthermore the British wanted an assured supply of weapons for immediate use against Soviet military capabilities which threatened their own vital centres, facilities and lines of communication.[45] Finally there were the usual questions of national pride and influence. Lord Cherwell commented that without nuclear weapons Britain would be just another European state. It was left to another distinguished scientist, Sir Henry Tizard, to suggest that the British – puffing themselves up like the frog in Aesop's fable – might suffer the same fate.[46]

THE WORSENING COLD WAR

Convenient as it is to date the militarization of the Cold War from the outbreak of the war in Korea in June 1950, warning signs of increasing East–West tension had occurred well before that crisis. Western confidence in 1949 was shaken by both the Soviet atomic test and the establishment of communist China. It is true that the British were more disposed to live with the reality of the new China than were the Americans, and to the annoyance of Washington they speedily recognized the new regime in Beijing. The next few months, however, suggested that neither approach was effective. The Chinese were not prepared to make any concessions. Indeed Acheson spoke of his increasing fears of China to the British ambassador, Sir Oliver Franks, as soon as 17 December 1949. He anticipated 'early expansion south and east beyond the borders of China'. Six months later Acheson indicated that the United States wished to keep Taiwan out of the hands of mainland China. The Korean War, perhaps, spared Anglo-American relations some difficult exchanges over the future of that island.[47]

In contrast it was the British, not the Americans, who were the first to express alarm at the wider implications of the communist challenge in French Indo-China. This lay uncomfortably close to British Malaya where communist guerrillas were already active. Thus the 'domino' theory, later articulated by the Americans, was anticipated by the British as early as 1948–49. There were the usual fears that American involvement might soon reduce the British to the status of a junior partner. But Malaya's value as a dollar earner (in 1950 it was responsible for one-quarter of the Sterling Area's dollar earnings) warranted some sacrifice of British influence and pride. Although the Americans were anxious not to become identified with 'colonial' authorities, aid was granted to the French from May 1950. Washington similarly acknowledged the value of Malayan dollar earnings to Britain.[48]

In the first months of 1950 both the British service chiefs and many influential figures in Washington complained that too little was being done to combat the communist threat in the Cold War. In the heart of Europe eight Western divisions were outnumbered at least three to one. In addition it was assumed that the Soviets could reinforce their front line much more rapidly than their opponents. Ideally Nato required at least 30 or 40 divisions at the start of hostilities. The Chiefs of Staff believed that some measure of West German rearmament was unavoidable. In May 1950 the Cabinet Defence Committee guardedly agreed that this should be 'one ultimate aim' of Nato.

In Washington there was even stronger pressure for action. The Policy Planning Staff supported the Joint Chiefs of Staff in arguing that Soviet over-confidence, fear or miscalculation might lead to conflict. The military gave it as their 'informal opinion' that the USSR 'could begin a major attack from a standing start so that the usual signs of mobilization would be lacking, . . . '[49] Acheson himself in the early months of 1950 set out to imbue the British and other members of Nato with a greater sense of urgency. 'We could not hold our position defensively', he insisted, 'we would slip backward'. He criticized Bevin for lack of imagination – surely an inverted compliment given its implication of positive contributions in the past. Dean Rusk complained that the British seemed to be making the solution of 'any specific problem' dependent upon 'the solution of many others'. Even when agreement was reached in principle with the British (and others) on the need for Western positions of strength, positive action did not follow.

Not surprisingly influential Americans again showed impatience at the apparent inability of Britain to recover from the war. The devaluation of sterling in 1949 had added to their pessimism. When was American aid going to show a return? In January 1950 Averell Harriman, a man whose international experience distinguished him from many of the more parochial critics, protested that the British chancellor of the exchequer's narrow economic vision was sabotaging Western European integration. Americans 'would not stand for this much longer. The American people and the Congress would not support an aid program which did not show a coordinated approach to Western European unity.' The complaints even led to talk of reducing Marshall Aid unless matters improved.[50] Yet increased defence spending could only injure Britain's economic recovery.

Nor were the British without defenders in Washington. These spelt out what was 'special' for the United States in the relationship with Britain. Apart from the efforts of the American embassy in London to explain British problems and points of view, the US Central Intelligence Agency (CIA) was active in promoting the view that – for all her weaknesses – Britain was an indispensable ally. She fared well in any comparison with the problems and demoralization to be found in much of Western Europe. The British were firmly anti–Soviet and pro-American, they enjoyed internal political stability, and were willing to bear a wide range of international responsibilities. British scientific research was of a high calibre. Among the armed forces of the Western allies, only the British were comparable in quality with those of the United States. The Royal Navy was the 'nucleus around which the naval defense of Western Europe' was being constructed.[51]

The CIA also added a cautionary reminder that the policies of even so reliable an ally could change unless it was adequately supported and encouraged. Conservatives as well as people of the left were anxious to find ways to reduce British dependence on the United States. Meanwhile American aid was needed to ease the dollar famine, and to sustain Britain's commitment to multilateral trade. Furthermore the British people might begin to clamour for drastic changes in foreign policy if they were asked to undergo yet more austerity. The CIA believed that the United States should be prepared to pay a high price given that Britain was America's 'only powerful ally'. In addition much of her extra-European influence was based upon the confidence and expertise of local British personnel rather than on physical power. Comparable American influence could probably be introduced only at greater expense and effort. It was thus in America's interest to subsidize Britain with her worldwide network of bases, territories and contacts. Finally the CIA itself benefited from its intimate ties with the British Intelligence community.[52]

The CIA also spoke highly of the British Labour government. The 'Attlee Government has on the whole been easy to deal with'. There was no reason to believe that a Churchill ministry would be more helpful. It might indeed make more difficulties. A socialist government was less vulnerable to communist propaganda, and was more acceptable than the Tories in the colonies. It also exercised influence among the non-communist left in Europe, and was more readily trusted in many countries than the United States. Thus policies presented jointly by Britain and the United States often proved more acceptable than if put forward by the United States alone. The CIA insisted on 7 December 1949, 'The United Kingdom is, by a vast margin, the most valuable and dependable' of America's allies. The United

States was receiving a good return on its investment.[53] The US embassy in London on 7 January 1950 offered a strong defence on similar lines.[54]

The British did not help themselves by continuing to try to make more precise and explicit in the relationship what – at best – certain American policy-makers were prepared to concede only in private. Nor were they interested in trade-offs whereby the British should be the senior partner in the Middle East in return for American leadership in the Far East. Acheson would agree to 'close and continued consultation on all the parallel interests' of the two powers, but he was not willing to spell this out on paper. Indeed, he often felt it expedient to hide from the British the degree to which he was willing to co-operate and listen to their views. Thus a secret US State Department memorandum could refer explicitly to 'a special relationship' (Acheson was reputed to have forbidden any such admission of this kind on paper) which should exist with Britain for the pursuit of common objectives. Indeed Anglo-American differences could themselves be evidence of the multiplicity and intimacy of contacts. Without the co-operation of Britain and her Commonwealth 'a whole reorientation' of American foreign policy would be necessary and with it the risk of a resurgence of isolationism at home. The State Department's main regret was that Britain would not go beyond her 'one foot in and one foot out' policy towards Europe.[55]

In the spring of 1950, therefore, Acheson encouraged French proposals for a European Coal and Steel Community in the absence of a British alternative. The appearance of a Labour party pamphlet, *European Unity*, in June 1950 added to the indignation in Congress and press alike given that it contained so little that was in tune with American hopes of European integration.[56] But American attitudes and behaviour could create equally bad impressions in Britain. Thus Cripps's patience snapped in one encounter with a top American official who, he complained, had wasted his time with a 'schoolboy lecture' on the complicated problems which afflicted Europe.[57]

But if Britain could not be moved towards European economic co-operation, Acheson continued to press for increases to the military strength of the West. If the alliance were not seen to make progress, it might go into reverse. The American public, in particular, might lose interest if East–West relations appeared to settle into an indefinite stalemate – even if the British and Europeans were satisfied with such an outcome.[58] For these and other reasons the US State Department and the armed forces tried to seize the initiative at home with their notable inter-departmental report (NSC 68) of April 1950. The current defence budget of less than $15 billion left the armed forces with virtually no reserves to meet any intensification of the Cold War. While the American hemisphere itself and the main trans-oceanic lines of communication were secure, there was – they claimed – only 'an inadequate measure of protection to vital military bases in the United Kingdom and in the Near and Middle East'.[59]

Acheson looked for an equivalent to NSC 68 from the Europeans – and more especially from the British. In the search for new initiatives one of his first moves was to seek the advice of the British ambassador, Sir Oliver Franks.[60] It was already Acheson's custom to meet Franks to engage in a weekly '*tour d'horizon*' of world affairs. Published American documentation captures something of the wisdom and judicious conduct which earned the ambassador so much respect in Washington. The British, however, responded cautiously to Acheson's pleas that Nato should be strengthened. They might agree in principle, but it was only after the invasion of South Korea by the communist regime in the North in June 1950 that some arms increases were approved. The same was true of the United States.

Korea itself was not a region of direct interest to Britain. But the brute fact of direct military action by a communist government outside its own territory was highly disturbing. Soviet direction was assumed, while it was feared that communist success in Korea might lead to similar moves elsewhere – including Europe and the Middle East. The British also had to send some aid to maintain their credibility and therefore their influence as allies of the United States. On the one hand the decisive American response – under the auspices of the United Nations – was reassuring. But on the other there were the usual fears that the United States might overreact or give too high a priority to the Far East at the expense of Europe. Careful British monitoring of Soviet conduct suggested that with delicate diplomacy a peaceful settlement might be possible. In any case the sooner the war was brought to a satisfactory conclusion the better. Instead their worst fears were confirmed in the winter of 1950–51 when the war spread to involve forces from communist China. American behaviour was soon being described as emotional and unpredictable – even 'insufferable'.[61]

The complaints were not all on the one side. The Americans were exasperated by the British readiness to talk to Moscow and – even worse – their continuing willingness to appease communist China. The British, it was said, had not lost the 'Munich mentality'. Nor was Washington pleased when the British resorted to their usual tricks in their search for influence over American policy. The tension was exemplified as early as July 1950 when bilateral political-military conversations were held in Washington. The chairman of the US Joint Chiefs of Staff, General Bradley, objected to a British proposal for a joint study of future Soviet moves. The British must not be allowed to discuss bilaterally what properly lay within the province of Nato. As he told colleagues:

> [The British] had pressed for some time for a continuation of a combined staff relationship and had only been convinced that we were serious in rejecting this when we moved their combined staff people out of the Pentagon and moved the standing group [of Nato] in.[62]

The British themselves at the end of the talks conceded the preeminence of the Standing Group. This did not put an end to their hunt for a privileged place in allied planning, nor did their efforts go unrewarded. Likely Anglo-American areas of co-operation in time of war could easily extend beyond the competence of Nato. Bradley, while still cool towards the British on certain issues, agreed that in the event of war some Anglo-American 'equivalent' of the Combined Chiefs of Staff of the Second World War would be necessary. The chiefs of staff of the two powers decided on 23 October 1950 that the Nato Standing Group would be supplemented by Anglo-American staff 'conversations in the event of global war'.[63] Meanwhile periodic joint meetings of the service chiefs continued, as did Acheson's 'tours d'horizon' with Franks.

Military planning, however, meant little without more military power. The Korean War brought some increases, but the Americans were soon pressing their allies to spend still more on armaments. In particular the crisis was seen by Washington as an opportunity to press for the rearmament of West Germany. Previous discussions had been inconclusive, and the initial response of the British cabinet in the autumn of 1950 was cool. The Chiefs of Staff, however, supported the American plea. In any case, the more Western defence planners began to think in terms of genuine forward defence in Europe against a Soviet attack, the more obvious it was that this could never be a realistic policy without a West German contribution. Forward defence also seemed more important in the age of nuclear weapons. The latter might preclude a second Normandy-type landing. If Western Europe could not be liberated from Britain, it would have to be defended. The Americans were looking even further into the future. NSC 68 had been influenced in part by the fear that the United States itself would be vulnerable to Soviet attack as early as 1954. American nuclear power might thereafter no longer deter a Soviet conventional attack in Europe. This was another reason for a massive expansion of Nato forces. Planning on these lines reached its climax at Lisbon in February 1952 when the target of no fewer than 94 divisions for the defence of Europe was agreed.

France, however, was putting an effective brake on West German rearmament. In the autumn of 1950 the French put forward the Pleven Plan, their aim being to ensure that any German forces were split into small units and integrated within a European Defence Community (EDC). France wanted no large independent West German forces. The EDC remained a subject of controversy and delay for four years, and was finally rejected by the French National Assembly in August 1954. It was then that the British gained much credit – especially with President Eisenhower – for their part in the creation of an alternative structure. German entry to Nato was finally agreed in 1955.

In the autumn of 1950 it seemed that the Korean crisis was well on the way to a solution. American-led UN forces had expelled North Korean forces from the South by the end of September. The question was whether to settle for a return to the status quo, or to try to unite the two Koreas and achieve a victory over the communists. Both Attlee and Bevin favoured reunification under the auspices of the United Nations – though perhaps with a buffer zone in the north to reassure the Chinese. British diplomacy, however, was speedily overtaken by events.[64] The Chinese, understandably, were not willing to tolerate unrestricted Western intervention in North Korea. Even the preference of the British Chiefs of Staff for an advance only to the waistline in North Korea (well short of Manchuria) might not have reassured them. By the closing weeks of 1950 it seemed that the Chinese might be about to win an outright victory in all of Korea. This was bad enough. Still worse was the fear that the Americans might respond with some desperate counter-stroke. The Cold War was reaching a point where, having reactivated the Anglo-American relationship, it was about to expose it to new strains and tensions.

NOTES AND REFERENCES

1. *DBPO*, I. iv. 67–9. Ritchie Ovendale, *Britain, the United States, and the End of the Palestine Mandate, 1942–1948*, Boydell Press, 1989, chapters 1–2.

2. *FRUS*, 1945, viii. 14–16; F.R. Harbutt, *The Iron Curtain: Churchill, America and the origins of the Cold War*, Oxford University Press, 1986, pp. 130–56. Forrestal, secretary of the navy and an early hardliner, was busily cultivating the press in his bid to push the United States into a tougher stance against the USSR.

3. H. Thomas, *Armed Truce: the beginnings of the Cold War, 1945–46*, Hamish Hamilton, 1986, pp. 393–4, 539.

4. *DBPO*, I. iv. 93–4.

5. See report from the British embassy (Washington), 10 March 1946, *DBPO*, I, iv. 154–6. For British opinion see Alan Foster in Anne Deighton, ed., *Britain and the First Cold War*, Macmillan, 1990, pp. 13–19.

6. Harbutt, pp. 247–79. For British controversy over policy towards the USSR see R. Smith in Deighton, chapter 2.

7. R.A. Best, *'Cooperation with like-minded peoples': British influences on American security policy, 1945–49*, New York: Greenwood Press, 1986, p. 22. See also pp. 31–9, and R.M. Hathaway, *Ambiguous Partnership: Britain and America, 1944–47*, New York: Columbia University Press, 1981, pp. 264–71.

8. Julian Lewis, *Changing Direction: British military planning for post-war strategic defence, 1942–47*, London: Sherwood Press, 1988, pp. 263–4, 272, 289–315.

9. *FRUS*, 1946, i. 1165; Best, pp. 121–2.

10. See early chapters in Best, especially pp. 37–8 on the naval co-operation.

11. I. Clark and N.J. Wheeler, *The British Origins of Nuclear Strategy, 1945–55*, Oxford; Clarendon Press, 1989, pp. 43–51.

12. *FRUS*, 1946, i. 1170.

13. Kent in Dockrill and Young, p. 49.

14. Hathaway, pp. 259–60. Anne Deighton conveniently summarizes British policy in Germany in 1945–46 in Deighton, chapter 3, especially pp. 63–9. For more detailed analysis of British efforts to influence the United States over Germany in 1946–47, see Deighton, *The Impossible Peace: Britain, the division of Germany and the origins of the Cold War*, Oxford University Press, 1990.

15. Lewis, pp. 285–9, 363–9.

16. Pollard, p. 56.

17. Bullock, p. 369. But see Louis, *British Empire in the Middle East*, p. 99, who cites evidence of British hopes of involvement from January 1947.

18. Hathaway, p. 303. V. Rothwell, *Britain and the Cold War, 1941–47*, Hutchinson, 1973, p. 434–6, comments on continuing Foreign Office fears of American unpredictability and unreliability.

19. See especially R. Smith and J. Zametica, 'The Cold War Warrior: Clement Attlee reconsidered, 1945–47', *International Affairs*, spring 1985, pp. 237–51; Louis, *British Empire in the Middle East*, pp. 27 ff; Lewis, pp. 272 ff.

20. *FRUS*, 1947, v. 578.

21. *FRUS*, 1947, i. 742; Etzold and Gaddis, p. 310.

22. *FRUS*, 1947, i. 750–8.
23. *FRUS*, 1947, i. 758; and E. Barker, *The British and the Super Powers*, Macmillan, 1983, pp. 99–102.
24. Louis, *British Empire in the Middle East*, pp. 110–12. For the 'Pentagon Talks' see *FRUS*, 1947, v. 488 ff. Note also *Records of the Joint Chiefs of Staff, part 2, 1946–53, Strategic Issues*, Microfilm Project of University Publications of America Inc., Washington DC, 1981 (hereafter JCSSI), reel 9, JCS 1259/41, 29 Sept 1947, encl F, summarizes US intentions to use Egyptian and UK bases against the USSR. See also R. Ovendale, *Britain, the United States and the end of the Palestine Mandate, 1942–48*, Boydell Press, 1989, p. 221
25. JCSSI, reel 9, JCS, 1826/1, 7 January 1948; see also JCS 1259/66, 17 April 1948. See also *Records of JCS, part 2, The Middle East*, Microfilm Project of University Publications of America Inc., Washington DC, 1980 (hereafter JCSME), reel 1. JCS 1887/1, 19 July 1948, which provides a military assessment of the Eastern Mediterranean/Middle Eastern regions. There is much of value on US defence thinking in Best, pp. 73 ff., 96 ff., 140–1.
26. JCSSI, reel 9, 1259/81, 20 July 1948; cf JCS 1259/86, 23 August 1948 for the navy's view.
27. The US Navy was more ambitious, but feared subordination to the British. See P. Ziegler, *Mountbatten*, Collins, 1985, pp. 508–20. Admiral Carney was full of Churchillian ideas of a counterattack to the Danube via the Ljubljana Gap. The JCS, however, gave the highest priority to Europe. For detail see JCSME, reel 1, January 1952.
28. W.R. Louis in 'American anti-colonialism and the dissolution of the British Empire', *International Affairs*, summer 1985, pp. 395–420, shows how the USA was broadly content with British policy in Libya, and was willing to play second fiddle as long as it believed that its interests were being protected.
29. See JCSME, reel 1, for JCS 1684/2, 19 June 1946; and 1684/3, 10 October 1947 for JCS assessments.
30. R. Ovendale, *The Origins of the Arab-Israeli Wars*, Longman, 1984, pp. 122–9.
31. At times British policy over the future of Palestine became so complex and devious that it angered Marshall and the State Department. See A. Shlaim, *Collusion across the Jordan*, Oxford: Clarendon Press, p. 368, and also pp. 175–8, 188–91, 245–8, 275–7, 294–5; also W.R. Louis and R.W. Stanskey, eds, *The End of the Palestine Mandate*, I.B. Tauris, 1986, pp. 40–56, 141–2.
32. W. Millis, *The Forrestal Diaries*, Cassell, 1952, pp. 182, 187–8, 244–5, 267, 277, 292, 300–1, 485, 488, 491.
33. T.G. Smith, *From the Heart of the American Desert to the Court of St James: The Public Career of Lewis W.Douglas of Arizona, 1894–1974*, Ann Arbor, Michigan, Microfilms, 1977, pp. 396, 424, 434.
34. Dobson, pp. 98–102.

35. Dobson, pp. 100–13. See also M.J. Hogan, *The Marshall Plan: Britain, America and the Reconstruction of Western Europe*, Cambridge University Press, 1987. A. Cairncross, *Years of Recovery: British economic policy, 1945–51*, Methuen, 1985, especially chapters 6–7.
36. For detail see Kent in Dockrill and Young, pp.57 ff.
37. For detail on Anglo-American economic relations, see Edmonds, pp.108–12; Dobson, pp. 119–25. A. Carew, *Labour under the Marshall Plan*, Manchester United Press, 1987, analyses US efforts to persuade British managers, trade unions and Labour ministers to replicate US managerial methods, and learn from US liberal capitalism.
38. P.M. Williams, *The Diary of Hugh Gaitskell, 1945–56*, Jonathan Cape, 1983, pp. 172, 175. But Gaitskell was still enraged when he found the USA again pressing for a larger UK defence effort in September 1951. See P. Boyle in J. Zametica, ed., *British Officials and British Foreign Policy, 1945–50*, Leicester University Press, 1990, p. 206.
39. Best (pp. 4–6) still singles out the creation of Nato as 'London's decisive contribution to postwar history'.
40. Best, pp. 155 ff. A. Shlaim, *The United States and the Berlin Blockade, 1948–49*, Berkeley, University of California Press, 1983, pp. 57–8. See also Jean Smith, *The Papers of General Lucius D. Clay; Germany 1945–49*, vol i, Indiana University Press, Bloomington, 1974, pp. 704, 1047.
41. The French found that they were still expected to provide the bulk of Western ground force.
42. See C. Greiner in O. Riste, ed., *Western Security: the formative years: Europe and Atlantic Defence, 1947–53*, Norwegian University Press, Oslo, 1985, pp. 150–7. At the end of 1949 the Joint Chiefs of Staff (JCS) calculated that operations on the Rhine would be feasible in 1957 at the earliest. Offtackle was not revealed to the Europeans, not least for fear of leaks to the USSR. (p. 152) Only the British and Canadians were fully trusted. Even in October the Americans described the defence of the Rhine as only an initial operation, and dismayed the French with their reliance on a defence based on 'successive positions' – ie a fighting retreat. (p. 156) The defence of the Rhine, followed by forward defence, had to wait for the build-up of Nato in the 1950s and the rearmament of West Germany.
43. Edmonds, pp. 187–9; Barker, pp. 112–55, 196–7; Best, pp. 178–88; D.C. Watt in *Foreign and Commonwealth: Occasional Papers no. 3*, November 1989, p. 43.
44. S. Duke, *United States Defence Bases in the United Kingdom*, Macmillan, 1987, pp. 31–56. See also N.J. Wheeler, 'The Attlee Government's Nuclear Strategy, 1945–51', in Deighton, pp. 137–40; and also his 'British nuclear weapons and Anglo-American Relations, 1945–54', *International Affairs*, winter, 1985–86, pp. 72–3; D. Gates, 'American Strategic Bases in Britain: the Agreements governing their use', *Comparative Strategy*, vol 8, 1989, p. 103. I. Clark and N.J. Wheeler, *The British Origins of Nuclear Strategy*, Oxford: Clarendon Press, 1989, p. 75, stress the role of strategic thinking in the acquisition of the nuclear force from the start.

45. Clark and Wheeler, pp. 75, 90–111.
46. For the later controversy on US bases in the UK, see below pp. 52–3, 73, 133.
47. W.A. Williams, T. McCormick, L. Gardner and W. Lafeber, *America in Vietnam: a documentary history*, New York: W.W. Norton, 1989, pp. 98–9. P. Lowe, *The Origins of the Korean War*, Longman, 1986, pp. 152–3.
48. R. Ovendale, *The English-Speaking Alliance, 1945–51*, Allen and Unwin, 1985, pp. 147–78. *FRUS*, 1950, vi. 154–5, 781; 1951, vi, part 1, 59 ff.
49. D.C. Watt in *FCO Occasional Papers* no. 3, pp. 43–5; *FRUS*, 1950, i, pp. 142–7 (PPS meeting of 2 February 1950).
50. See Boyle in Zametica, p. 197; R.A. Pollard, *Economic Security and the Origins of the Cold War, 1945–50*, New York: Columbia University Press, pp. 235–9; Bullock, pp. 761–5; Paul Gore-Booth, *With Great Truth and Respect*, Constable, 1974, pp. 177–8. See also *FRUS*, 1950, iii. 1609, 1629–31.
51. *CIA Research Reports, Europe, 1946–76*, Microfilm Project of University Publications of America, Washington DC Inc., 1983 (hereafter CIA), reel 1, reports to presidential office, 24 February 1949, 1 June 1949, 27 April 1950.
52. CIA, reel 4, report (ORE 79-49) 31 August 1949.
53. CIA, Reel 4, SR-25, 7 December 1949, ORE-9-50, 13 February 1950.
54. *FRUS*, 1950, iii. 1603.
55. JCS, part 2, 1946–53, Europe and Nato, JCS 2128, 4 May 1950, The Essential Elements of US–UK Relations. This includes the US State Department paper of 19 April 1950.
56. *FRUS*, 1950, iii. 1648–54. See also Clarke, pp. 208–10.
57. *FRUS*, 1950, iii. 1608.
58. *FRUS*, 1950, iii. 1628–32. On US estimates of Soviet policy, see *FRUS*, 1950, iv. 1083–4, 1099–101, 1150 ff., 1164 ff. Note Acheson on three senators who thought it might be necessary to force a showdown with the USSR before the H-bomb was developed. *FRUS*, 1950, i. 140–1.
59. J.L. Gaddis, *Strategies of Containment*, Oxford: Oxford University Press, 1982, chapter 4; *FRUS*, 1950, i. 235 ff.
60. *FRUS*, 1950, iii. 1628–32. M.L. Dockrill, 'The Foreign Office, Anglo-American Relations and the Korean War, June 1950–June 1951', *International Affairs*, summer 1986, pp. 459–76.
61. See Lowe in Dockrill and Young, chapter 6; Boyle in Zametica, pp. 198 ff.
62. *FRUS*, 1950, iii. 1655–6.
63. *FRUS*, 1950, iii. 1660, 1689. Further British probes for more intimate staff talks followed early in 1951, although they conceded that the CCOS had been superseded by Nato, *FRUS*, 1951, iv. 889.
64. Boyle in Zametica, p. 202; Lowe in Dockrill and Young, p. 128.

CHAPTER THREE
Similar Ends, Different Methods, 1950–55

THE KOREAN WAR AND STRAINS IN THE PARTNERSHIP

Despite major differences of opinion and emphasis, Britain and the United States had forged a remarkably creative and successful partnership between 1947 and November 1950. But the successful intervention of the communist Chinese in the Korean War proved to be the start of a period in which the British, while they clung of necessity to the Atlantic alliance, were often fearful of some impulsive or extreme action by the United States which would lead to an unnecessary intensification of East–West conflict and even, possibly, to the Third World War. Relaxation came only with the two Geneva conferences of 1954 and 1955. During these years the British were also pushing ahead with their own nuclear programme, while trying to ensure that American nuclear policies developed in ways which were compatible with or (better still) worked to the advantage of their own interests. The Americans, for their part, feared that British conduct in the Middle East was becoming increasingly heavy-handed and counter-productive. In their eyes the British were not adjusting sensitively enough to the emergence of potent radical Arab forces, and were therefore putting at risk Western interests and influence in this region. Not until 1953–55 was there a partial and fragile Anglo-American convergence of policy.

Unguarded remarks by Truman on 30 November on the possible use of nuclear weapons in Korea precipitated in Westminster what

Roy Jenkins has described as a 'mood of near panic' far worse than any he experienced throughout his entire political career.[1] Attlee promptly flew to Washington. The American military had indeed been giving some some tentative thought to the use of atomic weapons in response to the Chinese victories in Korea. Although Truman speedily allayed the worst of his visitor's fears, this simply cleared the way for other issues. Attlee was very anxious to prevent any extension of the war beyond Korea. This could be highly dangerous in itself, and might result in a weakening of the American commitment to Europe. Attlee also underlined the need for full consultation between the British and American governments.[2]

The prime minister did not achieve all his objectives, and he returned home to find that the new tide of anti-American criticism was still rising. American observers were hardly surprised by the outcry from sections of the British Labour party, but they were more disturbed by the attitude of influential Conservatives such as Lord Salisbury and Winston Churchill. The latter favoured a secret meeting at the 'highest level' before the Soviets could accumulate a stockpile of nuclear weapons.[3] The US State Department thought it time to look closely into the causes and extent of British criticism. Early in 1951, for instance, the first secretary of the US embassy in London probed Sir David Maxwell-Fyfe, an influential Conservative, for his views on the extent and character of anti-American feeling in Britain. Maxwell-Fyfe replied that virulent anti-Americanism was confined to a small minority, but he made the most of the opportunity to spell out the extent of British alarm over what the Americans were doing or might do in the Far East.[4]

The London embassy reported that, while the great majority supported the 'Anglo-Saxon "alliance"', there was a real fear of a bigger – even of a global – war. The activities of Senator McCarthy and other extremists in American politics might come to affect American policy-making itself. The British as usual were resentful and jealous because they were dependent on a stronger power. Washington was seen as insufficiently appreciative of British efforts, nor was its main ally always properly consulted before major foreign-policy decisions were taken which affected its interests. The embassy pointed out that the Attlee cabinet not only needed to reassure the left wing of the Labour party and the British public, but also wished to cultivate India and other Asian neutrals. It was anxious to preserve the unity of the Commonwealth and to nurture such anti-communist potential as existed among Asian nationalists. It was necessarily disturbed when the United States treated the United Nations as if it were its own exclusive 'club'.[5]

Despite these embassy warnings matters seemed in danger of coming to a head early in 1951. Opinion polls in January and February illustrated the extent of public alarm in Britain. Nearly 60 per cent thought there was a real risk of a general war. If 58 per cent expected the USSR rather than the United States (21 per cent) to be the guilty party, only 40 per cent approved of American policy and 35 per cent were critical. The usual hard core of some 22 per cent insisted that Britain and the United States should 'always stick together', while another 52 per cent (though favouring selective co-operation) were anxious to protect British independence and freedom of choice. It was at this time that a majority of the British cabinet was only with difficulty dissuaded from opposing an American UN resolution to brand China an aggressor and to introduce sanctions. Bevin, despite some fears of his own concerning American impulsiveness, argued that quiet persuasion, not public displays of dissent against 'the well-intentioned but inexperienced colossus', was the answer. Europe and the Commonwealth were too dependent upon American power to risk separation. Gaitskell also reminded the cabinet that Britain might soon require American economic help if there were a balance of payments crisis. Fortunately for the defenders of the American alliance the Chinese rejected proposals for a cease-fire, thus making it easier for the British government to support the UN's condemnation of Chinese aggression on 1 February 1951.[6]

Nonetheless the resurgence of anti-American feeling within sections of the Labour party – feeling which had been broadly silenced by Soviet moves from 1948 – persisted, and it was further stimulated by the sharp increases in British defence spending and the damaging effects these had upon the government's domestic programme. Ministers agreed, however reluctantly, that Britain's own condition and the international environment as a whole required the continuance of Atlanticist policies. Britain had to do whatever was necessary to maintain her position as America's premier ally (apart from the British and some Commonwealth forces, only Turkey sent troops to Korea to assist the Americans).[7] Further acts of aggression by the Soviet bloc seemed possible in a number of vulnerable regions such as Germany and Yugoslavia. The government did, however, try to insist that the added defence burdens should be equitably shared by all the Western allies. But they were unduly optimistic when they looked to Washington for assistance with their new defence programme.[8] The Americans not only were spending heavily on their own forces but they also were determined to wring the maximum defence effort from European allies.

In May 1951 the American ambassador in London summed up Britain's situation:

> British people realize that for better or worse their destiny is inextricably intertwined with that of the U.S. even though some of them may be reluctant to admit it.[9]

But critics who believed that the West was over-reacting were strengthened when Aneurin Bevan resigned from the British cabinet on 21 May accompanied by two other ministers. Bevan's action had various causes, but rearmament and its implications for domestic policy were understandably given great prominence in the following months. A Bevanite pamphlet appeared in July which argued – among other things – that the government was exaggerating the Soviet threat. Certainly the Bevanites could claim that rearmament was imposing too great a strain on the economy. Amid mounting political and economic problems Attlee decided that it was impossible for the government to struggle on with its tiny majority. In the ensuing election campaign foreign affairs were unusually prominent, with Labour trying to project itself as a better defender of the peace than the Tories. Indeed some observers thought this a major reason why the Conservatives won by so narrow a margin in October.[10]

Hugh Gaitskell, a leader of the strongly pro-American faction, later summed up his impressions of the relationship. Apart from those who were staunchly anti-American, many resented Britain's decline to the position of a 'poor relation' and were anxious for the nation to recover its former economic independence. In addition the closeness of the alliance and the sheer multiplicity of contacts were themselves a major cause of ill-feeling – as in a family. The British were tempted to behave as if the disparity in power between the United States and themselves was only of the order of two to one when seven to one would have been a more realistic figure. All these things had to be considered in addition to the criticisms of American policy and conduct. Nevertheless Gaitskell concluded, if somewhat tepidly, 'America is, after all, a free democratic country, while Russia is a cruel and ruthless dictatorship.'[11] Indeed, compared with all the enthusiasm for the 'special relationship' necessarily expressed in public by numerous British spokesmen between the 1940s and the 1990s, Gaitskell's cool summary is as broadly representative of British feelings and thinking as one is likely to find.

CHURCHILL FRUSTRATED

Churchill returned to office in October 1951 determined to increase British influence within the Anglo-American partnership. One of the most sensitive issues was the question of American air bases in Britain. Attlee had raised this issue during his visit to Washington in December 1950. While American war plans placed great reliance on these bases, the advance of the USSR to nuclear status was leading to reappraisals of the vulnerability of the British Isles to Soviet air attack. It was possible that Britain would be crippled by nuclear assault within 60 days of the start of a war. In contrast the American inter-service Harmon Committee concluded in 1950 that the Strategic Air Command had the capacity to destroy only about 30–40 per cent of Russia's industrial power. Soviet forces, meanwhile, were still expected to overrun much of Western Europe, the Middle and Far East.[12]

Attlee during his Washington visit of 4–5 December 1950 had been able to elicit no more than a promise that Britain would be kept informed of any developments which might lead to the use of nuclear weapons. This was not much of a promise, and Acheson himself was coming to the view that the British deserved some further reassurance. It was, he conceded on 6 August 1951, 'a life and death matter' for them. The United States could not properly insist on 'a blank check'. On the other hand he agreed that the Americans could not risk the destruction of their own forces in Britain by a pre-emptive Soviet strike or allow a major part of their bomber force to remain earthbound while British ministers tried to make up their minds. Given these competing interests, the best he could propose was that the two governments should try to come to a prior understanding concerning each other's needs and thereby avoid the formal commitments which the US Joint Chiefs feared might paralyse American forces at the start of hostilities. He also stressed the need to retain British confidence by showing that American policy was 'sober and responsible'.[13]

The British cabinet took up the subject again in Washington in September 1951.[14] The British foreign secretary did his best to argue that Britain should not be asked to face annihilation without representation. But it soon became clear that Washington was prepared to promise no more than a continuing exchange of views 'to bring our respective viewpoints as close as possible'. Franks devised the ingenious formula that the use of the air bases in an emergency naturally remained 'a matter for joint decision in the light of the circumstances at the time'. This was how matters stood when Churchill returned to office.[15] His own approaches, however, brought only the admission from Washington that the talks were designed to reach a better understanding of the respective positions of the two countries. There were no 'final and binding decisions'. If anything more was promised informally or verbally the American version remains classified.[16]

The question of an effective British veto on American use of British bases has surfaced on a number of occasions since 1952. In the end each successive British government was obliged to trust the Americans, and to hope that circumstances would not arise when it disagreed with American policy. Successive cabinets were compelled to weigh the dangers attendant upon the American presence on their soil against the implications of an American withdrawal. None in the end decided that the former outweighed the latter. They also had to accept that attacks on the USSR by weapons launched from American bases other than in Britain might still bring down nuclear strikes on this country as long as it remained a member of Nato or was linked to the United States in some way or other.[17]

While on the one hand Simon Duke describes the British commitment as 'perhaps the most important . . . made by one first-class power to another', he also notes the unique importance of Britain – especially before the development of inter-continental aircraft and rockets – in American grand strategy in Europe. Nor were the Americans merely interested in bomber bases in Britain. Reconnaissance and tactical aircraft were also deployed. Use was made of facilities for communications, intelligence gathering, and early warning systems. In return from the end of 1951 the British began to receive a small but increasing amount of information on American strategic air plans. The British defence chiefs also felt able to work on the assumption that the USSR would not feel strong enough to risk war for several more years. All this was precious time within which to advance the British nuclear programme.[18]

Nevertheless it is clear that Anglo–American relations had suffered a number of shocks since 1950, while Churchill was quite wrong in his expectation that the Americans would be happier to work with him than with Labour. Indeed over his three and a half years in office new problems were added as quickly as others were solved or eased. In any case the priorities of his government could not easily be reconciled in the context of British policy-making, let alone in conjunction with the United States.

The Conservatives had inherited numerous economic problems. Their small majority made them all the more conscious of the problems they needed to surmount to win the next election. They had to fulfil their election promises that the days of austerity were numbered. They had to defend the welfare state. At the same time they wished to protect and even advance British influence abroad. Churchill hoped to make a start towards the reconciliation of these objectives with an already over-burdened economy by making cuts to the defence pro- gramme he had inherited from Labour. The desire for defence econ- omies also increased his desire to see a relaxation in East–West tensions. But on neither count could he expect a very sympathetic hearing in Washington.

Churchill was genuinely hopeful by October 1951 that the Cold War would not become a 'hot' war. The prime minister even believed that a settlement of some kind might prove possible in Korea. In fact the conflict had nearly two years to run, but by October 1951 some movement was occurring even in Washington on the subject of rela- tions with the USSR. Western fears in general were receding that the USSR might be tempted to launch a pre-emptive attack before Nato had developed into an effective military force. There was less talk of preparing Nato for war by 1954. The West had now to adapt itself to a lengthy period of Cold War competition with the USSR rather than prepare for an imminent crisis.[19] If Churchill, even at the end of 1951, did not wholly discount the possibility of a pre-emptive attack by the USSR, he was beginning to see American impulsiveness as a more likely cause of conflict.[20]

His return to power was taken very seriously by the US State De- partment. The old warrior would have been flattered had he seen the care with which Washington prepared for his first visit.[21] There were various assessments of Anglo-American relations. The State Depart- ment's Policy Planning Staff noted on 20 November 1951:

> We have, in fact, at the present time a special relationship with the U.K. which involves consultation between us on a wide range of matters of joint concern.

While it recommended that the British should not enjoy even the hint of a veto in any form of consultative machinery, it did not think that Britain should be treated as a satellite. It welcomed the 'Slessor talks' (which had begun in 1951) as a model for non-military as well as defence issues – evidently hoping that greater frankness in informal meetings would satisfy British aspirations.

Leading US State Department and Defense personnel, however, were more wary. In their opinion the working of the 'special relation- ship' had been faulty since Bevin's illness and retirement early in 1951.

Hopes of an improvement under Churchill were qualified by the determination to prevent any return to the virtual parity which he had enjoyed at the height of his wartime partnership with Roosevelt. 'We all agree . . . on that', interjected General Collins, the army chief of staff. It was further understood that any arrangement with Britain would not preclude separate American talks with the French or the Canadians.[22]

The Americans were also anxious to nudge Churchill towards their way of thinking on a number of issues. This included a test of the new British government's policy on both the European Coal and Steel and the Defence Communities. Far and Middle Eastern issues similarly demanded attention. But the coded language of the joint communiqué issued at the end of Churchill's Washington visit of January 1952 showed that there had been little or no meeting of minds. It blandly stated that each government had 'gained a better understanding of the thoughts and aims of the other'.

The truth was revealed by Eden to the British cabinet when he indignantly reported:

> They [Truman and Acheson] are polite; listen to what we have to say, but make (on most issues) their own decisions. Till we can recover our financial and economic independence, this is bound to continue.[23]

At the actual meetings it was noted that Truman seemed deliberately impervious to Churchill's oratory, especially when he talked grandiloquently of Anglo–American co-operation. The Americans were also worried by the British tendency to take too mild a view of Soviet intentions, an attitude which they feared might give rise to false hopes among the public in the West, and lessen support for the build-up of Nato. Indeed some thought Churchill had little faith in Nato militarily, quite apart from his lack of interest in the creation of the European Defence Community. Finally, while the Americans were well aware of Britain's economic problems, they could not easily reconcile themselves to the need for actual defence cuts.[24]

The same was true of some of the leading policy-makers in Britain. While the Treasury was warning of a 'continuing mountain of difficulties' for some years to come, the Foreign Office argued that to reduce overseas commitments would only make matters worse. The Treasury insisted that living standards at home and even exports would be under threat unless Britain cut both defence spending and foreign commitments. It estimated in May 1952 that British overseas defence spending was ten times greater than the prewar figure. The Foreign Office retorted that the British economy would suffer from premature withdrawals. These could easily lead to the disruption of overseas markets and sources of raw materials. And it was equally insistent that a policy of retreat would cause dismay in Washington, thereby diminishing Britain's ability to exert influence over American policy. Allies received attention in proportion to their contribution to the Western alliance. Yet even the foreign secretary conceded that economic difficulties would in due course force a reappraisal of Britain's military commitments within Nato. When, however, a start was made on these lines in the mid-1950s there were indignant protests from Washington – just as the Foreign Office had forecast.[25]

Nevertheless even a stronger British economy might have had difficulty in satisfying American expectations. A Staff Study for the National Security Council of 22 August 1952 stressed the need for more easily mobilized reserves. At the same time it feared that Britain's vulnerability to modern weapons was such that her value as a base might be short-lived. A later estimate (21 November 1952), though it still graded Britain as the most important member of the Atlantic community, described her as in many respects a fragile and wrong-headed partner.[26] Once again British influence in Washington was enhanced by the greater weaknesses (political and economic) of the other leading European states, coupled with America's lack of effective and reliable allies in the Middle and Far East.

MIDDLE EASTERN DIFFERENCES, 1951–52

The Pentagon was interested in the role of certain Commonwealth countries as well as Britain herself, nor did it rule out separate arrangements with the more important of them if necessary. As the US Joint Chiefs of Staff commented on 22 October 1951:

> The security interests of the United States at this time would be greatly benefited if the British Commonwealth of Nations could achieve once more a state of political and military solidarity under strong and effective leadership by the United Kingdom; failing this, wholehearted support of United States military policies must be obtained from the several members of the British Commonwealth through other means.[27]

Similarly in the Middle East the Americans, while valuing the British presence (notably the base at Suez), were looking beyond it to a more comprehensive defence system. There was much interest in a broadly based Middle Eastern Command which would enlist the willing support of the Arab states. Turkey was also attracting attention, especially if British weaknesses should require another state to assume the 'primary leadership' in the region. The American services – other than the navy – were still reluctant or unable to send forces into the eastern Mediterranean. The available armed forces were expected to be fully committed to the defence of Italy in the first two years of a war.[28]

The US State Department was equally uncertain as to policy. While Acheson continued to support the British against Greek claims in Cyprus, elsewhere he was increasingly doubtful of the viability of existing policies and positions. There was a role for the British in the Middle East, but he hoped that they could be dissuaded from actions which would alienate Arab opinion. A draft NSC study of 27 December 1951 warned against trying 'to maintain and defend Western interests in the area in the 19th century fashion'. The British should adjust to the newly emerging regional political forces and interest groups. Unfortunately Britain had already run into major problems with Iran and Egypt. The return of Churchill to office threatened to make matters worse.[29]

A crisis had erupted between Britain and Iran in 1951 over the future of the Anglo-Iranian Oil Company. A great upsurge of popular discontent and nationalism led to the formation of a government headed by Mohammad Mussadeq. This promptly nationalized the British company. Quite apart from the economic implications, the British government feared that so drastic a move, unless effectively challenged, would encourage others in the Middle East – and even further afield – to act against foreign investments and interests. This seemed to be confirmed when in October 1951 Egypt unilaterally repudiated the 1936 treaty with Britain. Thereafter the important British base at Suez came under guerrilla attack.

Military action of some kind against Iran was discussed by the British cabinet in the summer of 1951. Herbert Morrison, the foreign secretary, was among the more belligerent. He was reputed to carry a copy of Philip Guedalla's biography of Palmerston around with him. But Attlee and others believed that Britain could not act without the support of or against the wishes of the United States. Franks was busily engaged in a damage limitation exercise in Washington.[30] Nevertheless London's resentment mounted against the Americans, not only on account of their efforts to restrain Britain, but also because of the growing influence and activity of certain American officials and businessmen in the Middle East. Numerous stories began to circulate of American machinations and claim-jumping at the expense of the British.

Among those to achieve notoriety was US assistant secretary of state George McGhee (the fact that he had been a Rhodes scholar seemingly counted for nothing on either side). As head of the Near East, South Asian and African Affairs Bureau he inherited (so he later claimed) little in the way of policy for a region where American involvement had been intermittent or localized. McGhee was not uncritically anti-British. Indeed he claimed that he sometimes drew upon his knowledge of British policies and methods – past and present – when developing his own ideas. But his enthusiasm and self-assurance meant that in practice he came to personify what Elizabeth Monroe in *The Economist* in London described as the American belief that with 'dollars and a wrench' one could transform the world.[31] McGhee himself later confessed:

> In retrospect I am amazed at our confidence, at the time, in our country's ability to help these people [Arabs and others] solve their enormous problems. Our role in defeating Germany and Japan, and in saving Greece and Turkey from Soviet take-over, undoubtedly gave us an exaggerated view of our capacity to help other peoples with quite different backgrounds.

On African issues he was more willing to listen to British views, helped by the fact that there was not the same fear of imminent communist penetration, nor were American interests so pressing. In the Middle East he believed quick and independent American action was justified, especially in Iran where he feared British economic pressure might destabilize the radical government to the advantage of communism and the USSR.[32]

In their dispute with Iran the British set out to close off all outlets for Iranian oil. American oil companies (fearful of the knock-on effects to themselves in the Middle East if Iranian radicals were seen to succeed) proved more enthusiastic allies than the State Department. The British, however, remained suspicious of American motives, and resentful of their advice. Eden's private secretary, Shuckburgh, thought it 'very offensive' when, following an unsatisfactory meeting on Anglo-American policy towards Iran, he was told by Acheson that the British had to learn to live in the world as it was. Yet Acheson's remarks were hardly surprising when his department was receiving so many reports of the strength of Arab feeling against the British. By 1952 he was becoming all the more determined that the United States should not be tarred with the colonial brush.[33]

Meanwhile the British remained under siege in their base at Suez. The US State Department, encouraged by the overthrow of the discredited Egyptian monarchy in 1952, set out to woo the young army officers who had seized power. Britain's current 'standfast policy' was deemed at best a short-term solution. A 'package deal' to provide for the future was imperative. The preferred solution was Egyptian participation in a Western-led anti-communist Middle Eastern defence organization. In January 1952 Acheson resorted to a vivid analogy as he tried to open Churchill's mind to the need for new policies.

> I said that we could have the most perfect mutual support and understanding, but that, if it were reached upon present policies, we would be like two people locked in loving embrace in a rowboat which was about to go over Niagara Falls. I thought we should break the embrace and take to the oars. This amused the Prime Minister.

Such light-hearted exchanges, however, had no effect on Churchill's thinking. He was, Acheson lamented, determined 'to live completely in the past'.[34]

The British, for their part, continued to follow American policy in the Far East with equal if not greater apprehension. Fears that American frustration over the continuation of the war in Korea might lead to some reckless form of escalation persisted.[35] But there was little the British could do. The new Republican administration under Eisenhower from 1953 was determined to bring the war to a speedy end. A cease-fire was finally agreed on 27 July, though in the absence of Soviet or Chinese documentation one cannot be sure what part was played by the American threats of intensified military operations. There is, however, some evidence of Eisenhower's own dismay when he found Anglo-American relations to be in such disarray in 1953. Furthermore, he did not seem entirely unmoved by Churchill's concern to improve relations with the USSR.[36]

ENTER EISENHOWER AND DULLES

The transition from Democrat to Republican administration in Washington in 1953 posed many problems for the British. Yet Acheson and Eisenhower were agreed on one thing. As Acheson had remarked in 1952, the world had moved on too far for Churchill and Eden to try to revive the sort of personal ties which had existed with President Roosevelt during the Second World War – this would be 'a classical example of the wrong way to do things'.[37] Eisenhower himself said much the same a year later. Certainly Churchill and Eden found that their dealings with Eisenhower and Dulles were no easier than they had been with the Democrats: in fact they often thought them worse. Indeed, during the presidential campaign of 1952 Churchill – and many others in London – were hoping for a Democrat victory. Republican talk of 'rolling back' communism had a particularly ominous ring to it, especially when (early in 1953) a shooting war was still in progress in Korea.

Eden and Dulles were never likely to be at ease with each other. Dulles combined the most austere characteristics of a lawyer and a Presbyterian minister. Eden was above all a diplomat of the classical school, though one whose command of his emotions was not always what it should have been. Dulles in any case made few friends among foreign politicians apart from the dour West German chancellor, Konrad Adenauer, and Jean Monnet (chairman of the European Coal and Steel Community who was doing more than any other figure to create the sort of Europe desired by Washington). Although Eisenhower and Churchill had worked together in the Second World War as military commander and prime minister, Churchill had now to remember that Eisenhower was president of the world's greatest power. The change was not without its difficulties.

Eden was soon complaining that, with the departure of Truman and Acheson, he had to deal with inexperienced people in Washington.[38] Churchill, when frustrated by Eisenhower, grumbled that the president was 'weak and stupid', and he later contemptuously dismissed him as Dulles's 'ventriloquist's doll'. As for the US secretary of state, he was 'a Methodist Minister' with the single text that 'nothing but evil' would come out of a meeting with Malenkov, at that time the leading figure in the USSR.[39] Such remarks, however, must be treated with some caution. Much was said in the heat of the moment. Around the same time Churchill was remarking that he would happily go to war with Egypt. There was no war. But Shuckburgh's long exposure to the whims and sensibilities of Eden and Churchill led him on at least one occasion to comment favourably on Eisenhower and Dulles as political leaders.[40]

Differences of economic interest added to Anglo-American diplomatic strains. As the Korean War eased, so the British became less and less sympathetic to the American desire to minimize East–West trade. Then there were the continuing problems with Washington over sterling convertibility, Imperial Preference and tariffs. The disunity of the Americans themselves over questions of trade liberalization did not necessarily help. Eisenhower as president battled against protectionists in Congress with only limited success. If the United States from 1956 became Britain's largest export market, the latter's dollar deficit still seemed as insoluble as ever. In the view of the British Treasury sterling convertibility, if accepted, would be feasible only with a floating pound. This was an anathema to the Americans. Britain's economic problems added to the sensitivity of her leaders, and to the conviction that the Americans were trying to undermine the British Empire just as they had destroyed that of the Dutch in Indonesia in the late 1940s.[41]

Of most importance, however, was the question of the conduct of the Cold War. The British wished to moderate and control East–West tensions: the Americans were more interested in success against communism. The death of Stalin early in 1953 was promptly seized upon by Churchill as an opportunity to test out the thinking of the new Soviet leadership. He urged Washington to act. The new men in the Kremlin might be unsure of themselves and their thinking open to outside suggestions. He also feared some new Soviet initiative on the future of Germany. The USSR must not be given the chance to persuade Germans that it had more to offer than the West on the subject of unification and neutralization. But Churchill's enthusiasm for a summit meeting was not yet fully shared by the Foreign Office and cabinet colleagues.[42] Much was made of the argument that the West should first reach agreement on the rearmament of West Germany and its integration into the Western alliance before overtures were made to Moscow.

Churchill, however, was 'an old man in a hurry'. At the Bermuda meeting with Eisenhower in December 1953 he tried to woo the president with a promise that, if the communists broke the cease-fire in Korea, Britain would agree to the use of nuclear weapons against military targets. He linked this with an impassioned plea for serious overtures to the USSR. Communism in the USSR might gradually be tamed by prosperity and the infiltration of Western ideas and trade. To this Eisenhower brusquely retorted that the USSR was 'a woman of the streets'. There was 'the same old girl' under the dress, whether new or patched, and despite a 'bath, perfume or lace'. The president noted in his diary that Churchill was preoccupied with the 'completely fatuous' dream of sitting on an 'Olympian platform' in relation to the rest of the world. Comments on Churchill by some in London at this time were no more flattering.[43]

At the start of his administration Eisenhower and his colleagues gave serious thought to ways in which the United States might be able to gain advantages in the Cold War. The president himself ordered studies of the feasibility of tougher policies than had been been pursued under Truman against the Soviet bloc. Under Operation Solarium three policy options were analysed. Two of these were variants on more aggressive strategies while the third was based on America's current management of the Cold War. In public hardline rhetoric also seemed appropriate at a time when McCarthy and his communist witch-hunt were riding high.

But there was another very important influence on policy. The deep interest in cuts in US government spending ensured that means as well as ends would drive policy. Eisenhower himself feared that a permanently mobilized nation must in time change its way of life for the worse. Thus from the start he was temperamentally disposed to look not only at strategies which promised to save money but also at those which offered at least some hope (if not of winning the Cold War) of making gains at the expense of the USSR.

Detailed studies, however, tended to produce cautious conclusions. As early as the autumn of 1953 the US National Security Council was coming to accept that the situation in Eastern Europe was unlikely to change in the foreseeable future. It could be transformed only by a Western victory in a Third World War or by a voluntary Soviet withdrawal. It was not long before the administration in practice became less dogmatic and less impulsive than its public rhetoric and even its diplomacy suggested. In 1953–54, however, it was often difficult for the British to evaluate just what risks the Eisenhower administration was prepared to run. It was easy for them to feel that they were struggling to restrain their ally from some madcap act.[44]

The secret deliberations of the Eisenhower administration show that allied (and especially British) advice and thinking received more attention than was realized at the time. As early as September 1953 Eisenhower was to be found ruminating, 'Abroad we and our intentions are suspect because we are known to be big and wealthy, and believed to be impulsive and truculent.' Allies could not be ignored. Others in Washington noted European charges that the Americans were obsessively and rigidly anti-communist. It was noted that allies were fearful both of the current American theme of 'liberation' and of a sudden lapse into at least some degree of isolationism. American foreign policy – allies believed – lacked the 'perspective' and 'confidence' of a great nation.[45] McCarthyism intensified the sense of unease. The famous British journalist and broadcaster, Alistair Cooke, recalled that at no time in his many years in the United States did he receive such a 'blizzard of disgusted mail' from the old country.[46]

On 12 May 1953 the American embassy reported with some concern that Churchill, in a wide-ranging speech on foreign affairs, had neglected to make the customary references to the Anglo-American alliance. Instead he had referred to the 'widespread disappointment and apprehension which now exists among the British with respect to the policies of the new United States administration'.[47] The following year there was even greater alarm in Britain. It seemed possible that American impulsiveness or ambition might ignite a powder train from the Far East to Europe and accidentally precipitate the Third World War. This fear was at its height in the spring and summer of 1954.

To the dismay of key figures in Washington, morale in France was crumbling under the strain of the colonial and anti-communist struggle in Indo-China. Massive American economic aid had failed to strengthen the French position. Influential groups in Washington began to urge yet more American involvement. They argued that a communist victory in northern Indo-China would help to relieve the economic problems of communist China (long-term Chinese weakness being an important assumption in American policy). Other areas (or 'dominoes') in South-East Asia would fall to communism, thereby adding to the credibility of the claims of communists that history was on their side. Even countries such as Indonesia, India and Japan, though they might not succumb to communism, could fall under the red shadow. Admiral Radford, chairman of the US Joint Chiefs of Staff, urged the use of American air (and nuclear) power to relieve the French force facing defeat at Dien Bien Phu.

Such militant talk was highly worrying to the British despite their own fears of communist expansion in South-East Asia. Contingency plans indeed were drawn up to intervene if necessary in southern Thailand to guarantee the security of Malaya. Nor were defensive measures in conjunction with the United States entirely ruled out, but the British Chiefs of Staff believed that in the worst eventuality they could hold the Kra Isthmus (to the north of Malaya) against the Chinese. Thus, although the British hoped that not all of Indo-China would fall to the communists, the scenario which haunted the government in London throughout the spring and summer of 1954 was of some reckless American action which might bring disaster throughout Eurasia. Already in October 1953 the British defence chiefs had warned that in a world war they expected the main and first Soviet nuclear assault to be directed against the British Isles. This would be a knock-out blow.[48]

Churchill commented that the 'British people would not easily be influenced by what happened in the distant jungles of South-East Asia; but they did know that there was a *powerful American base in East*

Anglia and that war with China, who would invoke the Sino-Russian Pact, might mean an assault by hydrogen bombs on these islands'.[49] From the spring of 1954 the British resisted all American proposals which threatened to intensify the conflict in Indo-China. The French, for their part, were interested only in American help to achieve some honourable compromise in Indo-China, whereas the militants in Washington were looking for combined military action to inflict a decisive defeat on the communists. Fortunately for the British opinion in the United States was far from united. The army chief of staff warned that naval and air action alone would not achieve Radford's objectives, while the troops which were needed to fight a land war were just not available. Radford himself early in March dropped his ideas for a 'quick fix'.

Disunity in Congress also compelled the administration to look for allies if it was to risk military involvement. This strengthened Eden's hand as he argued that the diplomatic options should be exhausted before attention turned to a possible defensive alliance to protect Western interests in South-East Asia. Dulles professed to be disgusted by such defeatism. Certainly he was determined to dissociate the United States from any settlement which made concessions to the communists. But, as James Cable and others have pointed out, it was often difficult to assess the seriousness of his more vehement statements, and how far they were made to test reactions and influence opinion at home and abroad. As it was, Eden was perhaps helped at the ensuing East–West negotiations by Soviet uncertainty and worries over American intentions, not least because of their awareness of the continuing nuclear superiority of the United States.[50]

Many, though not all scholars, have praised Eden's diplomacy at the conference which met in Geneva in April 1954 to discuss Far Eastern and especially South-East Asian questions. James Cable claims that without 'persistent British efforts the Geneva Conference would never have been held, allowed to continue, or permitted to end in even the limited measure of agreement actually achieved' over the future of Indo-China. Despite the Soviet (and probably the Chinese) desire to avoid a major crisis in the Far East, much bridge-building was undoubtedly necessary between East and West. The actual negotiation of a settlement in Indo-China was also difficult and complex, and was not completed until July 1954.

The settlement was, of course, a fragile one, and began to crumble once it was seriously tested. But from the British point of view at least a breathing space had been secured. Churchill in the cabinet in August 1954 expressed the fear that the United States, conscious that it must soon lose its nuclear lead over the USSR, might be tempted in the interval to try to snatch what advantages it could in the Cold War. In so doing it might by accident precipitate a general war, one from which the United States might emerge victorious, but which would leave Britain and Europe a radioactive desert.[51] From such comments as these one might infer that the British were anxious to buy time until the Soviets acquired sufficient nuclear power to persuade Washington to become more cautious. Nor is it unreasonable to assume that given a sufficient respite they hoped that Britain's own nuclear force might become strong enough to act as a deterrent to a Soviet attack on the home islands. More nuclear weapons, properly shared out, might decrease the risk of global war.

BRITISH DIPLOMACY AND AMERICAN BRINKMANSHIP, 1954–55

The American archives suggest that even in 1954 the British would have been somewhat reassured had they been able to eavesdrop on some of the discussions which were taking place in Washington. Admittedly they would have heard complaints against themselves as appeasers and compromisers, especially from the American hardliners. But if Eisenhower and Dulles were frustrated and disappointed, they were also impressed by the divisions of opinion within the United States and among their allies on the subject of Indo-China. Eisenhower's comments to reporters on the outcome at Geneva may hint at more than a desire to present a brave face to the world. He admitted that the settlement was 'not what we would have liked to have had. But . . . if I have no better plan I am not going to criticise what they have done.'[52] Indeed some scholars suggest that Eisenhower, from the start of the 1954 crisis, had never allowed his judgement to be warped by an obsessive desire to strike a decisive blow against the Vietnamese communist forces. Eisenhower was determined to intervene only with the full support of both Congress and adequate allies. In any case he seemed reluctant to become engaged in a ground war – except possibly to retain the rich prize of Malaya and its rubber.[53]

On 24 June Dulles himself – within the secret confines of the American administration and at the height of Anglo-American differences at the Geneva conference – conceded that, in contrast to the unpopularity of the 'tough' American anti-communist policies in the

free world, 'the British "soft policy" was gaining prestige and acceptance both in Europe and in Asia'. He added that few of America's
allies would have supported military action in Indo-China, and he believed that since the United States could not run the free world by
itself a reappraisal of its policies was necessary to retain allied support.
A week later he not only informed the National Security Council of
'basic' Anglo-American differences, but also added that 'it was essential
the US take [these] into account in the future'. He emphasized that
Britain's weakness and vulnerability robbed that country of the options
which the United States still possessed in dealings with the USSR;
hence the British interest in peaceful co-existence.[54]

A change in Eisenhower's thinking on the USSR can perhaps be
traced back to the visit by Churchill and Eden at the end of June
1954. Initially he had been an unwilling host. He had reluctantly
agreed 'to let the old man come over'.[55] Yet his mood mellowed a
little during the actual meetings. He even showed some interest in
Churchill's desire to undertake a personal reconnaissance to Moscow
(in 1953 Eisenhower himself had expressed interest in East–West co-
operation over nuclear issues). Admittedly there were still major reservations, not least the fear that an East–West Summit might generate
unrealizable public expectations, and so weaken popular support for a
strong defence against communism. But perhaps the most immediate
cause of the frustration of Churchill's hopes was a Soviet note of 24
July 1954 which was interpreted as presaging a new Soviet offensive
against the EDC.[56] Certainly some key figures in Washington continued to engage in quite open-minded discussion of American relations
both with allies and to some extent with the USSR.

Thus the closing months of 1954 found the US Joint Chiefs of Staff
arguing (exactly on the lines feared by the British) 'that the timely
achievement of the broad objective of U.S. security policy cannot be
brought about if the United States is required to defer to the counsel
of the most cautious among our Allies'. Admiral Radford on 24 November 1954 cited Indo-China as an example of European obstructionism and criticism. In contrast the US secretary of defense (Charles
E. Wilson) spoke out strongly in defence of the British. They had not
been timid. They had just not been prepared to support a lost cause.[57]
In December 1954 some members of the US National Security Council again pressed the case for a more dynamic foreign policy. Dulles
diplomatically expressed sympathy for their point of view only to warn
that such a strategy was unlikely to succeed unless the United States
expected to win a general war. Americans had to accept that the pursuit of more aggressive policies would 'almost certainly cause the disin-

tegration of the free world bloc'. This, he argued, would not be 'in the best interest of the United States'. Nato, he added, was still 'by all odds the greatest single US asset'.[58]

Indeed Dulles and George M. Humphrey, the secretary of the US Treasury, sometimes spoke in terms which were quite strikingly British in tone and content. To a plea from the military that the United States should engage in 'positive, dynamic and timely action' before the Soviets acquired 'atomic plenty',[59] Dulles replied that, short of preventive war which had already been ruled out by the administration, the Soviets were bound to develop a nuclear arsenal which sooner or later would threaten the United States with unacceptable levels of destruction. This was the 'heart of the problem' to which he could see no solution, or certainly no 'quick fix'. He stressed the constraints imposed on strategy by the American political and economic system, the weaknesses and attitudes of America's allies, and the solidity and invulnerability of the Soviet system in the face of anything short of general war. Humphrey backed up Dulles, not least because of his dread of excessive government spending. This argument was frequently used by Eisenhower given his fear that an arms race might ultimately lead to dictatorship at home, an American garrison state, and national bankruptcy or general war.

Dulles continued to develop the case for moderation in language that might almost have been scripted by the British. Nato was America's greatest asset. Excessive American militancy might put this at risk. Interestingly Dulles rated Middle Eastern oil in importance above South East Asia. The latter was a prestige objective save in so far as it was a stepping stone to Indonesia. The long-term prospects of the West were good. In time the Soviet bloc might begin to break up as nationalism reasserted itself among the satellite states. China, too, might pose problems to the USSR.[60] The Soviets were cautious and they preferred subversion to overt conflict. The parallel with Hitler was a false one.[61] There was much that the United States could do to counter communism in the Cold War. In the long run Dulles expected the superior economic strength of the United States to ensure its success against the USSR. Charles Wilson broadly agreed, while Humphrey spoke as if directly coached by the British (he also anticipated in striking fashion the language of Henry Kissinger in the early 1970s). He insisted that the United States would have to learn to live as other nations had lived for centuries – namely by co-existing with powerful rivals under the protection offered by the *balance of power*.

Although Eisenhower chose to sum up somewhere between Humphrey and the US Joint Chiefs, with each crisis being dealt with in the light of the prevailing circumstances, he agreed that if constructive talks with the USSR seemed possible at any time, it would be wrong to disappoint public hopes of some relaxation of the Cold War. On the other hand the United States should not write off in advance certain parts of Asia to communism without examining what might or might not be done.[62]

Yet even as these deliberations were going on in Washington, a new Sino-American crisis had developed in the Far East. The tiny islands of Quemoy and Matsu just off the coast of China were still in the possession of the Chinese Nationalists. Incidents there in 1954–55 led to renewed British fears of a war between communist China and the United States. As it happened both Washington and Beijing were learning some of the skills of crisis management (as well as 'brinkmanship'), although a biographer of Eisenhower writes that the United States 'came closer to using atomic weapons' in this crisis than at any other time in his presidency.[63] This episode demonstrated just how meaningless the special relationship could be. The British could only watch and hope, yet at the same time they provoked some American complaints that their instinctive reaction in an emergency was to look for a compromise. Even British participation in the new South East Asian Treaty Organization (SEATO), formed in September 1954, did not do much to reassure Washington.

Some aspects of American Far Eastern policy were thus object lessons in how little influence the British might have over their own fate. These scares helped to strengthen the case of those who argued that without nuclear weapons Britain had no hope of exerting sufficient influence in Washington. The interest of the British Chiefs of Staff in such arms was also increased by the seemingly prohibitive cost of adequate conventional forces – even with allies in Nato. As early as 1952 (the first British atomic test occurred in the same year) the defence planners produced a new and detailed analysis – the 'Global Strategy Paper'. They could now proceed in the knowledge that a small but growing number of nuclear weapons was becoming available to the British armed forces. It is true that the paper still gave considerable emphasis to conventional forces. These would be needed to control small incidents, to meet Britain's global commitments, and to buy time in an all-out conflict until the strategic nuclear forces of the West had crippled the USSR. Nor was it wise for the British to make precipitate and unilateral cuts to their conventional forces. The views of their allies had to be considered, while Britain's influence in Nato and in Washington depended upon the deployment of an appropriate mix of military units.

Certainly the initial American response to this British emphasis on nuclear weapons was unenthusiastic.[64] Already Washington knew that it was only a matter of time before the USSR was in a position to present a serious nuclear threat to the United States itself. Inevitably Americans began to look for ways to prevent a war in Europe from spreading to the American homeland. Part of the answer might lie in making the conventional defence of Europe more credible. But the British chief of the air staff, in particular, pressed for the steady implementation of the 'Global Strategy Paper'. Slessor believed that the new thinking met Britain's interests in both the short and long term. While the nuclear power of the Royal Air Force (RAF) would always be dwarfed by that of the United States, Britain needed to be able to strike at Soviet targets of prime importance to herself. As for the political importance of such a capability, this appeared to be of relevance in the short term mainly with respect to the possibility of American adventurism as long as the USSR could not strike effectively against the United States itself.[65] In the longer term, however, especially with the accumulation of thermo-nuclear weapons by both superpowers, the problem was likely to be one of nuclear stalemate. In such circumstances, the Americans, out of concern for their homeland, might falter in their commitment to Nato or look for ways to confine any war to Europe. In either case the American contribution to deterrence in Europe might be weakened. Moscow, however, might still be influenced and restrained by even a small British thermo-nuclear arsenal.

Churchill himself was interested not only in this but also in the wider implications of nuclear developments in the 1950s. The approach of the thermo-nuclear era with all its startling political and military implications increased his anxiety to see a relaxation in East–West tensions. While he shared the fears that the Americans might be tempted to try to take advantage of their current but waning nuclear lead, he believed that in the longer term the prospects might improve. The sheer destructiveness of the H-bomb could force the rival power blocs to negotiate and seek ways to avoid general war. It was also important to demonstrate the ability of nuclear forces to ride out a surprise attack. He argued in the cabinet in July 1954 that the credibility of the Western deterrent would be enhanced by the multiplication of nuclear bases. Britain's force could make a contribution here. He also spoke eloquently in the House of Commons early in 1955 of the value of invulnerable thermo-nuclear systems to both East and West. With such capabilities neither side should have an incentive to strike first. Thus safety might prove 'the sturdy child of terror, and survival the twin brother of annihilation'.[66]

Meanwhile it was not long before Britain's nuclear armoury began to make an impression in the United States. Washington was becoming more interested in some forms of nuclear co-operation. In particular it wanted to ensure that British nuclear thinking, planning, targeting and developments as a whole evolved along lines which were compatible with and were harnessed as far as possible to fit in with its own requirements. The Americans were also becoming increasingly interested in the potential of tactical or battlefield nuclear weapons. Even Washington as early as 1952 was beginning to count the cost of Nato's current defence plans. Throughout the alliance the will was lacking to create conventional forces on the scale needed to balance those of the Eastern bloc. Under Eisenhower as president from January 1953 America's own efforts to reduce defence costs accelerated. Planners in Washington began to put increasing emphasis on nuclear weapons as a way of saving resources without reducing firepower – the 'bigger bang for a buck' philosophy. The RAF strongly supported the new approach. By the end of 1954 Nato, though with not a little reluctance, was agreeing to the new strategy.[67] America's allies really had no choice as they fell further and further behind schedule in the build-up of conventional forces on the Central Front in Germany.[68] Finally, because the British were so much further advanced than the French in nuclear matters, they naturally received more information from the Americans, thus reinforcing their preferential position compared with other allies.

Detailed study of the effects of the use of battlefield nuclear weapons (notably in the starkly named Nato exercise Carte Blanche of June 1955 which resulted in huge civilian 'casualties') brought no practical change to allied strategy.[69] On the other hand the British government was disturbed to find, early in 1955, that the credibility of the nuclear deterrent in Europe might be weakened as the Americans tried to spell out differing roles for tactical and strategic nuclear weapons in the defence of the West. The British argued that the Soviets should be given no reason to think that an East–West war could be confined to Central and Western Europe. They wished to discourage anything which gave the superpowers reason to think that their homelands could acquire sanctuary status. Distinctions between categories of nuclear weapons should therefore be discouraged.[70]

As a corollary to the undifferentiated nuclear deterrent, the British became increasingly insistent from 1954 that Nato's forces in Central Europe should be limited to a trip-wire role. Churchill favoured having just sufficient troops to make it impossible for the USSR to attack without the need to make such large preparations that its intention to start the Third World War would be self-evident. It would then be up to the American deterrent to avert war.[71] But even this modest trip-wire strategy was dependent on the continuing presence of significant American forces in Europe. Much as he desired to make cuts, Eisenhower in the end decided not to risk a general crisis in the Atlantic alliance by precipitate unilateral action. He argued that the Europeans still needed time to arm and to build up their self-confidence. Ironically the British soon saw this as an opportunity to cut their own forces. [72]

Eden on 25 March 1955 gave the British cabinet his assessment of the international scene. Time was of the essence, he insisted. The future conduct of Russians, Germans, French and Americans alike seemed unpredictable. At one extreme he feared communist adventurism in the Far East, and at the other a resurgence of isolationism among the American public once the Soviets had acquired a significant nuclear capability targeted on the United States. He now favoured the earliest possible East–West talks. As prime minister from April and with a general election to be fought, he now pressed arguments which he had so often criticized when urged by Churchill.[73]

Fortunately for the British government even Eisenhower and Dulles were beginning to accept the need for a summit, not least because they were anxious not to lose the propaganda initiative to the USSR. The decline of McCarthyism, moreover, meant that they had less to fear from the American right. In Europe the occupying powers were at last able to agree on a peace treaty with Austria. Above all the future of West Germany had been settled to the advantage of Nato. The West, it was believed, was now in a better position relative to the USSR than at almost any time since the start of the Cold War.[74]

Unfortunately the July summit of 1955 in Geneva, for all the media talk of a 'Thaw' in East–West relations, produced no lasting results. Over the next few years, it is true, both the Eden and Macmillan governments devoted much time and energy to schemes for partial demilitarization, disengagement, or confidence-building measures in the heart of Europe, schemes which were sometimes linked to the question of German reunification. The US National Security Council in March 1956, though not mentioning the British by name, clearly numbered them among those allies who were allergic to high-risk Western policies, and who were all too eager to listen to the sirens in the Kremlin and to their 'soft' initiatives. Despite anxious calculations as to how quickly the United States was becoming exposed to Soviet nuclear attack, the Council was clearly not at one with the British over what constituted intelligent and realistic negotiations with the USSR.[75]

Yet paradoxically in 1956 it was the British government which chose to embark upon a high-risk and impulsive policy once it believed that fundamental national interests were at stake. It was then the turn of the Americans to see themselves as the party whose imperative task it was to rescue a friend from the consequences of her own folly.

NOTES AND REFERENCES

1. R. Jenkins, *Truman*, Collins, 1986, p. 178.
2. R. Foot, *The Wrong War: American policy and the dimensions of the Korean conflict, 1950–53*, Cornell University Press, 1985, pp. 116–17.
3. For details see eg B. Pimlott, *The Political Diary of Hugh Dalton, 1945–60*, Jonathan Cape, 1987, pp. 494 ff. Dalton was told by Callaghan that many of the party doubted if Britain should be fighting in Korea. There were fears of US policy, of Britain becoming a US 'satellite', and the danger of being dragged into a bigger war.
4. *FRUS*, 1950, iii. 1699. 1951, iv. pt 1, 891–4.
5. *FRUS*, 1950, iii. 1699–1703; 1951, iv. pt 1, 894–9, 904–5.
6. G.H. Gallup, ed., *The Gallup International Public Opinion Polls: Great Britain 1937–75*, New York: Random House, 1976, i. 237–42, and see also p. 269. For the cabinet debates, see M.L. Dockrill, 'The Foreign Office, Anglo-American Relations and the Korean War, June 1950–June 1951', *International Affairs*, summer 1986, pp. 466–7. The role of Franks is explained by Boyle in Zametica, pp. 203–5. See also Lowe in Dockrill and Young, pp. 130 ff; B. Heuser, *Western 'Containment' Policies in the Cold War; the Yugoslav Case, 1948–53*, Routledge, 1989, p. 137.
7. Plowden, p. 110. See also Attlee to cabinet, 30 August 1951, British cabinet memoranda and papers, PRO, London (hereafter CAB), 129/47 CP(51) 239.
8. Lowe in Dockrill and Young, pp. 128–9.
9. *FRUS*, 1951, iv. pt 1, 943. See also 896, 904–5.
10. The debate in the Labour cabinet and party can be followed in Dalton's diary, see Pimlott, pp. 498–505; P. Williams, *The Diary of Hugh Gaitskell, 1945–56*, Jonathan Cape, 1983, p. 282; also pp. 226–38; Richard Crossman, *The Backbench Diaries*, Hamish Hamilton, and Jonathan Cape, 1980, pp. 47, 52–3, 70–1, 176, 186–7, 216–17, 338.
11. P. Williams, *Gaitskell Diary*, pp. 316–20; see also pp. 226–38. Note A. Cooke, *The Americans*, Bodley Head, 1979, p. 13, and C.L. Sulzberger, *A Long Row of Candles*, Macdonald, 1969, pp. 523–4, for examples of British fears, warnings and criticisms in the winter of 1950–1.
12. Duke, pp. 31–56; Clark and Wheeler, pp. 122–30, 153, and chapter 6 in general.

13. Duke, pp. 64–9. *FRUS*, 1951, i. 803 ff., especially pp. 876–77. Acheson described as unrepresentative those 'vicious' American groups which seemed bent on war with the USSR, ibid, p. 848.

14. CAB 129/47 CP(51)239.

15. See *FRUS*, 1951, i. 898–9 and iv. pt 1, pp. 980–9 for US preparations for his visit. P. Boyle in J.W. Young, ed., *The Foreign Policy of Churchill's Peacetime Administration, 1951–1955*, Leicester University Press, 1988, chapter 1, offers a useful discussion of Anglo-American relations under Churchill.

16. D. Dimbleby and D. Reynolds (*An Ocean Apart: the relationship between Britain and America in the twentieth century,* Hodder and Stoughton, *1988*) suggest (pp. 192–3) that the British interpretation that London would indeed be asked for approval was probably accepted by Washington, though only in private. See also Duke, pp. 78–81 and p. 85, who cites President Reagan in May 1983 to the effect that he supposed a 'sort of veto power' existed. But see David Gates, 'American Strategic Bases in Britain: The Agreements Governing Their Use', *Comparative Strategy*, 1989, pp. 108–12, who concludes that in the last resort there was no British veto, or even if there were, only physical control would be effective in a real emergency, pp. 108–12, 117–19.

17. See Duke passim, and Gates, pp. 99–123.

18. Duke, pp. 72, 95–6; Clark and Winter, pp. 146–52.

19. The British Chiefs of Staff (memo to the cabinet, 12 January 1951, CAB 129/44 CP(51) 16) had never taken so apocalyptic view as their American counterparts. See also C. Keeble, *Britain and the Soviet Union, 1917–89*, Macmillan, 1990, p. 235.

20. M. Gilbert, *Winston S. Churchill*, Heinemann, 1988, viii. 663.

21. *FRUS*, 1952–4. vi. pt 1, pp. 695 ff. Mountbatten was among those to query the wisdom of very close ties with the USA, M. Gilbert, *Winston S. Churchill*, Heinemann, 1988, viii. 672–3.

22. *FRUS*, 1951, iv. pt 1, pp. 980–9.

23. A. Horne, *Macmillan, 1894–1956*, Macmillan, 1988, p. 347.

24. Evelyn Shuckburgh, *Descent to Suez*, Weidenfeld and Nicolson, 1986, p. 32. *FRUS*, 1952–4, vi. pt 1, pp. 860–1, 865 ff.

25. See eg Gilbert, *Churchill*, viii. 658, 726; CAB 129/52 CP(52)172–3.

26. *FRUS*, 1952–4, ii, pt 1, pp. 89–110, 146, 153, 191.

27. *FRUS*, 1951, i. 243–4.

28. *FRUS*, 1950, iii. 1693.

29. See eg *FRUS*, 1951, v. 4–11, 21–3, 27–42, 114, 257 ff.; also George McGhee, *Envoy to the Middle World*, New York, Harper and Row, 1969, especially chapters 3, 6, 27, 30.

30. Donoughue, p. 510; D.S. McLellan, *Dean Acheson: the State Department Years*, New York: Dodd and Mead, 1976, p. 388. K.O. Morgan, *Labour in Power, 1945–51*, Oxford: Clarendon Press, 1984, pp. 468–71, describes US pressure as 'overwhelming'.

31. Louis, *British Empire in the Middle East*, p. 610.
32. McGhee, pp. xx, 114–59, 323–42, 390 ff.
33. Shuckburgh, p. 27. See also *FRUS*, 1951, v. 372 ff; 1952–4, vi. pt 1, pp. 714 ff. For the temporary Arab–American honeymoon see T.G. Fraser, *The USA and the Middle East since World War 2*, Macmillan, 1989, pp. 60 ff.
34. *FRUS*, 1952–4, pt 1, pp. 714, 737–8, 861. For the time being the impasse between the British and both Egypt and Iran was complete. For Middle Eastern defence see also D. Devereux in Deighton, chapter 13.
35. Foot, pp. 154–5; Gilbert, *Churchill*, viii. 704–5, 715–16.
36. Foot, especially pp. 155, 166–72, 177–9, 200 ff, 242. See also P. Lowe, in Young, *Churchill's Peacetime Administration* (chapter 8, and pp. 142, 224), who is more impressed than Foot by Eisenhower's respect for the views of his European allies. Note also *FRUS*, 1952–4, xv. 1016, National Security Council, 13 May 1953. Lowe in Dockrill and Young, pp. 138–45, deals with the final phases of the war. The British ambassador reported on 31 July 1953 that Dulles was the most pro-British of the new administration, but warned that he could easily be soured by British criticism.
37. Dobson, pp. 136, 145.
38. D.C. Watt, *Occasional Papers*, pp. 48–9; Lester Pearson, p. 187. Shuckburgh, pp. 56 ff.
39. Gilbert, *Churchill*, viii. 936
40. Shuckburgh, pp. 329–31.
41. Dobson, pp. 137–54. Eden and Shuckburgh both complained that the USA was trying to undermine Britain throughout the world. Shuckburgh feared the British would be driven back into their own island – 'where we shall starve', pp. 63, 71.
42. Churchill's summit quest several times caused major strains in the cabinet, but he was not always friendless, and for a time in the summer of 1954 he seemed to be making an impression on Eisenhower. See Young, *Churchill's Peacetime Administration*, chapter 2. D.C. Watt, *Occasional Papers*, pp. 48–51, discusses Churchill's thinking relating to the USSR and West Germany in 1953–4.
43. *FRUS*, 1952–4, v, pt 2, pp. 1758–61. Gilbert, *Churchill*, viii. 917–23.
44. *FRUS*, 1952–4, ii. pt 1, pp. 464 ff.
45. *FRUS*, 1952–4, ii. pt 1, pp. 461–2, 499.
46. Cooke, p. 13.
47. *FRUS*, 1952–4, vi. pt 1, pp. 985–7, 997–1001.
48. *The Times*, 2 January 1984 and 2 January 1985; Duke, p. 106.
49. *The Times*, 2 January 1985. Churchill spoke on these lines to Radford on 26 April 1954, *FRUS*, 1952–4, vi. pt 1, 1030–2.
50. See G. Warner in Young, *Churchill's Peacetime Administration*, chapter 9. Note also Shuckburgh, pp. 171 ff., 193, 198.
51. CAB 129/70 C(54) 263 and 271. See J. Cable, *The Geneva Conference of 1954*, Macmillan, 1986, p. 2, for his assessment of Eden at Geneva.

52. Cable, p. 114.
53. Note conclusions of G. Warner and Rosemary Foot in *International Affairs*, summer 1989, pp. 516–18 and 594–5.
54. *FRUS*, 1952–4, ii. pt 1, 694–5, 707; for Dulles's comments on 1 July 1954, see vi. pt 1, p. 1136. Eisenhower also commented that he had been able to discuss nuclear strategy with his visitors 'in a realistic way' (ii. pt 1, p. 707). Dulles later in the year indicated some convergence in Anglo–American thinking over the Middle East (ii. pt 1, pp. 835–6).
55. *FRUS*, 1952–4, vi, pt 1, p. 1064. 1952–4, ii, pt 1, pp. 697–8. See also Shuckburgh, pp. 219–23.
56. John Young, 'Churchill's bid for peace with Moscow, 1954', *History*, October 1988, pp. 425–48. And see Boyle in Young, *Churchill's Peacetime Administration*, chapter 2. Finally French rejection of the EDC in August 1954 left the West in no position for a summit at that time.
57. *FRUS*, 1952–4, ii, pt 1, pp. 786, 796.
58. For NSC deliberations in December 1954, see *FRUS*, 1952–4, ii. pt 1, pp. 834 ff. Dulles thought present security was 'pretty generally adequate, save, perhaps, in Asia and in the Middle East'. See also NSC draft statement of policy, 30 September 1953, ibid, pp. 498–9.
59. *FRUS*, 1952–4, ii. pt 1, pp. 828–9.
60. *FRUS*, 1952–4, ii. pt 1, pp. 267–8.
61. *FRUS*, 1952–4, ii. pt 1, pp. 834–5, 841–2.
62. *FRUS*, 1952–4, ii. pt l, pp. 833–44.
63. Ambrose, p. 231.
64. Clark and Wheeler, pp. 170–6 and chapter 7. They also question (pp. 178 ff.) if Britain contributed as much to the formulation of Eisenhower's 'New Look' nuclear strategy as is sometimes claimed. See also L. Freedman, *The Evolution of Nuclear Strategy*, Macmillan, 1981, pp. 80–1.
65. Duke, p. 103. M. Gowing, *Independence and Deterrence: Britain and Atomic Energy, 1945–52*, Macmillan, 1974, i. 441. Churchill's first visit to the USA persuaded him that Britain needed nuclear weapons to be influential in Washington. Clark and Winter, pp. 168–9.
66. See Gilbert, *Churchill*, viii. 959, 961, 967–8, 1019–23; CAB 129/70 C(54) 263 and 271, for Churchill's thinking, February–August 1954.
67. Many Western defence experts in 1953 were estimating that even with a rearmed West Germany Nato would still be dependent on the American deterrent. *FRUS*, 1952–4, ii. pt 1, pp. 498, 585–7. See also T.H. Etzold in Riste, pp. 285–314.
68. A.J.R. Groom, *British Thinking about Nuclear Weapons*, Frances Pinter, 1974, p. 68.
69. Park, p. 57.
70. Memo from the foreign and defence ministers to the cabinet, 5 April 1955, CAB 129/74 C(55)95.
71. *FRUS*, 1952–4, ii. pt 1, p. 219. M.S. Navias in Deighton, pp. 153–4; J.W. Young, *The Foreign Policy of Churchill's Peacetime Administration*, chapter 3.

72. Eisenhower to the US secretaries of defense and state, 3 November 1954, *FRUS*, 1952–4, v. pt 1, p. 533.
73. CAB 129/74 C(55)83, 25 March 1955. The imminence of a general election encouraged other British politicians to press Washington for a summit. Macmillan argued that without it the Tories could lose power. See *FRUS*, 1955–7, v. 161, 304.
74. *FRUS*, 1955–7, v. 147 ff., 221–3, 236–7, 247–52, 268–73.
75. For NSC reactions to the approach of an East–West nuclear stalemate, and its belief that the USA must both sustain its military strength and convince allies of its serious desire for realistic East–West talks, see NSC, reel 4, NSC 5602/1, 15/3/56; reel 5, NSC Actions, 1510, 26/1/56.

CHAPTER FOUR
From Suez to Polaris

COMPETITION AND CO-OPERATION IN THE
MIDDLE EAST, 1953–55

In all the postwar crises in Anglo-American relations, none was so emotive or humiliating to the British as Suez. Yet, however serious the crisis seemed at the time, and for all the interest which it has subsequently generated, it was essentially a passing thunderstorm. Admittedly nerves were strained to breaking point and great passions aroused, yet what mattered in the longer run was the extent to which it caused the British to decide to draw even closer to the United States. Admittedly not all was forgotten or forgiven. There were some who could never bring themselves to attempt to take a dispassionate look at the reasons why American policy-makers (and above all Eisenhower) should have acted as they did. Yet most of the key figures in government concluded that they had no choice but to try to work even more closely with the United States, whatever their feelings on the subject of Suez.

What emerges from a study of the decade as a whole is the degree to which the British and Americans were able to co-operate in the Middle East despite many major differences of opinion and the cases of outright suspicion and competition which marred the relationship. At worst they could often act in parallel. Much of the mutual exasperation arose from disagreement over the appropriate routes to similar goals. Nor was the situation helped by the existence of divided views in Washington. These were important even in the run-up to Suez. It is thus possible to see why, although the Suez affair brought about so dramatic a collision between the two governments, the damage in practice was not lasting. It was the prelude to a period of closer co-operation in the Middle East which began to break up only in the later 1960s when the British government decided to retreat from most of its 'East of Suez' commitments. This time it was the turn of the Americans to experience feelings of profound dismay and disappointment.

That the Americans were often pushy, insensitive and inconsistent in their Middle Eastern policies is not in dispute. The British complained of arrogance and aggressive self-seeking. But they themselves could be self-centred, and often ignored or misunderstood well-meant advice. In particular it is important to appreciate that while the Americans frequently accused the British of old-fashioned colonialism, this did not necessarily mean that the spokesman or writer was wholly ignorant of the evolution of British imperial policies since Queen Victoria. Nuances were obscured by the use of shorthand. Indeed a precipitate British withdrawal was the last thing Washington wanted. Such an event would saddle the United States with new and expensive commitments. It was far better that Britain should remain primarily responsible for the defence of the region, and that the two powers should have working understandings where necessary – provided the Americans avoided guilt by association with 'colonialism' in the minds of the Arabs.[1]

The confusion over Anglo-American relations has been compounded by some influential Americans, including Richard Nixon and Henry Kissinger, who subsequently argued that the United States should have backed the British over Suez in 1956. These remarks were largely the product of hindsight and of their experiences in office from 1969. The reasons why the Eisenhower administration acted as it did in 1956 remain potent, especially when examined without the advantages of hindsight.[2]

The Republicans on taking office in January 1953 warned London that they were not prepared to 'gang up' with the British against Egypt. But a few months later, a US State Department official, in commenting on the tension in Anglo-American relations, reminded the US National Security Council that the British forces at Suez were the only effective Western fighting force in the Middle East.

> Accordingly we would have to play along with the British for the time
> being, and take the beating which inevitably results through our
> association with an ally whom the Egyptians and other Arab states hated
> as imperialists.[3]

Early in 1953 Britain and Egypt were still deadlocked over the future of the Suez base, while no settlement seemed in prospect to the dispute with Iran over the nationalization of the Anglo-Iranian Oil Company. Eisenhower commented in June that the British were so incensed by this question that he felt they would prefer to lose the oil, even to the USSR, rather than admit defeat. The US secretary of the treasury agreed that there was no easy way to 'get round' Churchill without injury to Anglo-American relations: the British feared 'world-wide damage to their prestige if they appeared to yield'.[4]

At least a little more flexibility was beginning to emanate from the British Foreign Office over the question of the Suez base. The British Chiefs of Staff followed suit. But Churchill was adamant, and did not disguise his racial contempt for the Egyptians.[5] He was unimpressed by suggestions that it would be sufficient if Britain could reactivate the base in certain emergencies. He was slow to recognize the extent to which the Suez garrison had become an expensive liability. To be of value in war it required Egyptian co-operation. In any case the vast base was vulnerable to nuclear attack. In the end even Churchill (though with much ill-grace) had to bow to the force of these arguments. With American diplomatic assistance a new agreement was slowly thrashed out with Egypt. The treaty of October 1954 included temporary provision for British re-use of the base in an East–West crisis. On this issue – it should be noted – it had been Churchill rather than Eden who had been tempted to proceed independently of the United States.

Nor had American diplomatic assistance been offered in a way that soothed British feelings. Washington tried to avoid any public impression of 'collusion' or any suggestion that Britain was entitled to privileged treatment. Eisenhower feared both American identification with British 'colonialism' and the use that Britain would make of any incautious American expressions of support. In any case the US State Department was not entirely sure of Britain's military value in the region. It doubted if the British could hold even the line of the Suez canal against a Soviet attack, while their own conduct and historical record might jeopardize the position behind them. The Americans were therefore busily looking for regional allies. But until these were secured and a new defence structure created, they had perforce to rely on the British. Consequently at a US National Security Council meeting of 9 July 1953, although note was taken of a report which recommended 'greater independence and greater responsibility in the area by the United States vis-à-vis Britain', it was still thought necessary to add an important rider:

> Capitalize on such elements of strength as remain to the British in the area by such support of United Kingdom positions as may be consistent with U.S. principles and policy objectives.[6]

Meanwhile some convergence had also developed in British and American interests in Iran in the course of 1953–54. On the American side the decisive development had been the loss of confidence in the radical regime of Mohammed Mussadeq as the best defence of Iran against communism. The political situation was becoming more volatile, and Dulles feared that there would be easy pickings for the communists if Tehran drifted into a state of political chaos. The administration also took note of the fears of American oil companies that their interests might suffer elsewhere in the Middle East as a result of the nationalization of the British company. The CIA (with some assistance from British intelligence and perhaps the Anglo-Iranian Oil Company itself) was poised to act against Mussadeq. The American armed services were considering how they might react to an appeal for assistance from an anti-communist government in Tehran, or how they should respond to a coup by elements which had the backing of Moscow.[7] American contacts with sections of the Iranian military multiplied as the political situation became increasingly unstable. This conspiracy, despite some initial setbacks, finally overthrew Mussadeq and his allies.

The new military regime was prepared to compromise on the oil dispute. Agreement was reached in October 1954, though, as the British had always feared, at a significant cost to themselves. They received only a 40 per cent stake in a new international oil consortium to handle Iranian oil (although there were other compensations). The United States was now the leading foreign oil power in the Middle East. Eisenhower was delighted by the outcome. If the Shah and the British showed good sense, he remarked, 'we may really give a serious defeat to Russian intentions and plans in that area'.[8] The British (and especially Eden) viewed the outcome with mixed feelings, and brooded over this and other examples of American expansionism. But at least the stalemate had been been broken. A 'common front' with the United States on some issues had its attractions, as is indicated by British disappointment when Washington declined to join the Baghdad Pact with Iraq, Iran and other Middle Eastern states in 1955.

In general, however, the British remained more conscious of American criticism than support in the Middle East. In any case each country at times preferred or was tempted to act independently of the other. Ideally the British wanted the Americans to be on call in reserve, not edging themselves into the premier position. Eden himself became more emotional, first as he waited for Churchill to stop teasing and bow out of Number 10 Downing Street, and later as his own premiership became increasingly plagued with problems at home and abroad. He was to be heard complaining in 1954 that the Americans wanted to run the world.[9] The Americans had already displaced the British in Saudi-Arabia and were now a major force in Iran. It is true that even as he complained and tried to protect the British position, so he could sometimes admit to the desirability of American support. He shared the disappointment when the United States did not join the Baghdad Pact in 1955. But on the whole he was less willing than his first foreign secretary, Harold Macmillan, to accept the importance of a 'common front' with the Americans on key Middle Eastern issues. Thus Eden remarked in October 1955 that, while American aid was desirable, Britain should not be inhibited by the lack of it. Macmillan and the Foreign Office thought differently.[10]

The difficulties of co-operation were well illustrated by the efforts to create a 'Northern Tier' and the Baghdad Pact. Both Washington and London were interested in the formation of a barrier to Soviet expansion in the Middle East, but it was more difficult to agree on the details. Joint studies in 1953 did produce agreement that the Zagros mountains (in Iran) provided the best line of defence given appropriate support on the flanks from Iraq to Pakistan. But Washington soon displayed more political sensitivity than London, especially with regard to the role of Iraq. Unfortunately for the West any move which seemed to strengthen that country created problems with its rival, Egypt. Indeed Washington was afraid on other counts that what might look attractive in theory might prove counter-productive in practice. Overt action had to be carefully considered in a region where, if the USSR were provoked, American power might be an inadequate deterrent to Soviet intervention. By the end of 1955, however, British and American hopes were growing that nuclear air strikes (or the threat thereof) might give some credibility to Western military strategy.[11]

The British were also prepared to take risks on their own. As Macmillan later conceded, they decided to take the gamble early in 1955 of concluding a new alliance with Iraq under the umbrella of the emerging Baghdad Pact. They hoped to retain the use of two key air bases in Iraq without – in the process – offering too many hostages to the radical Iraqi nationalists who were determined to break the British connection. Indeed Eden frankly conceded in the British cabinet on

14 March that the pact would cause annoyance in Cairo, and that the Americans were likely to stand aside.[12] This did not prevent subsequent British complaints that they had been let down by Washington.[13]

Nevertheless there were some encouraging signs. In October 1955 Macmillan noted Dulles's concern over increasing Soviet activity in the Middle East. The US secretary of state even asked if – in a crisis – Britain would reoccupy Egypt. Dulles, however, quickly backed off when Macmillan raised the question of actual Anglo-American pressure against Nasser, the charismatic Egyptian leader. Macmillan himself noted that Britain could do little by herself, but was encouraged by the general tenor of Dulles's remarks. The secretary of state even argued that the West had to demonstrate that '"Colonialism" was a fake charge', and underline the value of the British Empire, past and present, to the young nations of the world.[14]

For the time being Macmillan advised the cabinet that Britain should try to conciliate Egypt and persuade Washington to do the same. There followed a joint Anglo-American effort to outbid the Soviets for Nasser's favour (there had already been an Egyptian–Czech arms deal) by offering to help finance the ambitious Aswan high dam project. London and Washington even explored the possibility of Israeli territorial concessions to Egypt.[15] But at the same time the British greatly annoyed Washington by their abortive effort to draw Jordan into the Baghdad Pact in the winter of 1955–56 – an inept political move.

THE SUEZ CRISIS, 1956

It seemed, nevertheless, early in 1956 that Washington and London were drawing together in opposition to Nasser. Anti-Nasserite emotion was growing in Washington as the Egyptian leader went his own way. The Americans were now hoping to turn Saudi-Arabia into a contender for the leadership of the Arab world. By such means – so Eisenhower optimistically noted on 8 March 1956 – Egypt might become progressively isolated among the Arabs. With no ally in prospect except the USSR that country would soon 'join us in the search for a just and decent peace in that region'.[16] This was a disturbingly unrealistic assessment. Dulles and Admiral Radford later in the same month militantly argued for American intervention if Egypt –

equipped with Russian arms – were to attack Israel. Eisenhower, however, was persuaded by other advisers that there was no single or simple answer. Arms could be sent to aid a victim of aggression, Saudi-Arabia might be wooed, and the Arab world split away from Nasser. But he shuddered at the military and political repercussions throughout the Middle East of a Western bid to defeat or overthrow Nasser.[17]

In the spring of 1956 both London and Washington decided that all they could do for the moment was to allow the Aswan offer to 'wither on the vine'. Dulles also favoured American aid to members of the Baghdad Pact, though without American adherence. But the beginning of an Anglo-American dialogue was stopped short when the Egyptians suddenly pressed Dulles in July for an answer, yes or no, on the matter of financial aid for the dam. Dulles's 'no' was followed by Nasser's nationalization of the Suez Canal.[18] This provoked an almost universal howl of outrage in Britain. For Eden – and certain other key figures such as Macmillan (now chancellor of the exchequer) – this Egyptian coup was immediately seen as an opportunity to humiliate or better still to bring down Nasser. Military planning and preparations were begun, and as early as 5 August Eden was suggesting to Eisenhower that if Nasser could be compelled to 'disgorge his spoils' the 'secondary objective' – the collapse of his regime – might follow.[19]

Developments from August 1956 underline the extent to which any Anglo-American relationship in the Middle East was viewed by both governments as a 'conditional "alliance" of interests'.[20] In this instance the British wrongly persuaded themselves that the conditions extended to American benevolent neutrality if Britain chose to act independently of Washington. Admittedly the American signals were sometimes confusing, or sufficiently ambiguous for the British to read them selectively, especially those which continued to indicate deep American suspicion of Nasser. But it is clear that Eisenhower was not convinced that this was an opportune moment for any Western powers to risk a direct clash with Egypt even if his warnings to Eden to this effect were not perhaps sufficiently numerous.

Inevitably the approach of the presidential election contributed to the administration's desire to postpone a crisis (Dulles reminded Macmillan of this on 25 September). But Eisenhower was also powerfully influenced by international considerations. He had already received staff assessments of the difficulty of localizing any clash of arms. He feared the advantages which might fall to the USSR in the resultant confusion. He was deeply impressed by the degree to which Western Europe was dependent upon Arab oil. It was estimated that if the economy of Europe were to collapse 'the United States would be in a situation of which the difficulty could scarcely be exaggerated'.[21]

Furthermore Eisenhower and his staff were less disturbed than the US Joint Chiefs of Staff by the actual nationalization of the canal. The service chiefs favoured all military and political aid to Britain and France short of combat involvement. Eisenhower conceded that the West was suffering from 'the tyrannies of the weak', but in this instance he did not question the legality of the act of nationalization. Notwithstanding his own desire to deflate or remove Nasser, and his belief that Britain and France might with reason fear Nasser as a major long-term threat, this did not justify precipitate and premature action. Arab and world opinion could not be ignored, and especially not that in Saudi Arabia. Nasser must not be turned into a hero and gratuitously accorded the leading role in the Middle East. Eisenhower preferred to wait. Over time, he believed, economic pressure and Arab rivalries should interact to the advantage of the West. The British and French, he noted after the event, had hurt themselves 'immeasurably' by their action.[22]

As early as 31 July a presidential letter had bluntly warned the British prime minister that while 'initial military success might be easy . . . the eventual price might become far too heavy'. Eisenhower was also unmoved by the strongly anti-Nasserite and pro-British stance of several influential figures in Congress, notably Lyndon Johnson (a leading Democrat). Dulles, too, seemed more impressed than Eisenhower by the British arguments, and did not always hide his anti-Nasser bias. But the president warned Eden on 2 September that American opinion 'flatly' rejected the thought of force. It went on, 'I really do not see how a successful result could be achieved by forcible means.' While in talks with his own advisers the president did not necessarily rule out armed action at some later date, he vetoed a CIA plan to 'topple Nasser'.[23]

One pet scheme in Washington at this time was for an international board to supervise the running of the canal. The British replied that such a board must operate the canal, otherwise Egypt would be able to use the waterway as 'an instrument of national policy'. But Eisenhower and Dulles continued to work on the assumption that they could buy time with diplomacy, and with this object in view – especially in face to face meetings with the British – they were reluctant to lean too heavily on their ally. Meanwhile Macmillan and Eden (plus many ministers and much of the popular press) were insisting that for Britain it was a matter both of survival and of honour, a lethal compound. Macmillan noted on 1 August,

We *must* keep the Americans really frightened. They must not be allowed any illusion. Then they will help us to get what we want, without the necessity for force.[24]

Macmillan's personal meeting with Eisenhower in September is a classic example of how old friendships can have unfortunate consequences in diplomacy. 'His manner could not have been more cordial', recorded the president's visitor. 'It was just like talking to him in the old days in Algiers in Allied Force Headquarters.' Macmillan departed, convinced that he had persuaded the president that Britain's economy was too vulnerable to 'play it long', the tactic which Eisenhower clearly preferred. This was the meeting when, had Eisenhower been brutally frank or Macmillan less subjective, the course of events might have been altered. The British ambassador, who was present taking notes, was dismayed by the failure of both men to address themselves frankly and in detail to most of the key issues. Nor was he given an opportunity to present his own view of feeling in Washington when he returned to London.[25]

Macmillan himself confidently reported to Eden that Eisenhower favoured resistance against Nasser. The president had agreed that by some means or other Britain must gain a clear victory. This was a very different message from that which the British embassy in Washington had been delivering since August. Macmillan was reinforced in this view by expressions of sympathy from other leading Americans, and especially from influential figures in the Pentagon. Consequently, so he explained later in his memoirs, he anticipated only public protests from Washington. Behind the scenes there would be 'covert sympathy'. Even after the event Macmillan seemed unable to understand the reasons for Eisenhower's fundamental opposition to the use of force at that time. He over-simplified American reactions with his comment that they 'particularly resented the fact that we had acted on our own without American permission or concurrence.' The illusion persisted that the British might have succeeded if their diplomacy had been more sensitive and subtle, and if Macmillan himself had been more alive to the timing of the presidential election. But this was only a small part of the story.[26]

Once the Suez adventure began, and the Americans realized how totally they had been kept in the dark by London, an 'anti-British frenzy' developed in Washington. Eisenhower himself was dismayed and indignant when the Israeli attack on Egypt of 29 October was followed by the Anglo-French ultimatum (whose phraseology could not conceal its anti-Egyptian purpose) and as the determination to seize the canal by force became apparent. The several causes for his anger have been mentioned above, and one should not forget the concurrent crisis involving the USSR and Hungary. His protest that this was the worst kind of Victorian colonialism was short-hand for the conviction that the action had played into the hands of all the enemies of the West. It was they who would make full propagandist use of Suez as a blatant example of Western imperialism. Thus, when his secretary of the treasury ventured on one occasion to suggest that colonial rule was more efficient than the successor regimes in the newly independent states, the president brusquely retorted that it was his 'personal conviction that almost any one of the newborn states of the world would far rather embrace Communism or any other form of dictatorship than accept the political domination of another government even though that brought to each citizen a far higher standard of living'. But it is also noteworthy that once the Suez adventure had been stopped how anxiously, if in the greatest secrecy, the Eisenhower administration set about trying to reverse the damage which had been inflicted upon the Atlantic alliance and upon Britain.[27]

Eisenhower's feelings at the start of the Anglo-French action against Egypt were strikingly summed up in one notable outburst:

> I've just never seen great powers make such a complete *mess and botch* of things. . . . Of course there's just nobody, in a war, I'd rather have fighting alongside me than the British. . . . But – *this* thing! My God![28]

Other policy-makers were similarly torn between the desire to stop the crisis and to avoid a lasting rift with the British.[29] Dulles agreed that the United States must not be seen to aid colonialists. He noted on 1 November that in the future the United States would have to walk a tightrope between the newly independent states and the old colonial powers.

The administration lost no time in trying to regain the initiative for the United States. In the first place this meant action at the United Nations. The more the United States was seen to take the lead – especially at the UN – the better the prospect, so Eisenhower correctly calculated, of preventing yet more harshly worded motions in that forum. The United States on 2 November won a vote of 64 to 5 in support of its motion calling for a cease-fire. It was also determined, 'at all costs', to prevent the USSR from donning 'a mantle of world leadership through a false but convincing exhibition of concern for smaller nations'. Having grabbed the initiative, Washington brusquely rebuffed the USSR when, anxious to gain credit in the Middle East and to distract attention from its own armed intervention in Hungary, it proposed joint action with the USA against the Anglo-French operation. Eisenhower again gave vent to his feelings in private, threatening if necessary to hit the meddling Soviets 'with *everything* in the bucket'.[30]

Britain was subjected to formidable American economic pressure to bring about its withdrawal from the Suez canal. There was a moment when Eisenhower's eagerness to resume contact with Eden alarmed his colleagues and threatened to realign the United States prematurely with the British. But he then swung the other way, especially once he discovered that the appointment of a new British prime minister was a possibility. The inferences to be drawn from the exchanges so far identified between Washington and certain British ministers, however, hardly warrant the claim that American involvement in the Conservative party intrigues which led to Eden's replacement was 'somewhat analogous' to the Soviet role in the establishment of Janos Kadar in Hungary. Richard Lamb has more recently noted that once the terms of the British withdrawal from the canal had been agreed there was no further evidence of American involvement in Conservative party politics.[31] Perhaps there was no need. Finally, while Eisenhower indicated that he would be more co-operative with a new prime minister, many Conservatives had ample reasons of their own to try to make a fresh start.

Meanwhile the Americans continued to use their financial and oil leverage to force Britain to withdraw completely from the canal. In November Britain lost 15 per cent of her gold and dollar reserves. On the 28th Macmillan affirmed that Britain could avoid financial disaster only by regaining American goodwill. The cabinet bowed to American demands two days later. Scholars differ to some extent over the precise reasons why British ministers finally gave way. Although American economic pressure was probably the most important, the whole thrust of Eisenhower's policy was unmistakable. British ministers had to acquiesce if they wished to re-establish links with Washington. Furthermore the sheer intensity and persistence of American pressure on Britain hardly suggests that Eisenhower's policy would have been very different had there been no presidential election at the beginning of November.[32] At all times Eisenhower was guided by strong views as to what constituted the best interests of the United States and its allies – even if in pursuit of those ends he felt obliged to act so vigorously against Britain and France.[33]

THE RELATIONSHIP RESTORED, 1957–60

The American embassy in London reported on 23 November 1956 that 'anti-American feeling is at a very high pitch and yet is accompanied by the somewhat contradictory but nevertheless complacent assumption that the U.S. is bound to come to its senses and pick up the check'.[34] The US ambassador, who had marvelled at the readiness of the British to hazard so much in company with France (a nation which they were in the habit of disparaging), now saw that this had been no more than a passing flirtation. He was soon able to report that the British government was recovering from its 'kind of extreme retrogression to nineteenth-century attitudes'. Richard Crossman, a Labour Member of Parliament, also noted the determination of the 'liberal' establishment by the end of 1956 to rebuild relations with the United States 'without whom we could not survive', a conclusion with which he reluctantly concurred.[35]

At the same time the British leaders, although they soon realized just how much they would have to concede in order to regain American confidence and backing, were largely unshaken in their belief that in Middle Eastern affairs they were the true experts compared with the Americans.[36] At the turn of the year both the British Foreign Office and the cabinet even briefly considered the option of a closer association with the Western Europeans. But Macmillan (who became prime minister in January 1957) firmly decided that the special relationship could and should be rebuilt. He made a conscious choice to put transatlantic links above relations with Western Europe. His efforts to this end over the next three years were broadly approved by the British public. Doubts concerning American policy in any case were often offset by a higher regard for the Americans as a people. Thus, while those favourably disposed towards the United States government had fallen to around 52 per cent by October 1956 (just before the start of the Suez conflict) 64 per cent continued to think well of the 'American people'. There were plenty of favourable answers to the open-ended question 'What is your opinion of the United States?' in October 1958 (61 per cent) and February 1960 (66 per cent). Support dipped sharply to 51 per cent only when the Americans were held to be largely or in part to blame for the failure of the Paris Summit in May 1960.[37]

Good relations were re-established between Macmillan and Eisenhower at their meeting in Bermuda in March 1957. The Americans as well as the British were helping to bring this about. The US State

Department in its preparations for Bermuda reiterated the interesting claim that the two powers in combination, both in Europe and the Middle East, formed a 'more persuasive combination' than the United States alone.[38] Indeed the Americans soon found themselves moving yet closer to Britain, especially once they discovered that their own initiatives (not least their pressure on Israel) still left them at logger-heads with Egypt and the Arab radicals. Secretary Humphrey, for instance, spent time with Macmillan trying to find ways to protect Western oil companies from hostile action by Arab radicals.

The American government was also aware of the limitations of the recently proclaimed Eisenhower Doctrine (5 January 1957). This had asserted American interest in the Middle East and had given pledges of support to those states which felt threatened by communism. But such things were easier said than done. The Doctrine must be seen for what it was – a very political document which had been hastily cobbled together to try to fill the power vacuum caused by the Suez fiasco. It was also couched in language designed to satisfy or at least not to alarm a multitude of constituencies at home. Nevertheless it still had its American critics who asked what was really meant by the general references to aid programmes and to the use of American forces at the request of Middle Eastern states against 'overt aggression from any nation controlled by International Communism'.[39]

In practice the administration hoped the need for action would be diminished as a result of the bold tone of the Doctrine. Its main objectives were the creation of a pro-Western grouping centred on Saudi-Arabia, and the preservation of the stability of Lebanon, Jordan and Iraq. This suited the British, especially when pro-Egyptian groups appeared to pose a threat to Jordan in April 1957.[40] Secret contingency plans existed for intervention in Lebanon and Jordan if necessary, and a nervous watch was kept on communist activities in Syria. While the Americans had not entirely despaired of better relations with Nasser, they looked to the US 6th Fleet to remind possible trouble-makers of the power which the United States could immediately bring to bear against them in a crisis. The 6th Fleet had inherited the nineteenth and early twentieth century roles of the British navy in the Mediterranean. In addition Dulles was looking for ways to strengthen the Baghdad Pact. At one point he even went as far as to tell a group of American diplomats that he expected the United States to take over the 'primary role' which the British had hitherto held in the Middle East. Of recent British policy, Dulles privately remarked on 6 May 1957: 'It seems to us to have been characteristic of a nation which, realizing that it was weak, felt it had to act as though it was strong'.[41]

In practice there were so many calls on the United States throughout the world that Washington easily fell back into the habit of treating Britain as a modern 'Figaro' whose services could be called upon here, there and almost anywhere from Europe to South-East Asia. As a spokesman for the US State Department declared at an American chiefs of mission meeting in London in September 1957: 'The United States–United Kingdom relationship is at the core of the NATO alliance and is an important element in SEATO *and the Baghdad Pact.*' The existence of a 'special relationship' was again acknowledged, and this was done quite explicitly at the expense of France within Nato. As a result of Suez, 'tripartite consultation [with Britain and France] was quietly abandoned and replaced by bilateral consultation [with Britain] within the NATO framework'. The same document underlined British (and Commonwealth) usefulness in a vast segment of the world from Europe to the Far East.[42] Dulles on 12 December 1957 went as far as to describe France as 'a very weak partner indeed' and one which caused him a lot of anxiety.

Thus the very public display of Anglo-American unity at the meeting between Eisenhower and Macmillan in Washington in October 1957 was a true reflection of the state of relations as recorded in the US State Department and National Security Council files. While the Americans endeavoured to cultivate Arab support when and where they could, the British remained more reliable and useful partners, especially in the Persian Gulf. If preference was still given to diplomacy, force (alone or in co-operation with Britain) was not ruled out – especially in defence of oil supplies to Europe against any threat, Arab or Soviet.[43]

Towards the end of 1957 the London embassy put together a relatively encouraging report. The British, it was stated, had become more realistic as a result of the Suez setback, with Macmillan leading the push for better Anglo-American relations, especially in the Middle East. Britain still exercised 'considerable world influence'.[44] The restored relationship was soon put to the test in the summer of 1958 with the controversial British and American intervention in Jordan and Lebanon. Possibly the Americans exaggerated the supposed threat from Nasser and his supporters to those states. Certainly American Intelligence was unable to confirm the worst of the fears. Meanwhile some in London, apart from any particular worries of their own, appear to have seen this as an opportunity to mount a joint Anglo-American operation. This would demonstrate that the scars of Suez were fully healed and that the British decision to act against Nasser had been right all along. It was not, however, until the surprise overthrow of the pro-Western regime in Iraq on 14 July 1958 that Eisenhower decided to act. He concluded that a show of American strength in Lebanon gave the best promise of preventing a repetition elsewhere of the events in Baghdad. But at the same time the president refused to listen to the more ambitious suggestions emanating from London. The British were left to act on their own in Jordan, although Washington did persuade Israel to permit the British to overfly its territory. Both powers withdrew their forces from Jordan and Lebanon as quickly as possible.[45]

There has been no little debate over the wisdom and effects of these operations. Yet it seems clear that Eisenhower acted only when he was convinced that delay or vacillation might prove even more dangerous. Whether due to Anglo-American action or not, the Middle East became temporarily quieter than for some time. On the other hand British claims that the Americans had come to recognize the folly of their conduct in the Suez crisis depend as usual upon a simplistic interpretation of American policy from 1951, and ignore the fact that in 1958 the intruding powers were able to work with – not against – the grain of local politics. The British were also made uncomfortably aware of their dependence upon the Americans. Macmillan's dissatisfaction with the amount and certainty of American support was apparent in his complaint that policy in Washington had been 'fitful and uncertain'.[46]

Dulles at this time was also showing interest in the remnants of the European colonial empires in Africa. The policies of the metropolitan powers ranged from thoughts of withdrawal to the desperate efforts of the French to hold Algeria. Dulles did more than make the customary recommendations that the policies of the colonial powers keep abreast of local political aspirations. He argued that Europe needed Africa just as the east coast of America needed the west. Europe, with Africa, could 'develop into one of the greatest forces in the world'.[47] This could take place only if the two developed a good working relationship. His geopolitical (some would say his neo-imperialist) strategy similarly demanded the continuance of a strong British Commonwealth, especially given his doubts concerning the future of democracy as relatively backward peoples gained their independence.

Washington had to take account of the approach of a British general election – either in 1959 or 1960. Concern over the dangers of nuclear war – and over fall-out from nuclear tests – was adding to the strength of anti-American feeling among highly vocal sections of British opinion. The London embassy conjectured that Anglo-American relations might suffer if Labour returned to office.[48] But even under the Conservatives the Americans still found much to criticize. On the one hand the British were frequently too interested in East–West military disengagement in Germany, and on the other they showed too little interest in Western European integration. Dulles in January 1956 had bemoaned British 'coolness', arguing that integration was so important that it would justify 'some sacrifice of traditional US and UK interests to achieve it'. Greater British involvement was needed as a stabilizing influence to prevent a recurrence of historic Franco-German rivalries.[49] Consequently there was much disappointment in Washington when the European Community was established in 1957 without Britain, and when the latter went her own way as leader of the looser and less ambitious European Free Trade Area.

Anglo-American economic relations remained ambiguous. There were the first hints in the late 1950s of American balance of payments problems, and these strengthened the calls for higher tariffs. If the Americans could not agree among themselves as to the merits or otherwise of the Sterling Area, they were still troubled by the weakness of sterling, and by other evidence of the 'grave' economic problems which continued to plague their ally. Reports from London continued to promise 'jam tomorrow', but never 'jam today'.[50] Britain's economic dependence on the United States was again highlighted when a British cabinet dispute over government expenditure early in 1958 led to the resignation of the chancellor of the exchequer. To ease the fears of the money markets American help was sought – and given – to protect sterling. Meanwhile in the cabinet debate over spending cuts the chancellor's eye had inevitably fallen on defence.[51] His opponents predictably resorted to the traditional argument that it was 'debatable whether defence expenditure could be further reduced without engendering a lack of international confidence in this country as a friend and ally'. In fact the US Joint Chiefs were already describing the British as lamentably weak militarily.

From 1957 Macmillan and his cabinet tried to rectify this by drastic cuts to conventional forces as Britain's nuclear armoury expanded. The decision was not well received by those Americans who believed that their allies should concentrate on the provision of conventional forces. The British interpretation of Nato's 'trip-wire' strategy was already seen as disturbingly simplistic. Dulles had warned ministers in Paris on 11 December 1956 that Nato 'must have a measure of flexibility although our main reliance [about 90 per cent of cases] must be on atomic weapons in the event of a major attack'. At this time West German rearmament was only just beginning to gather momentum. The French were heavily engaged in Algeria. Britain's conventional forces in Germany thus remained of prime importance.[52]

Fortunately for the British these American worries were counterbalanced by the degree to which the two countries were being drawn closer together by nuclear and missile developments. The first generation of American nuclear missiles required bases in Europe. Early in 1957 Macmillan agreed to the stationing in Britain of 60 American Thor rockets. These were manned by British crews. While the Americans retained control of the warheads, the British in this instance enjoyed a definite power of veto over their use. Further deployments (with American crews) were not ruled out – though Washington did not in practice take up this option. On the other hand the British government declined to share information on its civil nuclear programme given the high (though misplaced) hopes which were then placed in its commercial potential.

The Soviet launch of the first satellite (Sputnik) later in the year caused consternation among many Americans. The launch suggested that the Russians must be in possession of effective inter-continental missiles. The Soviets had demonstrated unsuspected scientific and engineering skills. No comparable American rocket had yet been successfully tested. Eisenhower himself was less impressed. But the supposed 'missile gap' facilitated the revision of the McMahon Act in July 1958, the great legislative obstacle to significant Anglo–American nuclear interchanges since 1946. In practice Anglo–American co-operation had been increasing for some years, but this was now expanded. New American help included a nuclear submarine reactor and assistance with the Blue Streak missile programme. In return the Fylingdales radar installations in Yorkshire (in the North of England), completed in the early 1960s, greatly enhanced the American early warning network against Soviet attacks. In 1958 it seems that Eisenhower also hoped that his generosity in the nuclear field might encourage the British to transfer resources from their own programmes to a renewed conventional build-up. To American critics of his open-handedness he firmly replied that the British were 'true allies', but he was equally emphatic that he could see no reason for a French nuclear arsenal.[53]

Meanwhile there were those in the British government (notably Duncan Sandys, the minister of defence) who were convinced that a time might come when the United States, from fear of Soviet nuclear attack against itself, might hesitate in its support of Europe. The independent British capability must be retained.[54] The British successfully tested the H–bomb in May 1957, while Bomber Command was gradually acquiring aircraft which could strike at key Soviet cities. If critics, then and later, were able to point to many shaky assumptions and inconsistencies in British nuclear thinking, a personal adviser to Duncan Sandys subsequently argued that 'the unknowns were so great' that a number of options were essential to guard against the unexpected.[55] Successsive governments remained persuaded that an independent deterrent provided much more influence and security than could be obtained by spending the same money on extra conventional forces.[56] Although anti-nuclear protests were gathering strength in Britain at this time, the Labour front-bench in Parliament was strengthened by the switch of the charismatic Aneurin Bevan from unilateral nuclear disarmament to the view that the British bomb would enhance national influence in any disarmament talks. American fears of a possible Labour government after the next election lessened.[57]

In the autumn of 1958 there was another crisis involving the Chinese communists and the Nationalist outposts of Quemoy and Matsu, and consequently the United States. But the British, though fearful of serious escalation, had to draw what reassurance they could from their faith in Eisenhower's good sense.[58] Nor was Macmillan always happy with American responses during the renewed tension in Europe in 1958–59 as Khrushchev set deadlines and trumpeted warnings in his attempt to frighten the West into acceptance of a German peace treaty and a change in the status of West Berlin. Macmillan himself early in 1959 embarked on a reconnaissance to Moscow to appraise the mood and intentions of the Kremlin. At the same time he was urging the Americans to negotiate. In fact both Eisenhower and Dulles privately accepted the absurdity of a European war if all that was truly at stake was the status of East Germany and Berlin. But they could not ignore West German and French fears of Anglo-Saxon concessions, nor the possibility that one of Khrushchev's objectives was to foment divisions within the Western alliance.

Talk of a summit was not popular in Washington, but Soviet–American exchanges finally resulted in a decision to hold a four-power conference in Paris in May 1960. This became the summit that never was – ostensibly because of the dispute provoked by the American U-2 reconnaissance plane shot down over the USSR. It is possible, however, that Khrushchev had decided beforehand that the summit was not going to deliver what he required, and he therefore set out to wreck it or humiliate Eisenhower. Certainly he scored points at the expense of the Americans. Macmillan suspected that the Soviet leader was also under pressure from his own hardliners. He noted that Marshal Malinovsky adhered to Khrushchev like a leech in Paris.

NATIONAL INTERESTS AND PERSONAL
FRIENDSHIPS, 1961–63

The Berlin question remained in a state of suspense until after the American presidential election of 1960. The victor, John F. Kennedy, came from an Irish-Catholic family. Macmillan – worried by the age gap between himself and the young president – was careful not to take anything for granted. He meticulously prepared himself for his first meeting. Fortunately for him Kennedy had long been interested in British politics, and included Churchill among his heroes.[59] The two men, according to Arthur Schlesinger, 'found the same things funny and the same things serious' despite the generation gap. Averell Harriman, from his unique experience of Anglo-American relations over more than a generation, observed that while Roosevelt and Churchill had made the more far-reaching decisions, they were much less close than Macmillan and Kennedy.

Macmillan was quickly struck by the new president's habit of asking questions as a tool with which to develop policy. This gave him ample opportunities to put the British case. The president was anxious to expose the thinking of his own advisers to outside criticism and review. He was eager to listen to foreign – but not too foreign – opinion. British opportunities to pass on their views were enhanced when Sir David Ormsby-Gore (later Lord Harlech) became the British ambassador in Washington. He was a personal friend of the Kennedys. Admittedly their intimacy could have its dangers. Dean Rusk and others in Washington were not happy to find the British ambassador so often closeted with the president. Even so the president could do no more than test the reaction of the ambassador to some of the advice and conclusions of his own government machine. The opportunities of the British to make any impression were, as usual, largely dependent on the presence of others of like mind within the labyrinthine corridors of power in Washington.

Such divisions in fact provided Macmillan with exactly the sort of opening he required early in the Kennedy administration. American policy was in disarray over the appropriate response to the communist threat in the small South-East Asian state of Laos. Such contrasting figures as Averell Harriman and General MacArthur were among those to oppose direct American intervention in that country. Their case was strengthened by the fact that the support given by the Eisenhower administration to the militant anti-communists had succeeded only in intensifying the faction fighting in Laos. Kennedy was understandably wary and disposed to explore other options. The policy review was also encouraged by hints of a Soviet willingness to negotiate. The British were thus pushing against half-open doors when they recommended a compromise. Even so it was not until July 1962 that a precarious agreement was finally worked out between the factions in Laos, and one which was undone in due course by the intensifying conflict in Vietnam.[60]

Khrushchev re-opened the Berlin question in 1961. The Soviet sense of urgency was increased by the exodus of numerous East Germans by way of West Berlin to the Federal Republic. Unlike Eisenhower (who had argued in 1959, that if the Soviets really intended to make trouble they could be deterred only with the threat of nuclear war), Kennedy believed that Western diplomacy should be backed up by increased conventional forces on the continent. The British did not respond, partly because of their current involvement in the defence of Kuwait against an Iraqi threat. As it happened, though the tension continued for some time after the building of the Berlin Wall in August to stop the flight of East Germans to the West, the two sides had to settle for a stalemate. Furthermore, whatever Kennedy's disappointment over the lukewarm support from London, he was soon turning to Macmillan for advice and help on other questions.

Thus the Sino-Indian border disputes which led to a localized war in 1962 brought some joint Anglo-American action to try to deter China from further military action, and especially from air attacks on Indian cities. The British, it is true, thought the Americans were too eager to use the crisis to draw India closer to the West. This might do harm in dealings with a country which wished to remain non-aligned. Yet on balance in this case and many others the special relationship continued to operate.[61] As Kennedy's secretary of state, Dean Rusk (a man not usually given to sweeping statements) later commented: 'We can't break with Britain. We have to be able to discuss world problems with someone. . . . We and the British don't always agree. But we discuss.'[62]

Discussion, of course, could generate heat as well as light. Even strong Anglophiles could weary of British advice – it was so pervasive and often patronizing. Worse – as David Bruce, the US ambassador in London, asserted – the British were temperamentally predisposed to compromise, even at the expense of principle. They were jealous both of the United States and of the West German economic miracle, yet at the same time, 'joy through work' was not 'a British ideal' as it was in West Germany. Excessive domestic consumption and foreign commitments exacerbated the deep-rooted structural problems in the British economy. He thought its condition 'deeply disturbing'. Nevertheless, despite British reservations during the Berlin crisis of 1961, he believed that the Macmillan government – at the end of the day and despite the nation's moral and material weaknesses – would support American policy. There was, he believed, a large measure of 'informed self-interest' which maintained the 'solidarity . . . between the English-speaking peoples'.[63]

In October–November 1962 the world seemed on the brink of nuclear war when the United States suddenly discovered that the USSR was trying to position medium-range missiles in Cuba. The British ambassador in Washington was consulted on a number of occasions by Kennedy, and sat in on top-level sessions of the US National Security Council. Ormsby-Gore is credited with the suggestion that the American naval quarantine line around Cuba should be reduced from 800 to 500 miles to give approaching Soviet ships more time in which to react. On the other hand it is now accepted that Kennedy's lengthy telephone calls to Macmillan fell short of 'consultation' even if Macmillan's official biographer argues that they 'were certainly more than just "informative"'. A fair conclusion might be that Kennedy found it helpful – perhaps therapeutic – to talk to Ormsby-Gore and Macmillan whether or not they basically influenced his thinking. The president was still anxious to expose the recommendations of his own advisers to the reactions of others whose judgement he trusted.[64]

The British presence was much more persistent and important during the long negotiations which led up to the Partial Nuclear Test-Ban Treaty of 1963. The exchanges called for the utmost tact and patience. Given the strength of interested parties in Washington who strongly favoured unrestricted nuclear testing, there was always the danger that these would be strengthened if the British were too intrusive. The latter were again vulnerable to the charge that they were inveterate appeasers. Arthur Schlesinger, for instance, records one State Department complaint in January 1962: 'We can't let Macmillan practise this emotional blackmail on us.'[65] Although Kennedy himself was interested in some sort of test ban, there was at best in Washington a tendency to regard the issue as 'a bit of a sideshow'. No department was actively pressing for a treaty. Kennedy might thus have decided that the question was not worth pursuing had it not been for British persistence and Foreign Office assessments which suggested that the Soviets themselves hoped that an agreement of some kind might result. At least one American participant in the seemingly interminable East–West talks between 1958 and 1963 was impressed by the influence of the British over American policy despite 'their relative unimportance as a military force'.[66]

Doubtless progress would have been slower and might even have stalled entirely without the stark reminder of the implications of nuclear war provided by the Cuban missile crisis. Politicians were undoubtedly shaken by the experience, and felt the need to reassure world public opinion. It is true that even during the final talks in Moscow the American delegation had to keep a wary eye on those at home who argued against the surrender of the advantages which they expected the United States to derive from further tests above ground. In the end, however, the superpowers and Britain agreed by the treaty of August 1963 to conduct only underground tests in the future. Meanwhile Kennedy himself had strengthened hopes for a less hostile and competitive international environment with his American University speech of 10 June 1963, one which Khrushchev later described as 'the greatest speech by any American President since Roosevelt'.[67]

The most remarkable instance of British exploitation of the special relationship occurred in Nassau (18–21 December 1962) where Macmillan persuaded Kennedy to supply Britain with the Polaris missile. There had been American critics of Britain's pretensions to be an independent nuclear power in the time of Eisenhower. But in 1960 Britain's cancellation of her own costly and dubiously effective rocket project, Blue Streak, had been facilitated and offset by the American promise to supply the Skybolt stand-off missile. The weapon was still under development, but if successful it promised to extend the operational life of the British V-bombers. The aircraft would be able to launch the missiles at a considerable distance from well-defended targets. On the other hand this was also the year when the British government had reluctantly bowed to American pressure and agreed to the establishment of a base in the Holy Loch in the west of Scotland for American Polaris submarines. There was much protest from the anti-nuclear movements, and more unease because the Americans insisted on a base so near to a densely populated region with Glasgow at its heart. In the same year Eisenhower offered what Macmillan described as a 'gentlemen's agreement' or a 'half-promise' that Britain would be allowed to buy Polaris at a later date. Indeed, overall, a whole 'network of gentlemanly understandings' had been created.[68]

Yet only two years later these understandings were put at risk in one of the most serious trials experienced by the special relationship. What happened at the end of 1962 has been discussed at length by others.[69] In short, by 1962, the Americans were coming to regard Skybolt as expendable. But no one on either side of the Atlantic was eager to raise the question of the effect of American cancellation on

Britain. Doubtless there were some failures of understanding and communication – within as well as between the two administrations. US
secretary of defense McNamara's relations with his opposite number in
Britain were not good. Furthermore neither side fully grasped the
priorities, the political problems and the policy-making processes of
the other.[70] In addition there were those both in the State Department
and in the Pentagon who were determined to end Britain's special
nuclear status. For some it was an obstacle to better American relations
with West Germany and France. Interest was growing in the development of some sort of European multilateral nuclear force (MLF), albeit
one that was ultimately under American control. For others the main
objective was simply to restore central control of the nuclear armoury
of the West to the United States.

Washington could not but be uneasy when it heard the British (and
later the French) hinting (and sometimes stating more explicitly) that
their nuclear force might be used to trigger American use of nuclear
weapons in an East–West confrontation. In June 1962 Robert McNamara spoke frankly of the difficulties created for the United States by
'limited nuclear capacities operating independently'.[71] The British,
however, were determined to make the most of any argument or
'agreement' to protect their 'independent' deterrent, especially as Macmillan – quite apart from any strategic calculation – insisted that his
own political position and that of his government would be put at risk
if Britain were deprived of this great-power symbol.[72]

The Skybolt crisis of December 1962 has been described by some as
perhaps potentially more serious even than Suez, with the start of the
meeting in Nassau proving the 'angriest' of any Anglo-American postwar summit. Macmillan flew to meet Kennedy in the Bahamas determined not only to obtain Polaris but also to do so with safeguards for
its 'independent' use. His personal rapport with Kennedy was one
asset, but in addition, as on previous occasions, he could hope to play
on the contradictions in American policy, and exploit the fact that
Kennedy himself was by no means persuaded of the virtues of MLF.

The ideal American model of a strong Europe included Britain. Yet
too rigorous a pursuit of that objective might result not only in failure
but also in net losses to the United States. Macmillan worked on the
American fear that a crisis in Anglo-American relations might contrib-
ute to a Conservative defeat at the next election. A Labour government might then choose to sacrifice defence for welfare. It might even
drift towards a Scandinavian-style peripheral role in Nato as well as
distancing itself from the EEC. The message from the British, if coded,
was clear. Kennedy, according to Sorensen, took these warnings seri-

ously, especially the danger that a political crisis might jeopardize American hopes of British entry into the EEC.[73] In any case the Americans regarded the Nassau agreements as 'a monument of contrived ambiguity'.[74] The Polaris force was assigned to Nato: the British possessed the right in exceptional circumstances to use this weapon unilaterally in accordance with their own national needs. But the Americans might hope with some reason that these exceptional circumstances would never arise.

From the point of view of the British, Polaris had been secured at a knock-down price. The submarine force – over its whole lifetime – was often to absorb as little as 2 per cent of the defence budget, thus weakening the case of those who argued that Britain's conventional forces would have gained significantly from its cancellation. Furthermore Nassau met many of Macmillan's political needs. In terms of his own objectives it was a diplomatic coup – even if the 'independent' element was qualified in practice by the British desire to minimize the costs.

The Nassau agreement, however, did not silence those influential Americans who continued to believe that British policy and thus Anglo-American relations were in need of serious reappraisal. Dean Acheson had caused a storm in the British media with his suggestion that Britain's world role was just about played out. Although Washington promptly distanced itself from his speech, and publicized its own high valuation of relations with Britain, George Ball, deputy to the US secretary of state, privately noted that it was time the British gave up their 'not very healthy' illusions concerning the empire, the deterrent and the relationship with the United States.[75] Britain's position was further weakened early in 1963, when the French president, de Gaulle, vetoed the first British attempt to join the EEC, though George Ball later concluded that the veto would have been delivered sooner or later with or without Nassau. Close Anglo-American relations in general undoubtedly contributed to de Gaulle's decision, and Nassau doubtless influenced his timing.

Macmillan himself, when he had made his decision to seek entry to the EEC, had recorded his growing concern over attitudes in the United States. Britain, he wrote, was being treated 'now as just another country, now as an ally in a special and unique category'.[76] Nor could he ignore American enthusiasm for British membership of the EEC, in part to ensure a better balance among the states of Western Europe, but also in the hope that Britain would strengthen those in the Community who favoured more liberal and outward looking economic policies. Indeed de Gaulle would not have been in the least surprised had he known of Kennedy's assurance to Macmillan in April 1961 that Anglo-American relations would be strengthened by British entry.[77]

Opinion polls closely but not exactly mirrored the warmth of the personal relations between Kennedy and Macmillan. Polls in 1963 confirmed that in American eyes Britain was still the most dependable ally, but Gallup in July also recorded that West Germany (58 per cent) was now only 5 per cent behind Britain. Overall British backing for the relationship was apparently marginally less in 1963 (67 per cent) than in 1952, though when allowance has been made for differences in the questions asked it would seem that the proportion who were strongly pro-American had actually increased.[78]

The years 1961–63 were undoubtedly one of the peaks in the special relationship, and the successors of Kennedy and Macmillan in the 1960s failed to establish the same rapport. But as the next chapter will try to demonstrate, the feeling that the relationship had been seriously weakened – and perhaps even jeopardized – did not occur until the Americans became deeply involved in the Vietnam War and the British government decided to abandon the defence role East of Suez. There was no sense of a profound change until 1967–68.

NOTES AND REFERENCES

1. See, for instance, OSS/State Department: Intelligence and Research Reports: The Middle East, 1950–61, Microfilm Project of University Publications of America, Washington DC, 1977 (hereafter OSS/SD/ME), reel 1, no. 5980, The British position in the Middle East, 2 October 1952; and JCS/ME, part 2, 1946–53, reel 2, NSC Staff Study, 4 March 1952.

2. See Nixon in *The Times*, 28 January 1987, and *The Memoirs of Richard Nixon*, Sidgwick and Jackson, 1978, p. 179; also H.A. Kissinger, *International Affairs*, 1982, 'Reflections on a Partnership', pp. 583–4. Eisenhower's contemporary perceptions are in R. Griffith, ed., *Ike's Letters to a Friend, 1941–58*, University Press of Kansas, 1984, p. 190. For Nixon and Kissinger in the 1970s, see below chapter 6.

3. *FRUS*, 1952–4, ix. pt 2, pp. 2075–6, 20 May 1953. The British ambassador in Washington asked on 25 January 1954 if the USA was consciously trying to replace the British in the Middle East. W.R. Louis, 'Anti-Colonialism and the dissolution of the British Empire', *International Affairs*, summer, 1985, pp. 395–420.

4. *FRUS*, 1952–4, ii. pt 1, p. 439.

5. See Gilbert, *Churchill*, viii. 701–2, 719, 770, 800.

6. *FRUS*, 1952–4, ix, pt 1, pp. 394–5, 398, 401.

7. See JCS/ME, part 2, Middle East, reel 1, 0699–0777, for possible US military courses against Iran from 31 December 1952 to 6 October 1953. See R. Jeffreys-Jones for view that instability of Iranian politics put a question mark against Mussadeq, whatever the role of the CIA, p. 90.

8. S. Ambrose, *Eisenhower the President*, Allen and Unwin, 1984, pp. 109–30; Dimbleby, pp. 197, 200; Brian Holden Reid in Young, *Churchill's Peacetime Administration*, chapter 6.

9. E. Shuckburgh, *Descent to Suez: Diaries 1951–6*, Weidenfeld and Nicolson, 1986, p. 187.

10. Dimbleby, pp. 213–14. But note the Foreign Office view on 13 October 1955 on the need to co-operate with the USA: British oil needs were expected to treble in 20 years, with the volatile Middle East as the main supply source. CAB 129/78 CP(55) 152.

11. *FRUS*, 1952–4, ii. pt 1, pp. 835–6, provides evidence of Anglo-American fears of growing communist influence. OSS/SD/ME, reel 1, no. 7074, The Outlook for US Interests in the Middle East, 21 December 1955, indicates US interest in the Northern Tier, but underlines the lack of easy solutions. See also M.S. Navias in Deighton, pp. 150–1, W. Scott Lucas in Deighton, chapter 14.

12. Shuckburgh, pp. 298–9; CAB 129/74 C(55) 70.

13. See Reid in Young, *Churchill's Peacetime Administration*, chapter 6.

14. Horne, *Macmillan*, i. 369, 370, 373.

15. D. Carlton, *Britain and the Suez Crisis*, Oxford: Basil Blackwell, 1988, pp. 26–8. Eden was already showing signs of being prepared to act independently of the USA, though he preferred to co-opt the USA to support British interests (see Louis and Owen, pp. 103–4). Shuckburgh's diary is a very revealing source, not least because his own views were in a state of flux (see especially pp. 320–31, 350, 360 ff.) and he was becoming increasingly critical of British policy-makers.

16. Ambrose, p. 317.

17. Ambrose, pp. 317–18, 328–31. See also D. Neff, *Warriors at Suez*, New York: Linden Press, and Simon and Schuster, 1981, pp. 210–17.

18. Britain was not surprised by Dulles's decision.

19. Carlton, *Suez*, p. 126.

20. See W. Scott Lucas, 'Neustadt revisited: a new look at Suez and the Anglo-American "alliance"', in A.L. Gorst, W. Scott Lucas and L. Johnman, *Post-war Britain, 1945–1964*, London: Pinter Books, 1989, chapter 11, especially p. 186.

21. D. Reynolds, 'Eden the Diplomatist, 1931–56', *History*, February 1989, pp. 79–80. S.L. Spiegel, *The other Arab-Israeli conflict*, University of Chicago Press, 1985, p. 55 (for Eisenhower's diary entry of 13 March 1956). See also S. Adams, *First Hand Report*, Hutchinson, 1962, pp. 199–202.

22. Louis and Owen, p. 113; Neff, p. 287; Griffith, pp. 174–6.

23. Neff, pp. 287, 292–3, 301–2; Ambrose, pp. 330–3. Eisenhower's warning letters to Eden from 31 July 1956 are to be found in D.D. Eisenhower, *The White House Years, 1956–61*, Heinemann, 1966, pp. 664–71.

24. H. Macmillan, *Riding the Storm, 1956–59*, Macmillan, 1971, p. 106. See also Horne, *Macmillan*, i. 404–52; Ambrose, p. 334.
25. Horne, *Macmillan*, i. 420–1, 430–1.
26. Horne, *Macmillan*, i. 414, 420–5; Macmillan, *Riding the Storm*, pp. 134–5, 157. Amid the vast literature on British policy leading to the Suez intervention, see especially Adamthwaite in Dockrill and Young, chapter 10; Johnman in Gorst, chapter 10; Lucas in Gorst, chapter 11; and Carlton, *Britain and Suez*. On American policy see especially Ambrose, pp. 317–58; Bowie in Louis and Owen, chapter 10; Neff, passim. On Suez in general see Louis and Owen, passim.
27. Hughes, p. 217; Griffith, pp. 165, 174 ff.; Ambrose, pp. 377–8.
28. Hughes, p. 217, 30 October 1956. For other examples of Eisenhower's pro-British feelings see Neff, pp. 387, 396; and Griffith, pp. 175–6, for his comment (2 November 1956), 'Britain not only has been, but must be, our best friend in the world'. There is a reference in the same letter to his fear of Soviet gains.
29. Adams, pp. 212–15.
30. Ambrose, pp. 358–68.
31. Compare R. Lamb, *The Failure of the Eden Government*, Sidgwick and Jackson, 1987, pp. 299–300 with D. Carlton, *Eden*, pp. 456–61.
32. For the importance of American economic pressure on Britain throughout November 1956 see Kyle, Bowie and Kunz in Louis and Owen, pp. 129–30, chapters 10 and 11 respectively; Horne, *Macmillan*, i. 415–20; and D.R. Thorpe, *Selwyn Lloyd*, Jonathan Cape, 1989, pp. 251–2. Horne also stresses (pp. 440–5) the effect of American policy and attitudes as a whole on Macmillan. He detects a basic consistency in Macmillan's thinking throughout the crisis in that he always believed that Britain could not afford to separate herself significantly from the USA.
33. Ambrose, pp. 377–8. For US efforts at damage limitation see *FRUS*, 1955–7, iv. 107, 119. 133, 162.
34. Neff, p. 430.
35. Crossman, pp. 549–50; Neff, p. 430.
36. A. Horne, *Macmillan, 1957–86*, Macmillan, 1989, pp. 26–7.
37. Dimbleby, pp. 219–20. Horne, *Macmillan, 1957–86*, pp. 22–7. The polls are cited by Bruce M. Russett, *Community and Contention: Britain and America in the Twentieth Century*, Cambridge, Mass: MIT Press, 1963, pp. 128–43. See also below, note 78.
38. Dobson, p. 174. G. Wyn Rees (chapter 12 in Gorst, especially pp. 215–17) carefully explains the 'conditional' character of the Anglo-American alliance, especially outside Europe where neither wished to be tightly committed.
39. Crabb, p. 175.
40. See *Contemporary Record*, summer 1988, p 61.
41. *FRUS*, 1955–7, iv. 581–3.
42. *FRUS*, 1955–7, iv. 610.

43. *FRUS*, 1955–7, iv. 217, 610. See *Documents of the NSC, 1947–77*, for US worries over the advance of Arab radicals, and its consequent readiness to give full political and logisitic backing to the British in crisis betweenn Iraq and Kuwait in 1961; reel 4, NSC 5820/1, 4 November 1958; reel 5, NSC Action No. 2431, 29 June 1961. On the other hand, Anglo-American relations in the Middle East did not always correspond to the intentions expressed on paper in Washington. See, for instance, Bernard Burrows, *Footnotes in the Sand: the Gulf in Transition*, Michael Russell, 1991 (Burrows was Political Resident in the Gulf, 1953–58).

44. *FRUS*, 1955–7, iv. 615–17.

45. See Alan Dowty, *Middle East Crisis*, Berkeley: University of California Press, 1984, pp. 33–102, for a careful appraisal of US policy.

46. Horne, *Macmillan, 1957–86*, pp. 92–8.

47. *FRUS*, 1955–7, iv. 524.

48. Ibid, iv. 615–17, 638. Macmillan had been alarmed at the state of the British economy long before Suez. As chancellor of the exchequer he had pressed for defence economies, and British pleas for a radical review of Nato strategy had followed in the summer of 1956. *FRUS*, 1955–7, iv. 84–92. As prime minister Macmillan forced through drastic defence changes in 1957. Horne, *Macmillan, 1957–86*, pp. 45–51.

49. *FRUS*, 1955–7, iv. 183, 307–8, 399–400, 524, 586–7, 590–2, 605.

50. Dobson, pp. 161–4, 177–83.

51. See *The Times* of 2 January 1989 for a useful summary of newly released documentation.

52. *FRUS*, 1955–7, iv. 125–34, 152–4, 165–9, 592.

53. For the evolution of Anglo-American nuclear relations in 1957 see Wyn Rees in Gorst, chapter 12, and Horne, *Macmillan, 1957–86*, pp. 53, 56–7. For Eisenhower's thinking, see Ambrose, pp. 478–9.

54. *Observer*, 1 January 1989, and *The Times*, 2 January 1989. See also Duke, pp. 128–9.

55. *Contemporary Record*, winter 1988, p. 31, 'Defence Turning Point: the Sandys White Paper', report of a discussion chaired by L. Freedman.

56. Lord Carrington, *Reflect on Things Past*, Collins 1988, pp. 154–5, notes as defence spokesman in the Lords between 1959–63 that he could not say outright that Britain doubted if US protection would be forthcoming in all circumstances.

57. *FRUS*, 1955–7, iv. 616. Crossman, pp. 613–14, 633. 677–81. See also pp. 47, 52–3, 186–7, 385–97, 641–6, 659–62 for insights into earlier Labour debates.

58. Louis and Bull, pp. 315–17.

59. Horne, *Macmillan, 1957–86*, pp. 287–90. A. Dobson in 'The years of transition: Anglo-American relations 1961–67', *Review of International Studies*, July 1990, pp. 242–9, provides an excellent survey of the Anglo-American relations under Macmillan and Kennedy, including the contrary currents.

60. A. Schlesinger, *A Thousand Days*, Deutsch, 1965, pp. 299–304, 306–9, 449–53, notes that from the start of the Kennedy administration some, including the president, had reservations about existing US policy. Harriman led the US team in talks with the USSR, and was prepared to defy the diehards in Washington when necessary. See also R.B. Smith, *An International History of the Vietnam War, 1955–61*, Macmillan, pp. 244–51.

61. *The John F. Kennedy National Security Files: Western Europe, 1961–3*, Maryland University Publications of America, 1987 (hereafter JFK/NSC), reel 10, Kennedy to Macmillan, 13 May 1963; and Bundy to Zulueta, 17 May 1963.

62. Cited by N. Fisher, *Macmillan*, Weidenfeld and Nicolson, 1982, p. 303.

63. JFK/NSC, reel 9, Bruce to Rusk, no. 229, 17 July, 1961; see also embassy reports 15 July and 28 July 1961. Bruce advised US discretion over the resumption of nuclear testing at the time when Gaitskell was completing his victory over the unilateralists. The Conservatives were far from certain victors at the next election, and it was important that Labour should not fall into the hands of the anti-Americans. Bruce to Rusk, no. 3034, 16 February 1962.

64. Ambrose, p. 539: Louis and Bull, p. 100: Horne, *Macmillan, 1957–86*, pp. 362–85.

65. Schlesinger, p. 433.

66. Glenn T. Seaborg, *Kennedy, Khrushchev and the Test-Ban*, Berkeley: University of California Press, 1981, p. 113; Sorensen, pp. 558–9.

67. J.P.G. Freeman, *British Nuclear Arms Policy in the Context of Anglo-American Relations, 1957–68*, Macmillan, 1986, pp. 135–51; Horne, *Macmillan, 1957–86*, p. 525; Schlesinger, p. 826. Macmillan, by his own reckoning, thought it was his greatest achievement.

68. H. Macmillan, *Pointing the Way*, Macmillan, 1972, p. 255; Horne, *Macmillan, 1957–86*, pp. 275–7.

69. Horne, *Macmillan, 1957–86*, chapter 15. See also Freeman, pp. 161–73. P. Nailor, *The Nassau Connection: the organization and management of the British Polaris project*, London: HMSO, 1988, pp. 4–5, notes some Admiralty study of Polaris from July 1960, although 'unrelated perhaps to the preferences of the Naval Staff'. For the Holy Loch, see *The Times*, 1 January 1991.

70. S. Zuckerman, *Monkeys, Men and Missiles*, Collins, 1988, p. 258.

71. McNamara, despite assurances to the British that their force was not embraced by his remarks as it was not operating independently, had little time for independent deterrents. Kennedy in February 1962 had also spoken to Macmillan of his fear that the British force was encouraging France and even West Germany to take the same road (Schlesinger, p. 723).

72. Dimbleby, pp. 235 ff.

73. Sorensen, p. 566. Meanwhile both the US State Department and the CIA were evaluating the leaders of the Labour party, and the degree to which pro-American policies were likely to be followed. See JFK/NSC, reel 9, Rusk memo to JFK 7 July 1962 on visit by George Brown.

74. Zuckerman, pp. 258–9.
75. Dimbleby, pp. 238–9. See also US embassy, London, no. 1159, 10 September 1963, and no. 1206, 12 September 1963 (JFK/NSC, reel 10).
76. Macmillan, *Pointing the Way*, p. 324.
77. Washington was often critical of British strategy for entry to the EEC. Note JFK/NSC, reel 10, Ball to Kennedy, 10 December 1962. See also G.W. Ball, *The Past has another Pattern*, New York: W.W. Norton, 1982, pp. 209–21; Dobson, pp. 182–90.
78. *The Gallup Poll: public opinion, 1935–71*, New York: Random House, 1972, ii. 1266, 1464; iii. 1809–10; G.H. Gallup, *The Gallup International: Great Britain*, i. 269, 665, 673.

CHAPTER FIVE
The Weakening Relationship, 1963–69

THE UNITED STATES AND BRITAIN'S ECONOMIC PROBLEMS, 1963–66

The resignation of Macmillan and the assassination of John F. Kennedy followed each other in quick succession in 1963. But more than a change of personalities was complicating the American assessment of the relationship with the British at this time. There was the failure of Britain's bid to enter the EEC; there were yet more signs of the seemingly intractable weaknesses in the British economy; and finally there was the uncertainty occasioned by the need to hold a general election at some time in 1964. A return to office by Labour after thirteen years of Conservative rule was becoming a distinct possibility. Given Labour's stormy internal debates on foreign and defence issues since 1951 and despite the recent defeat of the unilateralists on nuclear disarmament, Washington was understandably anxious to gain some advance impressions of Labour's likely behaviour if it were returned to power. Shadow ministers who visited Washington thus found themselves at the centre of considerable attention, and were probed in detail on their thinking over a range of issues.[1]

Meanwhile presidential briefing papers prepared for a visit in February 1964 by Macmillan's successor (Sir Alec Douglas-Home) drew an interesting distinction between the American and British perceptions of the relationship. Whereas the '*close US-UK association* [was] the most important single factor in British foreign policy', for the

Americans it was sufficient to reassert the value of the 'association'. While this language might not have been chosen under Kennedy, the advisers of the new president, Lyndon Johnson, went on to cite specific grievances against Britain which would have arisen under any president. Britain's determination to trade with Castro's Cuba was a notable cause of complaint, the survival of his Marxist regime close to Florida causing particular affront to numerous Americans. Washington also contended that the grant of long-term credits to communist states in general was robbing the West of useful weapons with which it might hope to influence the conduct of both the USSR and China. Later there was no little discontent in Washington when Douglas-Home, in the run-up to the general election of October 1964, placed so much emphasis on Britain's 'independent' deterrent. Early contacts with leading Labour figures suggested that on this question at least they might prove more flexible than the Conservatives.

Labour won the election of October 1964 by a whisker, though the event itself was overshadowed internationally by the fall of Khrushchev in the USSR and by the first Chinese nuclear test. Washington soon showed its readiness to work with the new British government. The CIA commented somewhat tentatively at first on Harold Wilson, the prime minister, describing him as very much a loner in British politics. He was, however, a pragmatist and a realist who favoured close relations with the United States. By December 1965 the CIA was praising Wilson for his 'great political acumen' and his courage and flexibility in the face of an extraordinarily difficult political and economic situation. He had only a tiny parliamentary majority, and Britain was in the grip of another economic crisis. Dean Rusk remarked to Johnson as early as 15 April 1965, 'We have had an excellent degree of understanding and cooperation in critical foreign policy matters from the new Labor Government in Britain.' The difficulties had been less than expected. Wilson himself at his first meeting with President Johnson seems to have struck the right note with his claim that his was a forward-looking government with none of the imperial nostalgia of its predecessor. He also thought it expedient – for domestic and international reasons – to speak of a 'close', not a 'special relationship', one based on matters of substance.[2]

James Callaghan, the chancellor of the exchequer, was pleased by the American interest in the smoothest possible transition from Conservative to Labour in all that related to sterling. Earlier, as shadow chancellor, he had contacted and won assurances of help from the president of the Federal Reserve Bank of New York if a Labour victory precipitated a run on the pound. Help was duly forthcoming – if only for the practical reason that the dollar was bound to suffer in the event of a sterling crisis. Callaghan also found the Americans sympathetic (in contrast to the Europeans) to Labour's attempt to ease the 1964 balance of payments crisis with a temporary 15 per cent import surcharge.[3]

Other circumstances as well as the interplay of national interests ensured that Britain was at first able to retain her special position in America's network of alliances. Thus, while the French economy (as well as that of West Germany) was clearly pulling ahead of the British, de Gaulle was eager to go his own way and even defy the United States (not least in economic matters) wherever it seemed appropriate. West German attention remained centred on the affairs of Central Europe – nor had the Germans either completely liberated themselves from or lived down their own past. A Gallup Opinion Poll of 17 March 1965 found that Americans ranked Britain not only as their most reliable ally, but also as the most influential country in the world after the United States, the USSR and China. This was at a time when British opinion was becoming evenly divided over the pros and cons of seeking prominence on the global stage.

Anglo-American relations therefore early in the Wilson–Johnson era gave little hint of the extent of the decline that was about to take place. If ground had been lost since 1963, it had been lost before Labour took power. As we have seen, in so far as Washington valued the special relationship it was essentially for hard-headed reasons of self-interest, and in the mid-1960s three issues in particular were to bring about a marked weakening of the old ties.

In the first place Washington desired sterling to be maintained at its current parity of $2.80. This would help to protect the dollar at a time when the United States was experiencing balance of payments problems. American interests required prevention or at least control of any sterling crisis. And just as sterling was welcomed as a junior partner to the dollar as an international currency, so too was British aid in resistance to any threats to the Bretton Woods agreements and the liberal international economic order as a whole.

Secondly the United States desired British military support outside (as well as inside) Europe for its self-assumed role of world policeman. The interest in Britain's retention of bases and the deployment of troops, ships and aircraft in the Persian Gulf, at Aden and Singapore, and in the Indian Ocean deepened as the United States became ever more deeply and uncomfortably involved in war in South-East Asia from the mid-1960s.

The third requirement grew out of this – namely, as America became more involved in this conflict, so it looked to Britain to send at least a token force to assist in the war in Vietnam, or failing that to give strong diplomatic backing to the United States.

In the course of 1966–68 all three of these major props to the relationship were to be removed. By the beginning of 1968 Britain was ceasing to be regarded by many Americans as either a powerful or a special ally.

The Wilson government inherited serious economic problems in October 1964, but made matters worse by its own decisions. Most ministers at first were more interested in spending money than in getting to grips with the nation's economic problems. George Brown, minister of the ill-fated Department of Economic Affairs, even believed that with American aid the British economy could quickly be restored to health. Lasting and faster growth would ensue. Although the sterling crisis which followed the budget of 11 November 1964 alerted more ministers to the economic realities, Labour's tiny majority and the need to go to the country again as soon as possible meant that all too often electoral considerations were given priority (as they had been by the Tories earlier in 1964) over economic policy. Key figures, for instance, argued that devaluation would cripple Labour's chances of re-election. The wooing of electors similarly limited the scale of deflationary action until Labour won a large majority in the general election of July 1966.

The postponement of uncomfortable decisions was also facilitated by the scale of American aid. While dependence on American assistance in 1964–65 might seem to have left the British government dangerously exposed to American influence (or even dictation), in practice it is just as reasonable to argue that the Wilson government was able to turn American self-interest to its own advantage. Clive Ponting qualifies his own claims concerning American leverage by acknowledging that Wilson was wholly opposed to devaluation, and differed at most from the Americans over the details of the British role East of Suez.[4] In effect Washington was subsidizing the Wilson government to pursue policies which the latter wished to pursue in any case. Roy Jenkins fails to see anything 'either sensational or sinister' in the American role. Himself a minister from 1964 and an advocate of devaluation, Jenkins contends that 'if they [Wilson and Callaghan] could get American support for what they wanted to do anyway this could be regarded as serving a British interest and, from the point of view of the 1966 election, even a Labour Party interest'.[5]

It is true that policy-makers in Washington often saw themselves as using financial inducements to compel the British to act as they desired. Similarly those reporting on their negotiations with the British may at times have been tempted to exaggerate their success. They may also have naively failed to distinguish between genuine British opposition to American demands and a tactical stance designed to wring aid from Washington. George Ball, for instance, had two tough and vital sessions with Wilson on 8–9 September 1965, during which he battled for agreement to link American defence of the pound with Britain's maintenance of her overseas commitments. A year later, however, he warned his president not to be misled by Wilson's apparent reluctance to stay East of Suez. Ball had come to distrust the arguments he had himself encountered in London in 1965. If economic weakness exposed the British to American leverage, it also gave them bargaining power, given the anxiety of the Americans to achieve certain objectives. Washington's fear of devaluation is reflected in Johnson's decision to set up a Special Study Group in the middle of 1965 to examine the implications of the weakness of sterling for the dollar and the Bretton Woods international monetary system. The president was looking for at least a four or five-year breathing space before the United States had to confront the implications of a sterling crisis and a British withdrawal from East of Suez.[6]

American analyses of Britain's ills and the strain of her overseas commitments at this time make interesting reading. Many accepted that Labour was not uniquely responsible for Britain's plight. Some suggested that a Conservative government would not necessarily do better. The embassy in London had been sending disturbing accounts of Britain's over-stretched economy and defence forces well before Labour took office. For too long the British had sought incompatible economic objectives: full employment, price stability, economic growth, long-term foreign investment, and the preservation of sterling as a reserve currency. The result had been a succession of balance of payments crises, deflationary countermeasures at home, and consequent interruptions to economic growth. Thus Labour was seen to have inherited 'a very difficult [economic] problem' in 1964, whatever degree of guilt could be attached to its own mismanagement and doctrinaire behaviour. Indeed it was possible that the obstacles to change in Britain were too deeply ingrained for any government to effect significant improvements. These embassy and other American appraisals concluded that if Labour were too much swayed by the unions and its own socialist shibboleths, the Tories might prove even more fearful of a popular backlash and thus be even less willing to introduce adequate deflationary policies. Tory remedies, in any case, might include the devaluation of sterling.[7]

The embassy analysts were also troubled to find how few in Britain seemed aware of or – if aware – troubled by the scale of the economic problems. Radical structural reform of British industry was needed. Decayed and declining industries had to be shut down, and vast capital investment directed to the new sectors. There was a general want of enterprise and innovation. Business people had succumbed to the lure of 'gracious living'. Higher education reinforced the cultural barriers to economic growth. Not surprisingly the British economy had been growing at only about half the average annual rate of 5.4 per cent for the EEC countries since 1953.[8]

The US Treasury, in a brief for the president on 26 June 1965, darkly concluded that Britain required an austerity programme of almost wartime stringency. This, it conceded, was politically unthinkable. The secretary of the treasury himself (28 June) also noted that Britain's problems were now too large for the United States to solve with its own resources. Britain's financial withdrawals from the IMF had been on an unprecedented scale. Thus he favoured co-operation with other major industrial states in the hope that sterling might be restored to health over a period of three or four years. A year later (14 July 1966) he was more pessimistic – even alarmist. Britain's problems were now so acute that they posed a threat to American interests and the free world's financial system. It was imperative that the British take decisive deflationary action to save themselves and others.[9]

EAST OF SUEZ AND THE VIETNAM WAR

Some major reappraisals of policy beyond the narrow financial sphere were clearly called for in London, but Wilson and key members of his cabinet refused to make cuts to their fundamental home and foreign programmes until they were forced to do so by circumstances. Labour, for instance, had taken up Britain's role East of Suez in 1964 with no little enthusiasm. Indeed in its 1964 election campaign this had been merged with Labour's ambitious promises to develop a multiracial Commonwealth as an alternative to membership of the EEC. It was also presented as a contribution to the strengthening of the United Nations. Once in office Labour chose to stand by their predecessors' commitment to the newly created Malaysian Federation. This entailed the maintenance of a large military presence in and around Singapore to combat and deter Indonesian efforts to break up what President Sukarno described as an instrument of neo-imperialism.

It is true that Callaghan in 1965 underlined the importance of a healthy British economy when warned by McNamara (US secretary of defense) that Americans were not prepared to play the role of world policeman by themselves. But another British cabinet minister, Richard Crossman, was reminded of defence policy in the days of Ernest Bevin. Wilson, like Bevin, was willing to accept over-commitment in the world in order to sustain the special relationship. The latter was needed both for its general utility and so that 'we can survive outside Europe'.[10] Similarly Labour's minister of defence, Denis Healey, an early exponent of Britain's continuing police-keeping presence East of Suez, had reported with apparent satisfaction to the cabinet on 11 December 1964 (after a visit to Washington) that the Americans wanted Britain to keep footholds – not huge bases – in Hong Kong, Malaya and the Persian Gulf.

> [These would] enable us to do things for the alliance which they can't do. They think our forces are much more useful to the alliance outside Europe than in Germany.[11]

Admittedly one can begin to detect suggestions of new thinking as early as 1965. Healey dropped hints in Washington that Britain – in the long run – might decide to give up the Singapore base. Some of his planners were already comparing the potential and costs of seaborne forces with those generated by large land bases. The British also indicated that more American (and Australian) aid in the Indian Ocean would be welcome. In reply the American military cautiously expressed a preference for joint action within existing alliances such as Nato or Seato rather than any new bilateral arrangements. Interest, however, was growing in the development of American bases on some tiny British controlled Indian Ocean islands.

Not surprisingly the British achieved little with their request for direct American support in their dispute with Indonesia over Malaysia. Yet it was privately admitted in Washington that American interests might suffer if British and Commonwealth forces ultimately failed to contain the Indonesian threat, and in December 1964 both governments agreed to acknowledge the importance of each other's military efforts 'in support of legitimate governments in South-East Asia, particularly in Malaysia and South Vietnam'. As it happened a political upheaval in Indonesia in 1965–66 (in which American contacts with the military in Indonesia may have played a part) brought an unexpectedly early end to the confrontation with Britain. Large British forces had been tied up in an expensive operation to which there seemed to be no obvious military solution other than counter-guerrilla operations in Sabah and Sarawak and the deployment of large forces to discourage further escalation of the conflict. It was the cost of this operation which helped to persuade ministers to re-examine the basic premises of their East of Suez policy.[12]

There had been other setbacks. Political extremists in Aden and the neighbouring protectorate had turned the local British base into a liability. In 1967 the British presence in the Middle East obviously failed to offer any protection to British oil interests during the Arab–Israeli war. Business people no longer believed that gunboats and garrisons were vital for the protection and promotion of their activities. Finally hopes for a dramatic improvement in trade with Commonwealth members were not realized. India and some other states were showing less interest in the Commonwealth as an organization.[13]

Meanwhile the Vietnam War was imposing a growing strain on the Anglo-American relationship. The souring of relations, however, was taking place gradually. Lyndon Johnson's searing complaints against the British have been much quoted, yet for the first year or two the president was not insensitive to the political realities in London. There were measured assessments, too, from American officialdom, while the embassy in London advised Washington on ways in which the Wilson government might be helped to manage the increasingly outspoken British critics of American actions in Vietnam. The British foreign secretary, Michael Stewart, was warmly praised for his defence of American policy in the highly charged and much publicized Oxford Union debate of 16 June 1965. In general Wilson and Stewart were complimented on the political assistance they were providing in what for them was an 'agonisingly difficult' situation. The US embassy even suggested that a Conservative government might find it more difficult to keep public protest within bounds. From the spring of 1965 an understanding of a sort emerged whereby Britain would give general diplomatic support in return for advance information of major American military moves in Vietnam. Britain, as co-chairman of the Geneva Conference of 1954, was also allowed to explore possible peace initiatives, but only in ways acceptable to Washington.[14]

By 12 July 1966, however, the US embassy feared that the limits of British tolerance were being reached as the struggle in Vietnam intensified. The first American bombing of the outskirts of Hanoi and Haiphong had taken place a month earlier. Over 100 Labour Members of Parliament began to urge the government to dissociate itself entirely from the war. Public opinion moved sharply against American action in Vietnam in the summer of 1966. A Gallup Poll in August found only 31 per cent support for the United States with 49 per cent against. No less than 87 per cent favoured peace talks. Ministers had no choice but to distance themselves from the bombing. An increasingly desperate president unavailingly demanded that at least a token British force should be sent to Vietnam. American complaints intensified. One adviser, for instance, protested to Johnson on 28 July 1966, 'In short, we are up against an attitude of mind which, in effect, prefers that we take losses in the free world rather than the risks of confrontation.' Even so a loose diplomatic understanding survived after a fashion, while British opinion polls in 1967 suggested that only about 25 per cent were firmly of the view that the government was too close to Washington.[15]

Briefly in the winter of 1966–67 it seemed as if the British might be making some progress towards a cease-fire agreement in conjunction with the USSR. An abrupt change of position by the United States ostensibly wrecked what some have claimed was a promising diplomatic move. But Sir Paul Gore-Booth, the permanent undersecretary in the Foreign Office, later expressed his doubts. He thought that the Americans were right in their estimate that any truce would have been abused by the North Vietnamese to strengthen communist forces in South Vietnam.[16]

NO LONGER A 'POWERFUL ALLY'

In the mean time many issues, separately or in conjunction, continued to keep the lines busy between Washington and London, a point regularly noted by Crossman.[17] The talks ranged from the Caribbean, over much of Africa and the Middle East, to relations with China, India and Pakistan, as well as the central questions in Europe, policy towards the USSR and the free world economy. When a crisis blew up between Israel and Egypt in 1967, London and Washington briefly took the lead in what turned out to be an abortive attempt to organize an international naval force to re-open the disputed Straits of Tiran.[18] Britain also sought American help in dealing with the unilateral declaration of independence by the whites of Southern Rhodesia in 1965 in the face of the Wilson government's insistence on safeguards for the rest of the population. Washington agreed that a military solution was not an attractive option, and recognized that Britain dared not risk the economic repercussions of a break with South Africa. It gave some backing to Wilson's much-publicized but largely ineffective policy of economic sanctions against Rhodesia. At the same time Wilson was bluntly told that the United States would not make good any losses that the British economy might suffer.

The economy continued to stagger from crisis to crisis. The election of July 1966 at least returned Labour to power with a large majority, while government economic policy soon became somewhat tougher. Wilson no longer saw American aid as politically practical or desirable. But growing American unease over Britain's plight was still neutralized by the determination of most of those at the top to try to prevent devaluation or the end of the role East of Suez. Further American aid was offered, although the US Treasury no longer believed that the United States alone could find the resources to remedy Britain's problems. Indeed some Americans were beginning to question whether either government was making the right choices. Perhaps Britain had to undergo painful shock treatment if she was ever to become as economically dynamic as France or West Germany. Perhaps the United States itself would benefit in the long run from a more flexible policy on sterling and other matters.[19]

The London embassy made its own attempt at crystal-gazing on 26 May 1966. In a lengthy study of Britain it addressed in particular what it described as the 'rather fashionable' debate on the imminence of change and decline in the Anglo-American relationship. It contended that on 'most "hard" calculations' the British appeared to have a limited future on any measurement of international power, especially if they continued to over-commit themselves. Should the United States, it therefore asked, allow Britain to adjust naturally to a lower level of power – defined by some as that of a 'comparatively lesser middle state' ?

It was essential, the US embassy report argued, to separate the substance from the sentiment surrounding the relationship. It noted the many differences in historical experience, in values and in interests. Yet it was a simple matter of fact that the United States consulted more regularly with Britain than with any third state. Anglo-American policies were 'made to fit' in numerous areas by a series of compromises. Co-operation at a variety of levels was often natural or habitual. With the appropriate reservations it was possible to talk of 'a special kind of Anglo-American relationship'. The embassy was convinced that, at least in the short term, the United States would be much embarrassed without the services of such a partner. It could not act everywhere by itself. Times might change, but as matters then stood Britain, the Commonwealth and sterling were still of importance to the United States.[20]

The US secretary of state himself reached similar conclusions a year later. Although he anticipated a change in the relationship as Britain gradually concentrated on its roles in Europe, for the present the two countries continued to take 'a broadly similar view of the world'. The British played 'a constructive part in helping to maintain world order', even if they now had to rely on 'ideas and dexterity rather than military might'.[21] George Ball, however, believed that a change of policy was becoming essential in response to the more pessimistic diagnoses. He argued that Britain's role in the world should be thoroughly reappraised by Washington.[22] Where he had formerly regarded British devaluation or a retreat from East of Suez as totally contrary to American interests, he now believed that the damage to those interests would be tolerable if the British – by their own choice – embarked upon a long-term and systematic attempt to put their economy to rights. Britain's salvation lay in the EEC. Only through membership would her economy be sufficiently exposed to the rigours of competition. Only then would ministers steel themselves to introduce the unpleasant but indispensable reform measures.

Ball also set out the pros and cons of the commitment East of Suez. On the one hand, although he now thought that the Commonwealth was 'little more than a figure of speech', he acknowledged America's continuing interest in a British presence in the Indian Ocean. On the other he argued that it was 'basically unhealthy' for the United States to continue to press the British to live beyond their means. Indeed he now questioned if the United States itself had earned an adequate return from its investment in the special relationship. He believed the relationship should be redefined to facilitate as large a British role as possible within the EEC. This would counter the activities of Charles de Gaulle and put a brake on the inward-looking tendencies in the Community. Britain should give the EEC the sort of leadership that France would not and West Germany could not provide. In time not only might the Americans receive more help from Britain, but also other European states might follow her lead in assisting the United States in its role of world police-officer.[23]

By the autumn of 1967 the British government itself could no longer avoid the issue of devaluation. The point had been reached where further procrastination on this issue – and on the role East of Suez – had ceased to make sense economically or politically. Nevertheless these were conclusions which some ministers – including Harold Wilson – reached with the utmost reluctance. Devaluation was announced on 18 November, and this was followed in January 1968 by the decision to recall most of the British forces from East of Suez by the end of 1971.[24] Even these measures, however, coupled with rigorous deflationary steps, failed to bring a speedy restoration of international confidence in the British economy until the autumn of 1969. Furthermore, de Gaulle delivered a second veto against British entry to the EEC shortly after the decision to devalue.

British standing in Washington plummeted in the winter of 1967–68. Thus the US ambassador in London dismissed the special relationship as little more than 'sentimental terminology' while the US secretary of defense wrote off the British as a 'powerful ally'. Yet such criticism and dismay were in themselves testimony to the degree of reliance which the Americans had come to place on the special relationship – especially outside Europe. As will be shown later, subsequent problems in the Persian Gulf – notably when the fall of the Shah of Iran robbed the Americans of a hoped-for substitute regional ally – prolonged the American sense of dismay and betrayal. Anglo-American co-operation resumed in the Gulf only from the late 1980s.

MEANWHILE IN EUROPE . . .

The many setbacks suffered by the Wilson government, however, should not be allowed to obscure the extent to which Britain was able to exert influence in Nato in the years 1964–70. Various developments in the later 1960s helped to make this possible. The United States was increasingly distracted by Vietnam, while in 1966 France began to disengage itself militarily from the alliance. In these circumstances the British were able to exert more influence over the development of defence thinking than their physical strength strictly warranted. The policies pursued were not always pleasing to Washington, and showed that the British could have a mind of their own. At the same time in certain areas Britain was still proving the most significant of all America's allies in Europe. Overall the positive effects tended to outweigh the negative ones – whatever the American perceptions of the situation.

In the mid-1960s Washington was pressing for decisions on a number of defence issues affecting Nato. Indeed in 1964 it briefly entertained hopes that Labour might prove more helpful over nuclear policy than the preceding government. But Harold Wilson's talk of renegotiating the Nassau agreement on Polaris was soon shown to have little meaning in practice. Denis Healey demonstrated the strategic and political value of this force to the cabinet. He also made much of its cost-effectiveness, especially as an instrument with which to earn influence in Nato and in future East–West arms talks, quite apart from the military impression it might make on the USSR. Ministers were as anxious as their predecessors to preserve Britain's privileged position in the Western alliance.

Admittedly in public Harold Wilson did his best to argue that Britain did not possess an 'independent' deterrent with his insistence that the British Polaris force was dependent on some American components and other assistance.[25] Nevertheless the British government refused to assign its Polaris submarines permanently and unambiguously to Nato, or to include them in any of the current multinational or multilateral (MLF) schemes being floated by the Americans. As early as 1967 an inner group of ministers was examining proposals for the modernization of Polaris to prolong its credibility into the 1990s. The only significant change of policy was the reduction in the number of submarines from five to four.

Washington was also disappointed to find that once in office Labour was determined to oppose any proposals, however ingenious, to give West Germany access to nuclear weapons. Fortunately for the British government the West Germans themselves were divided or uncertain on the question of MLF, while its proponents in Washington were also losing ground. Thus MLF began to disappear from the agenda.

On the other hand in the early and mid-1960s the Americans remained determined to push ahead with the newly formulated strategy of flexible response. The Berlin crisis of 1961 had, if anything, intensified the American fear of nuclear war. Later that year McNamara pressed for a conventional build-up by all the members of Nato so that a Warsaw Pact attack in the heart of Europe could be resisted long enough (without recourse to nuclear weapons) to persuade the USSR of the gravity of the situation and to encourage it to negotiate. The British and the West Germans, however, remained convinced that the USSR would be more effectively restrained by the belief that Nato would use tactical nuclear weapons almost from the start of a war. The West could not fight a conventional war in Europe with any hope of success. Although McNamara conceded that this might be the case, he insisted that the search for more options in Nato's strategy should continue.

But the Europeans refused to be convinced by American arguments that the credibility of the overall American guarantee to Europe would in fact be increased if sufficient forces could be deployed to make the the strategy of flexible response a reality. Many feared the reverse, namely that increased reliance on conventional arms might lessen superpower fear of war in Europe. A conventional war would still cause unacceptable devastation. As Denis Healey commented, Europeans wanted to prevent a war, not fight one. In Britain both Conservative and Labour cabinets insisted that only the threat of early use of nuclear weapons could stop a major Soviet offensive. They were sceptical of claims that the Soviets might be checked by the selective use of nuclear weapons in Europe – escalation to all-out war was almost inevitable.[26]

Naturally there were many differences of opinion among the European governments, but basically all were trying to find an answer to the same problems. Underlying the strategic variants were similar fundamental objectives: the prevention of war in Europe; the denial of sanctuary status to the superpower homelands lest Moscow and Washington should become too trigger-happy in Europe; a continuing guarantee from the United States – but ideally one which was accompanied by overall American restraint in the conduct of the Cold War; and the avoidance of major increases in Western European defence budgets. Whatever the differences among the Europeans themselves, those with the United States were much more important.

Denis Healey soon saw himself in the role of bridge-builder between the West German government (which particularly feared any decline in the credibility of nuclear deterrence) and McNamara who hoped to avoid the first – or at least the early – use of nuclear weapons. Healey had already outlined some ideas in a lecture at the University of California in February 1961. He had then spoken frankly of the need to restore European confidence in the United States. This would require improved planning and consultation within Nato. Since conventional fighting on any scale was quite unacceptable to the Europeans, flexible reponse should be used essentially to deal with localized crises. At best in a major conflict it would give allies time to reach agreement on how to use nuclear weapons. Once in office Healey pressed his Nato colleagues to accept that no conflict was possible in Europe at any level between that of a local skirmish and all-out war. The alliance should prepare for a conventional war lasting no more than a few days.[27]

The debate over the respective roles of nuclear and conventional arms was inevitably bound up with questions of authority and influence within Nato, especially in so far as they related to the possible use of nuclear weapons, and to their proliferation within the alliance. As it happened progress proved possible in three directions in these years – the formation of Nato's Nuclear Planning Group; an agreed if rather fuzzy definition of flexible response; and the negotiation of a

Nuclear Non-Proliferation Treaty with the USSR. In all these negotiations the British were surprisingly active notwithstanding the shocks
to the special relationship caused by devaluation and the withdrawal
from East of Suez, and the on-going concern over the state of the
British economy.

Thus the British were able to make the most of their supporting
role in the superpower talks which led to the Non-Proliferation
Treaty of 1968 to try to prevent further nuclear proliferation in
Europe. J.P.G. Freeman credits them with a 'modest' influence when
they helped to persuade the Americans that agreement with the USSR
was dependent on the exclusion of West Germany from direct control
over nuclear arms. For the time being the aspirations of the West
Germans were met by the creation of the Nato Nuclear Planning
Group. This gave them access to deliberations on nuclear strategy and
tactics in Europe. The Non-Proliferation Treaty, however, was the last
occasion when the British sat at the top table to discuss nuclear questions with the superpowers. The talks which led to the first Strategic
Arms Limitation Agreement (SALT I) were confined to the Russians
and Americans.

Progress towards a new version of flexible response was also possible
once it became apparent that there would be no major increases to
Nato's conventional forces, especially since the Americans could not
lead by example as long as they were mired in Vietnam. In any case,
despite the continuing growth of the armed forces of the USSR,
tension in Europe had markedly declined since 1961 (this was paradoxically confirmed when the Soviet intervention in Czechoslovakia
in 1968 resulted in only a limited and temporary upset in East–West
relations). The West Germans were becoming increasingly eager to
cultivate relations across the Iron Curtain, and both sides were hinting
at new arms talks. In this environment Healey could be sure of an
audience when he argued that Nato should plan on the basis of the
forces that would definitely be available.

In December 1967 Nato officially replaced the strategy of massive
retaliation with that of flexible response, but without the enlarged
conventional forces which McNamara and other American proponents
of this strategy had originally envisaged. Flexible response was defined
as the use of force against an attacker at an appropriate level on an
escalating scale, starting with conventional arms and with strategic nuclear forces as weapons of last resort. This conceded something to the
Americans, though if Nato were seriously pressed it was evident that –
short of surrender – nuclear weapons would have to be used in some
way or other. Attempts were made in the Harmel Report to allay

West German fears that flexible response would turn their territory into a battlefield. Here the need to pursue detente with the Eastern bloc was underlined as well as the maintenance of Western defences. Even so the most ingenious phraseology could not truly reconcile the many disparate concerns of the allies. Fortunately East–West tensions had lessened sufficiently in Europe for the allies to live with these unresolved questions for the time being.

Denis Healey was again in the forefront of the efforts to devise satisfactory guidelines for the use of tactical nuclear weapons. He bluntly argued on the basis of a series of tactical nuclear war games in the mid-1960s that most of Nato's doctrine was politically unacceptable and militarily unsound.[28] Early in 1969, in company with the West German defence minister, he drafted new proposals. The intention was to try to use tactical nuclear weapons politically rather than militarily – that is, as signals to the USSR if and when a conventional collision in Europe was reaching an unacceptably dangerous level. These guidelines were submitted to Nato in May 1969. They did not – it seems – win general assent. Certainly the Americans continued to look for alternative strategies, both to raise the nuclear threshold and (because they felt the Europeans left them too few military options) to ensure that small nuclear weapons could still be used for war-fighting. On the subject of the 1969 guidelines, William Park cryptically concluded in 1986 that the status of the proposed 'demonstration shot' in Nato's nuclear strategy still remained 'unclear'.[29]

Healey's influence had been further enhanced by the resignation of McNamara as US secretary of defense in 1968. He briefly (until 1970) became the leading figure in the Nuclear Planning Group. In public he continued to argue that Nato's conventional forces were needed essentially to handle a small incident – the most likely kind of military crisis in his view. Above that level it was a question of deterrence, not war-fighting.[30] Lord Carrington, Healey's successor in the British Ministry of Defence from 1970, warmly commended what had been achieved since 1964. If nothing else flexible response as adopted in December 1967 had caused the planners to concentrate on actual rather than target forces. Western strategy had become a little more credible. Similarly Healey had persuaded the Eurogroup to challenge American complaints that the Europeans were doing too little to defend themselves. Evidence was put together to demonstrate just how large a proportion of Nato's current force was actually provided by the Europeans. Publicity of this kind was much needed against the campaign being waged by Senator Mansfield and others in favour of major reductions to American forces in Europe.[31]

Close collaboration continued between Britain and the United States in many other areas. American strategic interest in the British Isles had shifted from land-based nuclear forces to the Polaris facilities in the Holy Loch. The multi-capable F-111 aircraft were to arrive in 1970, while the departure of France from Nato necessitated the redeployment of some American units to Britain. The British Isles were still valued as an emergency base. The nuclear deterrent gave Britain access to valuable American military intelligence. In addition there were comprehensive links between the two intelligence services. British stations around the world, especially in Cyprus and Hong Kong, filled gaps in the American network, while Britain herself was one of the main intelligence centres of the Western alliance. Co-operation continued to flourish between diplomats, members of the armed forces, and between sections of the bureaucracies. Nor should enduring personal contacts be forgotten. Just how far these could go in some cases is illustrated by George Ball in 1968. Despite his sharply critical memoranda on Britain in 1965 and 1966, he could write as if the relationship were still at its peak:

> [The British and Americans] to an exceptional degree, . . . look out on the world through similarly refracted spectacles. We speak variant patois of Shakespeare and Norman Mailer, our institutions spring from the same instincts and traditions, and we share the same heritage of law and custom, philosophy and pragmatic *Weltanschauung* . . . starting from similar premises in the same intellectual tradition, we recognize common allusions, share many common prejudices, and can commune on a basis of confidence.[32]

Such ties and feelings, however, could not indefinitely resist some erosion as material national interests and priorities began to change. The United States itself was soon driven to reappraise its global thinking as a result of the Vietnam War. A.P. Dobson heads the final chapter of his study of Anglo-American economic relations, 'Terminal Decline? The Special Relationship, 1967–87'. For him the 'special' economic ties ended with the devaluation of sterling and the cessation of Anglo-American co-operation to uphold the Bretton Woods system in 1967. Devaluation increased the vulnerability of the dollar, although the seriousness of the situation did not become fully apparent until 1971–73. At least the easing of the Cold War lessened Anglo-American tensions over trade with communist countries.

It was another sign of changing times when the British from 1967 began to embark upon more joint defence procurement programmes with the Europeans – notably the multinational collaborative effort which produced the Tornado fighter-bomber. The precariousness of personal ties was demonstrated by the gradual reduction in the numbers of those in positions of influence in both countries who had gone through the great co-operative experience of the Second World War and the early stages of the Cold War. Devaluation, the retreat from Suez and Vietnam had, of course, provided the main shocks to the relationship in the 1960s. But the world was moving on, and national agendas were changing both in the United States and in Britain, a fact soon to be underlined by a British prime minister who was to make a conscious effort to grade Western Europe above the United States in Britain's list of national priorities.[33]

NOTES AND REFERENCES

1. See *L.B. Johnson National Security Files, Western Europe*, Maryland University Publications of America, 1987 (hereafter LBJ/NSC), reel 6, memos by the US assistant secretary and secretary of defense, 18 February and 24 March 1964. Denis Healey (Labour's minister of defence, 1964–70) found American defence experts more preoccupied with 'abstract concepts' than human and political realities. D. Healey, *The Time of My Life*, Michael Joseph, 1989, pp. 243–6.

2. LBJ/NSF, reel 10, Rusk to Johnson, 15 April 1965.

3. J. Callaghan, *Time and Chance*, Collins, 1987, pp. 159, 171, 176, 189–90. The Americans were understandably wary of any longer term trends towards protectionism.

4. C. Ponting, *Breach of Promise: Labour in Power 1964–70*, Hamish Hamilton, 1989, pp. 53–4; see chapter 3 passim.

5. Jenkins's review of Ponting in the *Observer*, 5 March 1989. See also Dobson, pp. 213–19, and his 'The years of transition: . . . ' in *Review of International Studies*, July 1990, pp. 250–1, where he doubts the existence of any effective quid pro quo between American aid and the British role East of Suez. See Ponting, pp. 69–71, for the mid-November 1964 economic crisis and ministerial reactions. Wilson declared devaluation would ruin Labour's election hopes.

6. LBJ/NSC, reel 8, Ball to Johnson, 22 July 1966. Note Dobson's argument (pp. 213–19) that the relations of Harold Wilson and Johnson were initially satisfactory.

7. JFK/NSC, reel 10, nos 1159 and 1206, 10 and 12 September1963. LBJ/NSC, reel 7, London embassy, 27 July 1965. See also *Central Intelligence Agency Research Reports: Europe, 1945–76*, Microfilm Project of University of America Publications Inc., Washington DC, 1983 (hereafter CIARRE): reel 4, staff memo, no 26–65, 25 June 1965.

8. See LBJ/NSC, reel 7, London embassy, 24 June and 3 August 1965; CIARRE, memo: 'The British Economy and its Implications', 25 June 1965.

9. LBJ/NSC, reel 7, Treasury briefing, 26 June 1965; US secretary of the treasury to LBJ, 28 June 1965; reel 8, secretary of the treasury, 14 July 1966.

10. Richard Crossman, *The Diaries of a Cabinet Minister, 1964–70*, Hamish Hamilton, 1975–7, i. 117; ii. 181–2.

11. Crossman, i. 95. For Washington talks, see NSC/LBJ, reel 9, State Department memo, 7 December 1964.

12. See LBJ/NSC, reel 7, Office of Current Intelligence, no. 1771/65, 7 June 1965, which reveals some US awareness of the impact of Britain's East of Suez role on the balance of payments.

13. C.J. Bartlett, *A History of Postwar Britain, 1945–74*, Longman, 1977, pp. 201–2, 232–6.

14. LBJ/NSC, reel 8. The director of intelligence and research (US State Department), 27 July 1966, commended Wilson's skill and courage amid great political and economic difficulties.

15. LBJ/NSC, reel 7, US embassy (London), 12 July 1966; see also reel 8, US embassy, 23 May 1966, and reel 10, Rostow to Johnson, 28 July 1966. It was noted by some American officials that much British criticism was not based on principle but on doubts of the possibility of success. A *Guardian* editorial of 17 February 1967 attributed moral responsibility for the tragedy of Vietnam to Hanoi, and saw American policy as in line with its responses over Berlin, Korea and Cuba – but in this instance it believed the Americans were engaged in 'a hopeless task'. G.H. Gallup, *Gallup International: Great Britain*, ii. 871, 882–3, 919, 925.

16. Ponting, pp. 222–6. P. Gore-Booth, *With Great Truth and Respect*, Constable, 1974, pp. 357–62. See also Wilson, pp. 345–66.

17. *Crossman Diaries*, i. 94–5, 117, 354; ii. 156, 181–2.

18. Ponting, pp. 226–9.

19. LBJ/NSC, reel 10, Bator to McGeorge Bundy, 29 July 1965.

20. LBJ/NSC, reel 8, London embassy, 23 May 1966.

21. LBJ/NSC, reel 10, Rusk to Johnson, 31 May 1967.

22. LBJ/NSC, reel 8, Ball memo to Johnson, 22 July 1966. Note also Ball's view in 1965 that a British evacuation from East of Suez would be worse than devaluation since it would leave the USA with permanent commitments (Ball memo, 6 Aug 1965, LBJ/NSC, reel 10).

23. LBJ/NSC, reel 8. The US State Department expressed its belief to European embassies, 3 February 1967, that British membership of the EEC would not prove incompatible with the East of Suez role.

24. Ponting, pp. 103–6, 288, 306–9; Callaghan, p. 211; *Crossman Diaries*, ii. 418, 437, 645–8. Roy Jenkins claims (*Observer*, 5 March 1989) that US pressure effectively ended in the middle of 1967. For American reactions to Britain's economic problems and to devaluation see Dobson, 'The years of transition . . . ', *Review of International Studies*, July 1990, pp. 254–7.

25. S. Zuckerman, *Monkeys, Men and Missiles*, Collins, 1988, pp. 375–6. D. Healey, pp. 302–4, 307; J.P.G. Freeman, *British Arms Control Policy in the Context of Anglo-American Relations, 1957–68*, Macmillan, 1986, pp. 183–5; G. Rumble, *The Politics of Nuclear Deterrence*, Cambridge University Press, 1985, p. 84.

26. D. Healey, p. 308. See also JFK/NSC, reel 9, nos 1159 and 1206 for General Norstad's dissatisfaction in October 1961 with the strength of BAOR. This had been decreasing since 1956, and BAOR was too reliant on nuclear weapons. Note Paul H. Nitze, *From Hiroshima to Glasnost*, Weidenfeld and Nicolson, 1989, pp. 203–6.

27. Bruce Reed and Geoffrey Williams, *Denis Healey and the Politics of Power*, Sidgwick and Jackson, 1971, pp. 141–3, 254–5. W. Park, *Defending the West: a history of Nato*, Brighton: Wheatsheaf, 1986, pp. 132 ff.

28. P. Buteux, *The Politics of Nuclear Consultation*, Cambridge: Polity Press, 1983, p. 51.

29. Park, pp. 138–9. Healey (p. 311) agreed that nuclear options were listed only in 'very general terms' in his day, and he doubted if any real progress was made subsequently.

30. Reed and Williams, pp. 254–63.

31. Carrington, pp. 231–2; Reed and Williams, pp. 254–63.

32. George Ball, *The Discipline of Power*, Bodley Head, 1968, p. 91. Note McGeorge Bundy's informal exchanges with Burke Trend, the cabinet secretary, to try to prepare the ground, anticipate problems, and generally oil the wheels of inter-state relations. See for example his communication to Trend, 3 November 1965 (LBJ/NSC reel 7).

33. Dobson, pp. 228–30, suggests from 1964 to 1967 that there was more joint activity over international monetary issues than on defence questions.

CHAPTER SIX
A Muted Relationship, 1969–81

THE EEC VERSUS THE SPECIAL RELATIONSHIP

January 1969 found a new president, Richard Nixon, in the White House with Henry Kissinger as his national security adviser. Both men hoped to work closely with the British. Kissinger in particular, both before and after his years in office, seemed to go out of his way on several occasions to underline his interest in Britain as a player on the international stage. She was, he claimed, an example of a country which, through the exercise of outstanding diplomatic skills, enjoyed more influence than her physical power strictly warranted. Similarly, and not least in his memoirs, Kissinger made several references both to his desire to co-operate with Britain and to his disappointment that the relationship had not been more intimate during his years of power between 1969 and 1977. It may be, as one scholar has claimed,[1] that Kissinger was always sceptical concerning the worth of the special relationship to the United States, and it is obviously essential to test all his remarks on the subject against his underlying strategies. He had no time for sentiment. But there is still reason to suppose that he felt it important that Britain should if possible retain special links with the United States whatever – and perhaps because of – her ties with Western Europe.

In practice Britain did not come up to the expectations of the Nixon administration. Nixon was disappointed even on his first tour of Europe in February 1969. Yet Kissinger still recorded of the 1969 visit that the British and Americans, whatever their differences, were able to discuss problems and exchange ideas in a friendly, frank and open-ended manner. In contrast he found the West Germans and Italians too lacking in self-confidence to address issues which were not of immediate concern to them. De Gaulle had no such inhibitions, but his beliefs concerning the future of Europe and East–West relations were too distinct and strongly held to permit any genuine dialogue with his visitors. Kissinger described Harold Wilson as a good friend to the United States and one who was eager to discuss and to seek out solutions to 'definable' problems. British pragmatism stood out in welcome contrast to the doctrinaire attitude of the French. Kissinger was able to develop a useful working relationship in the longer term with Sir Burke Trend who, as cabinet secretary, co-operated in the maintenance of discreet channels of communication between the two capitals.[2] Nevertheless this first visit to Britain, however interesting the exchanges, did not produce results of substance. Kissinger returned home complaining that the British and Europeans wanted an alliance with the United States which was largely defined by themselves: that is, they wanted to be free to negotiate unilaterally with the USSR from the shelter of the American deterrent. They also wanted the Americans to play as large a part as ever in the Western alliance so that the Europeans would not have to increase their own contribution to defence.[3]

The Nixon administration suffered from contradictory desires of its own, as well as from the contradictions which existed within the alliance. It wanted to economize on defence, and yet at the same time it did not want to lower the nuclear threshold in Europe – the obvious corollary to cuts to conventional forces. The Europeans remained as fearful as ever of anything which raised the threat of war on their continent. Equally understandably the Americans continued their search for strategies which would minimize the threat of disaster to their own homeland. Nixon was soon underlining his country's dilemma. In both his 1970 and 1971 presidential foreign policy messages to Congress (17 February 1970 and 25 February 1971) he asked whether a president could be left with a single military option – one which could only result in the mass slaughter of Americans. His answer, not surprisingly, was in the negative. Other choices were needed beside mutual assured destruction. Washington therefore tried to persuade the Europeans that the more secure Americans felt at home the more likely they would be to honour exisiting Nato commitments. But such arguments and proposals only added to the worries of America's allies. To Kissinger this inability to devise a satisfactory defence strategy was particularly frustrating when the combined gross national product of the members of Nato was several times that of the USSR and its allies.[4]

Nevertheless it seems that Kissinger philosophically resigned himself to these transatlantic differences. He concentrated upon the identification of those problems which, if not soluble, at least lent themselves to management. Thus, while he believed that the separate use of nuclear weapons by Britain and France was almost inconceivable, he tried to draw what advantages he could from the existence of these 'independent national' forces. An important element in nuclear deterrence was uncertainty in the mind of an opponent. The British and French nuclear arsenals would also add to the complications in Soviet nuclear planning. All this should help to enhance Western nuclear deterrence.[5]

In the realm of politics and economics Kissinger accepted that it was no longer possible to ignore America's relative decline in the global economy. Although the output of the six members of the EEC was only half that of the United States, they had double the share of world exports. Increasing balance of payments problems meant that Americans were becoming even more fearful of economic competition from the EEC. European protectionism was an obvious cause for complaint, and as early as 1969 there were American threats of a 'full-scale attack' on the non-tariff barriers employed by the EEC. Talk of an 'economic Cold War' followed.

In 1970 the Conservatives returned to power in Britain. Briefly, until the new prime minister, Edward Heath, sensed that France was warming to the idea of British membership of the EEC, Anglo-American relations went on much as before. Indeed Kissinger for a time entertained the hope that some sort of British military presence might be maintained both in the Far East and in the Persian Gulf. In practice he found that the only durable agreement was confined to the development of the Anglo-American base on Diego Garcia as a precaution against the growing Soviet naval presence in the Indian Ocean. The planned British run-down East of Suez proceeded apart from the occasional despatch of small mobile forces to show the flag and for exercises.

In the Persian Gulf the United States now turned to Iran in the hope that it could replace the British as the main stabilizing force in the region. Even so Kissinger regretfully reflected in his memoirs:

> [In the early 1970s Britain] still possessed the experience and intellectual resources of a great power and was governed by leaders of vast goodwill towards the United States. But with every passing year they acted less as if their decisions mattered. They offered advice, usually sage; they rarely sought to embody it in a policy of their own. British statesmen were content to act as honored consultants to our deliberations.[6]

Nixon shared his sense of disappointment, and traced the British loss of nerve in the wider world back to Suez and Eisenhower's failure to support Eden. Among the special research studies commissioned by the US government at this time was one on the UK's changing concept of her worldwide responsibilities.

There was further dismay in the White House when Heath's campaign for membership of the EEC began to erode still further what remained of Anglo-American contacts at the highest level. Heath warned Nixon that Britain could not allow herself to be seen as America's Trojan horse in the EEC. The prime minister no longer sought preferential treatment from the United States, despite, according to Kissinger, some tempting offers from Nixon. Kissinger continued to argue the Atlanticist case, though he agreed that in any future relationship sentiment would play a small part compared with self-interest. He was struck by Heath's cool, calculating attitude, and detected little emotional attachment to the United States. Heath himself spoke of a 'natural relationship', a subtle demotion of Anglo-American relations to somewhere below special but seemingly rather more than ordinary.[7] Kissinger, however, still hoped that the United States would benefit from British membership of the EEC.

The final stages of British entry to the Community coincided with a crisis in America's economic relations with the rest of the world. Its gold reserve, for instance, had fallen by more than a third in the 1960s. A variety of financial and economic strains developed with the Europeans. Finally the dollar crisis of August 1971 resulted in the unilateral suspension of dollar convertibility into gold and a 10 per cent surcharge on all American imports. The British response was to move still closer to the Western Europeans. When Heath visited Washington in December 1971 he pointed out that it was now the practice to formulate an agreed European position in the first place, and only then to try to reconcile that with the interests of the United States. He acknowledged that European unity would mean competition – though he trusted not confrontation – with the United States. Kissinger began to characterize Heath as a 'more benign' version of de Gaulle (especially on questions of defence). Yet Britain still had a slight edge over West Germany and France. Even a successful meeting between Brandt and Nixon in the same month showed that the West German leader still had no wish to discuss global issues. Similarly, helpful as Pompidou of France proved at some stages in the talks to end the Vietnam War, only Heath was willing to back Nixon at the time of the controversial American bombing of the North in December 1972.[8]

The New Year at last brought a temporary settlement in Vietnam, and this, with the steady progress towards detente with the USSR, tempted the American administration to try to reassert its influence in

Western Europe. Kissinger proceeded to launch his ambitious 'Year of Europe' in 1973 and with it the idea of a new Atlantic Charter. Heath alone of the European leaders, it seems, was consulted in advance. Nixon went out of his way to cultivate the British prime minister during the latter's February visit. Nevertheless the signal favour of a full day at Camp David failed to fracture Heath's reserve. There was even a temporary interruption in April 1973 to Kissinger's regular and useful meetings with Sir Burke Trend. Gradually the painful realization began to dawn in Washington that in so far as the British continued to discuss European affairs with them, they were doing so largely for the sake of appearances. When Franco-American relations became particularly soured at a Western Summit in Reykjavik (31 May–1 June 1973) Heath assumed the guise of a 'pained bystander'. And when Kissinger was at last able – at the end of July – to resume contact with Trend he was offered only sympathy and no promise of more meaningful contacts in the future.[9]

Overall Kissinger was driven to conclude that his bid to make 1973 the 'Year of Europe' had only highlighted and exacerbated the prevailing divisions within the Atlantic Community. Heath, for his part, suspected that Kissinger was trying to play off one European state against another. 'None of us were prepared to play that game.' For their part the Europeans agreed at the Copenhagen European Summit of July 1973 that no member of the EEC should enter into individual dealings with the United States until an overall European view had been constructed. Greater European unity, it seemed, was only adding to America's international problems.[10]

There were other instances of Euro-American friction. Even as East–West relations found some relief in detente, so Kissinger tried to demonstrate to the Europeans that they could not profit from unilateral overtures to the USSR since, 'in any competition for better relations with Moscow, America had the stronger hand'. The Nixon administration similarly sought leverage in Europe by trying to establish links between the scale of its military presence in Europe and the liberality of European treatment of American exports.[11] In practice such moves only added to transatlantic tensions. Yet Nato of necessity survived. Co-operation continued to outweigh controversy, but with the difference that Edward Heath now tended to regard Britain as 'just another European country'.[12]

OUT OF STEP IN THE MIDDLE EAST, 1973–74

Even this degree of unity did not operate outside Europe as was demonstrated when Kissinger tried to orchestrate Western policy when Egypt attacked Israeli forces on the east bank of the Suez Canal in October 1973. Other Arab states intervened with the oil weapon – an effective combination of embargoes and more especially of price rises. In contrast to previous crises the United States was no longer in a position to make good some of the interrupted supplies from the Middle East so that the Europeans, who now drew some 80 per cent of their oil imports from that region, were highly vulnerable to Arab pressure, and responded accordingly. British development of North Sea oil was in its infancy. Petrol ration books were printed and distributed. Thus economic interests as well as Heath's desire to sustain the confidence of his EEC partners in the European-mindedness of his government dictated a policy of caution in the Middle East. There was in any case rather more sympathy than before in Britain for the Arab case. On 26 July 1973 Britain had been one of seven on the Security Council to compose a motion calling for an Israeli withdrawal to its 1967 frontiers. This was vetoed by the United States with the claim that it did not make provision for all-round security.

In October 1973 the United States, for foreign and domestic reasons, could not allow Israel to suffer a serious setback. At the same time Nixon and Kissinger were interested in a Middle Eastern settlement which, while guaranteeing Israeli security and strength, would do something to assist and conciliate the more moderate Arab regimes. They received reassuring signals from President Sadat of Egypt that he was fighting a war with limited objectives – not the destruction of Israel. This reinforced the hopes of Nixon and Kissinger that the United States might emerge as the leading superpower. From such a position it should be able to influence the outcome of the war and its aftermath, and to reduce Soviet influence in the region.

By 12 October Kissinger seemed about to gain the diplomatic initiative. The Israelis had recovered from their early setbacks in the war, but were still dependent upon American supplies of arms. Kissinger hoped to use this dependence to push Israel towards a moderate peace. When Israel expressed interest in a cease-fire, Kissinger looked to the British – given their satisfactory relations with both the main parties in the war – to take the lead at the United Nations. But the British were not prepared to act without consulting Cairo. Above all they were afraid, as one official later remarked, of becoming a 'fall guy for the

US'. Nor were the Egyptians yet ready to talk.[13]

Sadat's refusal meant the continuance of the war. Within days, however, Egypt was facing a major military disaster, and Washington on 24 October, fearing unilateral Soviet intervention, placed its forces on an 'alert'. Nixon's powers and standing as president had already been seriously weakened by the Watergate Scandal. This made Kissinger all the more determined to demonstrate American weight and resolve in order to retain the initiative in the Middle East. During this second stage of the war the Americans were also engaged in a frantic military re-supply of Israel, and were angered by the refusal of the British and their other European partners (except Portugal) to assist in the process. Even the American decision to inform the British of the 'alert' ahead of the other allies did not improve matters as London made no attempt to influence the Europeans in favour of American policy. To the Americans this was an abuse of its privileged position.[14]

American disappointment and frustration at the time was very real. The United States temporarily ceased normal intelligence-sharing with the British. On the other hand Kissinger went out of his way in his memoirs to compliment the British foreign secretary, Sir Alec Douglas Home. He notes that Home was critical of the cease-fire proposals of 12 October as being unfair to Egypt, and praises him throughout for his prudence and integrity. 'There was quite literally no one we trusted more.' In addition his colleague, the US secretary of defense, later thought it an error not to have consulted (rather than simply to have informed) the British before the 'alert' was ordered – especially given the implications surrounding the American bases in Britain. He did not agree that there had been no time. Meanwhile an indignant British government insisted in Parliament that while the Americans could put the bases on 'alert' they could not use them without British permission.[15]

Yet with respect to the crisis as a whole Kissinger had cause for satisfaction. His aggressive diplomacy had given him the leading position in the subsequent negotiations between Israel and the Arabs, while the standing of the USSR in the Middle East was sharply reduced for some years to come. The Europeans, admittedly, still wished to preserve and demonstrate their independence. The Brussels Declaration of November 1973 signalled the Community's intention to devise a policy of its own on the Palestinian question. The episode was another ironic commentary on the 'Year of Europe', and it also revealed the limitations of inter-allied consultative agreements (including those between the British and the Americans) in a time of crisis when policies diverged.

Heath himself underlined the transatlantic policy differences in a speech to American reporters on 28 November 1973, while Home put the British case more diplomatically to Kissinger the following day. Nato was still the linchpin of British foreign and defence policies, but Home argued that Britain's value as an ally to the United States would decline if she were seen to be following uncritically in the footsteps of Washington. The British and the Europeans had views on the Middle East which were worthy of American attention. Both Heath and Home believed that circumstances were compelling the Europeans to draw together. The Americans sharply retorted that they would continue to support only 'the right kind of united Europe'. They made it plain that European unity should be compatible with a higher loyalty to Atlantic solidarity. When the Community, early in 1974, again publicized its desire to develop closer relations with the Arab states, Nixon decided that the time had come for some blunt speaking. On 15 March he warned that the Europeans could not expect to enjoy American support on 'the security front and then proceed to have confrontation and even hostility on the economic and political fronts'. The Americans and Europeans would have to sit down and decide whether to act together or go their separate ways.[16]

In fact it soon became evident that only the French were really attracted by the independent road, particularly when the major oil consumers were forced to consider how they could respond to the energy crisis. Indeed, Kissinger felt he had made useful progress with Home as early as the Washington Energy Conference at the start of 1974. The American economy was less vulnerable than the European to the Arab oil weapon, and Washington had some surplus oil with which to bargain. Nor could the Europeans ignore Nixon's warning that security and economics were two sides of the same coin. The Community's declaration of December 1973 on its identity had already included an acknowledgement that there was no alternative to the security provided by American military power. Thus, after much horse-trading, the International Energy Agency was set up in November 1974.[17]

LABOUR AND THE UNITED STATES, 1974–79

Anglo-American relations improved a little when the British general election of February 1974 led to the formation of a minority Labour government. Harold Wilson did not share Edward Heath's depth of commitment to Europe, and, while struggling to preserve his party's unity by renegotiating British terms of entry with the rest of the Community, he was happy to broaden his options by moving closer to the United States. His foreign secretary, James Callaghan, informed the House of Commons in March that the new government repudiated 'the view that the new Europe will emerge only out of a process of struggle with the United States'. It would resist consultations within the Community which took on 'an anti-American tinge'. Callaghan set out to reduce the 'mutual needling' between the EEC and the United States. But in the same year Harold Wilson, from his observations on a visit to the United States, was struck by the extent to which Britain had fallen in American esteem.[18] Nor did Denis Healey, the chancellor of the exchequer, find the American Treasury of much help during the major British economic crisis of 1976.[19]

Fortunately the new British inclination towards the United States coincided with the development of a rather more sensitive and sympathetic mood than had existed of late in Washington. The Ottawa conference in June 1974 acknowledged that Soviet–American strategic nuclear parity was giving 'a different and more distinct character' to the defence problems of Europe, and that both the French and British nuclear forces were adding to the credibility of the overall Western deterrent. The Americans promised that their relationship with the USSR would not be allowed to develop in any way at the expense of their European allies. Kissinger also found the Wilson government helpful during his 'shuttle diplomacy' to reduce tension between Israel and its Arab neighbours, while rising communist influence in Portugal and Italy in the mid-1970s led to frequent exchanges of views between London and Washington. Wilson at times shared Kissinger's pessimism, but he gave what encouragement he could to the Portuguese socialists and other democrats. Britain co-operated with the EEC in the supply of aid with the proviso that this would continue only so long as Portugal remained a democracy. The American scholar, Raymond Garthoff, commends British and European handling of the crisis compared with the more alarmist responses in Washington. The worst was over by the end of 1976.[20]

Troubles between Turkey and Greece over Cyprus, and the influence of the military in both states were not so easily handled. Again Washington was more obsessed than the Europeans with possible communist gains. The Cypriot leader, Archbishop Makarios, was labelled 'the Castro of the Mediterranean', and there was talk of the eastern Mediterranean becoming 'a Russian lake'. American support for the military in Greece and Turkey, and the last-minute backing of Greece against Turkey in the Cypriot crisis in July–August 1974 damaged American (and Nato's) relations with both states. Once again Wilson's policy was of some assistance to the Americans. He opposed any effort at centralized European foreign policy-making. 'It would make nonsense of our relations with the Commonwealth . . . and US.'[21]

These episodes in the mid-1970s demonstrated the precariousness of the East–West detente which had aroused so many hopes at the start of the decade. Indeed, even when detente was at its most promising Soviet sources indicated that it did not mean the end of the class war or a lack of interest by the USSR in the Third World. Some Soviet diplomatic moves in the context of detente could also excite profound suspicion. Kissinger recounts an interesting example of Anglo-American co-operation in 1972. This was in response to Soviet suggestions for an agreement on the prevention of nuclear war. To both Washington and London this had the hallmark of a Soviet move to decouple Europe as well as China from American nuclear protection. It could also be variously interpreted as a bid to encourage European neutralism at the expense of Nato, and as another variant on the much feared theme of Soviet–American condominium. In the preparation of the American response Kissinger worked closely with a British Foreign Office specialist on the USSR, and wrote glowingly of the latter's contribution in his memoirs.[22]

Fundamental questions of strategy continued to haunt Nato. Thus on 17 January 1974 Nixon signed a new strategic memorandum, NSDM-242, which provided for the selective use of strategic nuclear weapons in a global war. The intention was to give the enemy 'opportunities to consider his actions' and to ensure that valuable enemy targets were temporarily spared to serve as hostages in the hope of forcing an accommodation.[23] This re-opened for the Europeans the old fears of sanctuary status for the superpower homelands. Nevertheless Nato continued to grapple with the question of fighting a war in Europe. Further studies were undertaken as to what might be done if the 'demonstration shots' (as proposed in 1969) failed to stop an aggressor.[24] But basically the allies were continuing to circle around the old problems. The Europeans feared both American inaction and overreaction in a crisis. The Americans persisted in their search for ways to prevent a conflict in Europe leading to devastation of their homeland, and to escape from the scenario crudely summarized by a former American official two years earlier:

the Nato doctrine is we will fight with conventional forces until we are losing, then we will fight with tactical nuclear weapons until we are losing, and then we will blow up the world . . . indeed, that is what the Europeans think it [the doctrine] ought to be.

Whatever the difficulties experienced by the British in the Nixon-Ford era, the presence of Henry Kissinger had ensured continuity and a remarkable measure of cohesion in American foreign policy. From 1977, under the presidency of Jimmy Carter, there was much more uncertainty, not least because of the rivalry between the national security adviser, Zbigniew Brzezinski, and the secretary of state, Cyrus Vance. Their approach to policy also differed, with Brzezinski inclining to a more assertive and geopolitical approach. In a critique of the Kissinger era – written in 1975 – Brzezinski had called for more 'architecture' and fewer 'acrobatics' in American foreign policy. In practice, because of divisions within the administration and Carter's own ambiguity and hesitations, foreign policy – in the words of Raymond Garthoff – bore more resemblance to 'acrobatics, while the architecture of the structure of peace erected in the Nixon years crumbled'.[25] From the very start of the Carter years, the British feared or perceived weaknesses and confusion. Worse, from 1979 policy often seemed shrill and unduly alarmist.

A meeting between Brzezinski and the British ambassador late in 1978 sums up British impressions of the first half of the Carter term. The ambassador (so Brzezinski recorded), 'representing a Labour government not noted for its martial fervor, pressed me at some length on whether our Administration had the will to apply American power . . . Jay specifically asked whether Carter had the "guts" to invoke America's might.' Carter's personality and his religious and moral convictions compounded his problems. Thus, although Brzezinski rated him highly as a negotiator in small meetings, Callaghan's political adviser, Tom McNally, writes of his 'initial puzzlement' on such an occasion.

[The president proceeded to expound] certain values, about God and the family and the American pioneer spirit and to talk about national and international problems in ways which would have been mawkish and embarrassing coming from other lips. In the end, I came to the conclusion that Carter was for real: but I can well understand how he unnerved some of the old Washington professionals.[26]

The new administration was also less inclined – than had been the case under Kissinger – to distinguish the British from the other West Europeans. There was of course a great and notable exception – the readiness to supply Trident missiles to extend the life of the British nuclear deterrent for another generation (though by then – 1980 – the renewed Cold War was well established). Otherwise Britain's growing economic and political problems in the 1970s, together with the power and behaviour of its trade union movement, excited a mass of critical and disparaging comment in America. Cyrus Vance, in a foreign policy survey which he prepared for Carter in October 1976, thought Britain worthy of special mention only on account of the scale of her current political and economic problems.[27] Similarly in his chapter on 'Key Players' Brzezinski singles out no British politician for mention in contrast to his admiration for the French president, Giscard d'Estaing, a judgement which was fully shared by Carter. The German chancellor, Helmut Schmidt, also receives notice, if only because of his increasingly turbulent relations with the president.

James Callaghan, at the start of his premiership in 1976, believed that the power of the super-states had become so great that the Europeans would be able to make their voices heard only if they were able to work to some extent in unison. Similarly he believed that if the anti-EEC elements in Britain had their way the outcome would be just as obnoxious to the left wing of his own party – it could only result in increased British dependence on the United States.[28] Nevertheless he persisted with efforts begun during his spell at the Foreign Office to cultivate close relations with Washington, especially in foreign and defence matters, and to discourage anti-Americanism in the policies of the EEC.

Carter himself, to judge from his memoirs, seems to have been unaware of (or unimpressed by) Callaghan's efforts. Margaret Thatcher, in contrast as premier from 1979, was unforgettable. She was tough, 'highly opinionated', and quite unable to accept that she did not know something.[29] Brzezinski, however and despite his omission of Callaghan from his list of 'key players', credited the Labour prime minister with no little diplomatic skill and influence.

> In fact, I was amazed how quickly Callaghan succeeded in establishing himself as Carter's favorite, writing him friendly little notes, calling, talking like a genial older uncle, and lecturing Carter in a pleasant manner on the intricacies of inter-allied politics. Callaghan literally co-opted Carter in the course of a few relatively brief personal encounters.[30]

The British also continued to make their presence felt in the prestigious Bureau of European Affairs (BEA) within the US State Department, a fact underlined during the later Falklands crisis in 1982 when the Anglophiles prevailed against the Inter-American Affairs Bureau. Yet even in the BEA West German tours of duty were coming to be regarded as more important by rising Europeanists.[31] Nor can one ignore Brzezinski's own interest in and hopes of France as a partner, or his claim that he consulted French colleagues more frequently than any in Britain or West Germany. France was full of vitality. Here, in his opinion, was the most authentic nation on the continent and therefore the one whose material and moral power most merited attention in his search for an appropriate American policy towards Europe.[32]

In other American accounts of the Carter administration it is rare to find Britain distinguished from Western Europe. There were, in any case, relatively few episodes (such as the efforts to find a solution to the Rhodesian question) in which Britain's activities, while intermingling with those of the United States, separated her from partners in the EEC or Nato. Other reasons help to explain Britain's relative lack of prominence. More American attention was being given, for instance, to the Far East. There was growing concern in the United States at the seemingly irresistible advance of the Japanese economy. The American defence establishment, especially the navy, was much preoccupied with perceived communist threats in the Western Pacific. Within the United States itself, the political and economic influences of the Anglophile elements of the East Coast were declining in relation to interest groups in Florida, California and other sun-belt states. Indeed Europe as a whole no longer loomed so large in the American consciousness as in the 1940s and 1950s. When it did the reasons were often negative ones. Transatlantic economic differences were acutely felt, with American exporters fretting over European tariffs and restrictions even when a weak dollar increased the competitiveness of their goods. Protectionism was a serious matter as the American economy became more dependent on exports. On the European side, whereas in the 1960s they (including the British) had feared American economic power and domination by American multinational corporations, they now shared the American concern over the Japanese industrial challenge.

The net effects of the changing American agenda and the tendency to see Britain as a museum piece, enlivened only by strikes and a newsworthy royal family, meant that Britain's standing in the United States reached its lowest point in the postwar era – despite the fact that Wilson and Callaghan were both more willing than Heath to work with Washington. Cyrus Vance, for instance, deals specifically with Britain at some length in his memoirs only with reference to the

Rhodesian question. Washington was increasingly anxious to see the beleaguered white minority come to terms with the black majority, and concede one man one vote. The collapse of the Portuguese empire in the mid-1970s brought the customary American fears of Soviet and other communist exploitation of new openings in Africa. Callaghan thought the Americans were being unnecessarily alarmist. He joked about these new 'Columbuses who lately discovered Africa'.[33]

At the same time his government sought American diplomatic support in Rhodesia, especially when it was faced with the possibility of a UN move to impose sanctions on South Africa, the main prop to the white regime in Rhodesia. British economic interests in South Africa would suffer if she supported such sanctions: her trade with a number of other states would suffer if she did not. The Commonwealth itself might be put at risk. The British government's anxieties and lack of confidence at times were such that the Americans felt that they were being asked to assume too much responsibility. The 1979 election, however, brought the Conservatives back into power, and the new government of Mrs Thatcher soon showed that it preferred to do things its own way, even if it continued to welcome American help from the sidelines. Furthermore real progress was at last being made towards a settlement – much to the surprise of most people. By the last months of 1979 both South Africa and Mozambique, each for reasons of its own, were urging restraint on the political groups which it had hitherto supported in the Rhodesian struggle.

TOWARDS A SECOND COLD WAR

By the late 1970s West Germany was often more prominent than Britain in East–West security issues. Despite the decline of detente since 1975, the Europeans could not overlook the possibility that the superpower SALT II talks might still result in an arms deal at their expense. Thus from October 1977 Helmut Schmidt, the West German chancellor, while expressing his support for SALT, warned of possible dangers to the 'Eurostrategic' balance. The more comprehensively the superpowers cancelled out each other's inter-continental nuclear capabilities, the more the existing military disparities in Europe might be magnified to the disadvantage of the West.[34] Western Europe had to be involved in the arms limitation process, and might, depending on its progress, require more – not fewer – forces for its defence. Schmidt was particularly troubled by the new Soviet SS-20, an intermediate-range missile with no comparable Western equivalent. Its range allowed it to strike at the heart of Europe from launch sites beyond the reach of any allied weapon system based in West Germany. In any case improved Warsaw Pact air defences were putting question marks against the effectiveness of Nato's nuclear strike aircraft. Doubts concerning the reliability of one vital rung in the ladder of flexible response naturally placed an additional onus on the next – namely the American strategic nuclear forces. Again the question surfaced as to whether an American president would dare to use these in a European war, and whether the Kremlin would find this a credible threat.

With respect to defence as a whole, Nato had already agreed in 1977 that each member should increase its spending on arms by 3 per cent in real terms per annum between 1979 and 1985. The extra American forces assigned to Europe included a doubling of the number of F-111 bombers stationed in Britain. Yet at the same time the Europeans were often troubled by the aggressive moral tone of the Carter administration. Moscow as well as the Europeans had difficulty in reading its real intentions. Within a few months of Carter's inauguration both Callaghan and Schmidt were asking Washington for a more sensitive and constructive response to what they believed to be a genuinely co-operative mood in the Kremlin.[35] The Soviet conception of detente was, of course, highly selective. It was also, apart from the question of the SS-20s in the later 1970s, more acceptable to the Europeans than to the Americans. In contrast the Europeans were complaining – even in the early Carter years – that the American approach to detente was too competitive or was being presented in ways (as on the question of human rights) which actually strengthened the position of the hardliners in the USSR.[36]

Nevertheless it was the Europeans in the newly established High Level Group (a branch of the Nuclear Planning Group formed under West German and British inspiration) which pleaded early in 1978 for an 'evolutionary upward adjustment' to Nato's long range theatre nuclear forces. At the Guadeloupe summit in January 1979 they persuaded the Americans to take the first steps along what became known as a 'dual-track' policy for the deployment of intermediate-range American missiles in Europe in conjunction with arms negotiations with Moscow.[37] Although there were some in Washington who welcomed this opportunity to modernize the Nato nuclear armoury, it appears that the final decision to deploy was not taken until the early 1980s.[38] Meanwhile this was an occasion when, initially at least, the Europeans made the running. On the question of Nato nuclear strategy as a whole, William Park argues: 'The point here is that for all its power, the US has not been able to ensure the adoption of an Alliance posture more to its liking, or even to ensure that this is clearly understood.' All too often the Americans, in his view, were driven to engage in 'the construction of nuclear use options because their friends in Europe have left them with few alternatives'.[39]

But there was a further American dilemma. While a 'European pillar' of the alliance had its theoretical attractions with its promise that the continent would be better able to stand on its own feet, this self-same 'pillar' could also lead to more independence from and even more competition with the United States.[40] Hence some on both sides of the Atlantic noted that a continuation of the existing policies of muddle and improvisation was not without its attractions. There existed in Nato's defence policy, according to McGeorge Bundy (an adviser to both Kennedy and Johnson in the 1960s), a condition of 'doctrinal confusion' which was apparently and handsomely offset by 'pragmatic success'. He described strategic ambiguity in European defence as 'a fact of life', and thought a foolproof deterrent superfluous given that war in Europe presented the USSR with unacceptable risks.[41]

Ambiguity was also a fact of life for the British, the increase in their military contacts with Europe since the 1960s (such as the joint Tornado fighter project) being accompanied by only a partial diminution in their transatlantic links.[42] Thus against the exclusion of Britain from the Russo-American talks on nuclear weapons after the 1960s must be set the Anglo-American exchanges which led to the agreement of 1980 whereby Britain would be supplied with Trident as a successor to Polaris. Although SALT I, by minimizing superpower anti-ballistic missile deployment, had prolonged the effectiveness of the British Polaris force, its life could not be extended beyond the mid-1990s. Discussion of the question of a successor therefore had to begin under the Callaghan ministry in the late 1970s. The British needed to sound out the attitude of the Americans. They could not automatically assume that there would be a sequel to the Nassau (Polaris) agreement of 1962. In the heyday of detente, for instance, there had always been the possibility that the United States would give priority to its relations with the USSR.

But in 1979 assurances arrived from Washington that no concessions would be made to the USSR in the SALT II talks on the subject either of the British deterrent itself or of the American relationship with it.[43] Carter went on to assure Callaghan that he favoured the continuance of both a British and French deterrent (this was also the

view of Helmut Schmidt of West Germany) and he promised sympathetic consideration if the British became seriously interested in Trident.[44] The ground had thus been prepared for a new Conservative
government under Mrs Thatcher to make the final decision. It was
agreed in mid-July 1980 that the United States would supply Trident
missiles, equipment and support services on terms similar to those which
had governed Polaris.[45]

The election of a Conservative government in 1979, especially
given the leadership of Mrs Thatcher, was a matter of some consequence in Anglo-American relations. It is true that Labour, had it
been returned to office, might not have moved so far to the left as it
did in Opposition, but American policy in Latin America and Africa
had already alarmed sections of the party. It is also reasonable to assume that the course of events elsewhere in the world in the early
1980s would have caused greater strains in Anglo-American relations
under a hypothetical Labour ministry than in fact occurred under the
Tories.

This change of ministry took place at a time when the Carter administration was desperately trying to fashion a tougher policy abroad.
The ill-starred American attempt to build up Iran as a friendly regional
power in the Persian Gulf had collapsed with the overthrow of the
shah in January 1979. The seizure of the American embassy and the
beginning of the long 'hostage' crisis followed in November. Already,
in August 1977 American fears of Soviet and other communist activities in Africa and the Middle East had produced the Presidential
Directive, PD-18, which ordered the creation of special units for rapid
deployment in regional danger spots. The events in Iran and worsening relations with the USSR, accelerated the American military build-
up in the western Indian Ocean and the search for local base facilities
even before the Soviet intervention in Afghanistan at the end of 1979.
The seriousness of the situation was underlined by the customary
American response to a new crisis, the articulation of another doctrine.

The Carter Doctrine of 1980 stepped back from the emphasis in
the Nixon Doctrine of 1969 upon the responsibility – in the first
instance – of regional countries for their own security against aggression. It reasserted the role of the United States in the containment of
the USSR on the lines set out in the Truman and Eisenhower doc-
trines. For the British and Europeans this more militant approach was
in some ways as worrying as the earlier Carter ambiguities in East–
West relations. But impatience with apparent Soviet foreign successes
had been mounting in the United States since the mid-1970s – especially among the more extreme right. In 1979 the president's domestic

enemies scented blood. Carter had to try to roll back both his foreign and domestic opponents.

European sympathy for his problems was further strained when Carter asserted to Congress on 8 January 1980 that 'the Soviet invasion of Afghanistan is the greatest threat to peace since the Second World War'. It was also one thing for the Europeans to join in criticism of and diplomatic protests to the USSR, but trade sanctions and the denial of export credits at the expense of the West European economies was a different matter. Cyrus Vance himself later accepted that Washington was failing to take adequate account of the views of its European allies. Its actions were often precipitate – even excessive. He could understand the allied desire that American policy should be less erratic. Meanwhile British sales to the USSR rose sharply (French and West German exports increased even more) at a time when the Americans were savagely cutting theirs.[46]

At least the British Conservative government was able to earn more credit than other Europeans with its support of the United States on a number of issues at this time. London used its influence in the EEC to secure added sanctions against Tehran in the spring of 1980. The British also agreed to improve the air and sea facilities on the island of Diego Garcia in the Indian Ocean and were among the participants in the international consortium which gave financial assistance to Pakistan as it tried to handle the flood of refugees from the Afghan conflict. Britain similarly came to show more sympathy in general for America's policy on Afghanistan. Within Nato, the Thatcher government announced its intention in January 1980 to permit the deployment of 160 cruise missiles in Britain (a step which a Labour ministry might have had particular difficulty in taking).[47]

But American complaints persisted that the Europeans could not compartmentalize Western security, demanding American support in Europe while leaving the Americans to deal with communist challenges elsewhere. Nor was Washington pleased when the European Community used the Venice Declaration of 1980 to signal its interest in the inclusion of the Palestinians in future peace talks between the Arabs and Israel. The Declaration also spoke of the Palestinian right to self-determination. The British foreign secretary, Lord Carrington, persevered with the argument that the United States should recognize that the Arab moderates were entitled to some show of Western sympathy.

Overall, by 1980, there had been some improvement in Anglo-American relations compared with the Heath period of government. The improvement had begun under Labour from 1974, and increased again under the Conservatives. But clearly different outcomes to either or both of the British and American elections of 1979 and 1980, or indeed the presence of different tenants in Number 10 Downing Street and the White House whatever the party in power, might well have denied Anglo-American relations the remarkable – if sometimes squally – Indian Summer which they were about to experience in the 1980s under Margaret Thatcher and Ronald Reagan.

NOTES AND REFERENCES

1. A.G. Andrianopoulos, *Western Europe in Kissinger's Global Strategy*, New York: St Martin's Press, 1988, p. 27.
2. H. Kissinger, *The White House Years*, Weidenfeld and Nicolson, 1979, pp. 91–111. Kissinger refers to Nixon's distrust of Wilson, but the working relationship was satisfactory, with Britain, for instance, exerting some influence over American policy on the Nigerian civil war (p. 417).
3. Kissinger, *White House Years*, pp. 94, 392.
4. G. Rumble, *The Politics of Nuclear Deterrence*, Cambridge University Press, 1985, pp. 54–5; Kissinger, *White House Years*, pp. 391–2.
5. Adrianopoulos, pp. 27, 40–1, 75–7, 109–10, 117–18.
6. Kissinger, *White House Years*, p. 421.
7. Ibid, pp. 932–8; Adrianopoulos, pp. 155–7.
8. Kissinger, *White House Years*, pp. 950–66; *The Years of Upheaval*, Weidenfeld and Nicolson, 1982, p. 137.
9. Kissinger, *Years of Upheaval*, pp. 143,151, 171, 189–91.
10. Dimbleby, pp. 262–3. See also W.L. Kohl, 'The Nixon–Kissinger Foreign Policy System and US–European Relations', *World Politics*, October 1975, pp. 15–19.
11. R. Garthoff, *Detente and Confrontation: American–Soviet Relations from Nixon to Reagan*, Washington DC: Brookings Institution, 1985, pp. 321–2. See also Kohl, pp. 15–18.
12. W.C. Cromwell, 'Europe and the "Structure of Peace",' *Orbis*, spring 1978, pp. 11–36. Note also the Senate defeat in May 1971 of Mansfield's bid for a 50 per cent cut in US forces in Europe in May 1971.
13. Cromwell, p. 22.
14. Garthoff, pp. 401–5; Dimbleby, pp. 264–6.
15. S. Duke, *United States Defence Bases in the United Kingdom*, Macmillan, 1987, pp. 165, 166; Kissinger, *Years of Upheaval*, pp. 516–17, 590–3, 709–14; Garthoff, pp. 401–3; Dimbleby, pp. 264–6.
16. Kissinger, *Years of Upheaval*, pp. 720–32; Cromwell, pp. 24–5, 29.
17. Cromwell, pp. 11–36, especially pp. 25–6.

18. Cromwell, p. 30. H. Wilson, *Final Term: the Labour Government*, 1974–76, Weidenfeld and Nicolson, and Michael Joseph, 1979, p. 113. See Dobson, p. 237, who notes that Britain in her latest economic crisis received no separate aid from the United States. She had to rely on the International Monetary Fund.

19. D. Healey, *The Time of My Life*, pp. 429–32.

20. Garthoff, pp. 489–96. See also Cromwell, pp. 30–1.

21. See Barbara Castle, *The Castle Diaries*, Weidenfeld and Nicolson, 1980, pp. 227, 390–1, for American unease over Labour's proposed defence cuts.

22. Kissinger, *Years of Upheaval*, pp. 277–86; Cromwell, pp. 20–1.

23. Rumble, pp. 55–8.

24. Park, pp. 99–101, 142; P. Buteux, *The Politics of Nuclear Consultation in Nato, 1965–80*, Cambridge University Press, 1983, pp. 149–51. Note Park's comment (pp. 138–9) that in 1986 thinking on a 'demonstration shot' still seemed 'unclear'.

25. Garthoff, pp. 564 ff.

26. See review by Tom McNally in *International Affairs*, 1983, p. 465.

27. C. Vance, *Hard Choices*, New York: Simon and Schuster, 1983, p. 442.

28. Callaghan, pp. 305, 319–20. Callaghan adds that America's own problems made Schmidt of West Germany Britain's most useful friend (pp. 326–30, 429–47, 487–93).

29. J. Carter, *Keeping Faith*, Collins, 1982, p. 113.

30. Z. Brzezinski, *Power and Principle*, Weidenfeld and Nicolson, 1983, cf chapter 1 and p. 291.

31. B. Rubin, *Secrets of State*, Oxford University Press, 1987, p. 135.

32. Brzezinski, p. 313.

33. Brzezinski, p. 321.

34. Helmut Schmidt, *Men and Power*, Jonathan Cape, 1990, pp. 64 ff. Note also Healey, pp. 453–7, 513, and his fear of any situation or decision that might tempt the USA to withdraw those inter-continental forces which were committed to a deterrent role in Europe.

35. Brzezinski, p. 165. The British ambassador in Moscow (1978–82), Sir Curtis Keeble, commented that the 'Carter morality . . . did not make for predictability in relationships with the Soviet Union, and America's allies could not avoid being caught up in the confused waters . . . ', *Britain and the Soviet Union, 1917–89*, Macmillan, 1990, pp. 290–1.

36. For a useful summary of the early Carter years see S.R. Ashton, *In Search of Detente*, Macmillan, 1989, pp. 141 ff.

37. Ashton, p. 149.

38. Park, pp. 110–11. Note also Healey, pp. 453–7, 513.

39. Park, pp. 139, 197.

40. Michael Howard, 'A European Perspective of the Reagan Years', *Foreign Affairs, 1987–8: America and the World*, p. 482.

41. P. Williams, 'The United States' commitment to Western Europe: strategic ambiguity and political disintegration?', *International Affairs*, 1983, p. 199, and see pp. 195–209 passim.

42. J. Baylis, *Anglo-American Defence Relations, 1945–84*, Macmillan, 1984, pp. 169–70.
43. Vance, pp. 97–9.
44. Callaghan, pp. 553–8.
45. Baylis, p. 182.
46. Vance, pp. 392–407. See also A.J. Blinken, *Ally versus Ally: America, Europe and the Siberian Pipeline Crisis*, New York and London, Praeger, 1987, p. 92.
47. Carter, pp. 465, 486, 501–2

Co-operation and Controversy, 1981–89

THE START OF THE REAGAN ERA

In the course of Ronald Reagan's eight years in the White House it became evident that a very special personal relationship was developing between the president and Mrs Thatcher. That this was of real political moment was demonstrated on a number of occasions – not least when the USSR and Britain's partners in the EEC employed Mrs Thatcher's good offices to assist them in some of their own dealings with Washington. On the other hand the precariousness of the relationship was underlined with the ending of the second Cold War and the presence from 1989 of a new president in the White House. It required a crisis in the Persian Gulf in 1990–91 to bring Britain back into the limelight.

Even in the Reagan era it is important to note that personal ties could operate in a highly selective fashion. There were occasions when the president himself seemed to forget their existence, and when the British were affronted by American neglect of their interests. Ostensibly successful meetings with the president did not always result in obvious gains for Mrs Thatcher as the Byzantine American government machine continued on its own mysterious ways. On the other hand Reagan finally overruled those in Washington who opposed aid to Britain in the Falklands War, while Mrs Thatcher risked great unpopularity at home when she permitted American aircraft based in Britain to bomb Libya in 1986.

Claims that the Reagan–Thatcher personal relationship was at least as close as that between any pair of American and British leaders since 1940 may prove correct, but it is important to remember the degree to which contemporary impressions of the state of Anglo-American relations in the Roosevelt–Churchill and Kennedy–Macmillan eras have been modified with the growing availability of primary sources. In the case of Reagan and Thatcher, the story is likely to be complicated by the looseness of and the divisions within the American administration, a situation which could sometimes (but not always) be turned to their advantage by the British.

From the start of her premiership in 1979 Mrs Thatcher was determined to show that she had no intention of being inhibited by British membership of the European Community (EC). Indeed for much of the 1980s Britain's relations with her partners in the EC were such as to encourage London to cultivate its American ties. The start of the Thatcher era was marked by a number of acrimonious exchanges with the Community. France and West Germany were more often in agreement with each other than with Britain. The Thatcher government had a long struggle before a major British grievance – the unfair distribution of national contributions to the Community's finances – was met. It also stood by the decision of the previous government not to become a full member of the newly established European Monetary System (EMS). It was not until 1989 that Mrs Thatcher's pugnaciously nationalistic approach to the EC began to provoke serious criticism at home. It was only in 1990 that Britain joined the Exchange Rate Mechanism within the EMS.

The prime minister's friendship with Ronald Reagan predated his election to the presidency, but this in itself did not bring an immediate change to the inter-state relationship. This had in any case staged a small recovery since 1974. A British opinion poll taken early in 1981 found that 70 per cent regarded American world leadership as 'fairly desirable', a clear sign that the legacy from the 1970s had not been entirely negative. American impressions of Britain's importance, however, were more guarded. In 1982, when the long-term future of Mrs Thatcher's government was still in doubt and when she herself was still in the process of gaining frontline status among the world's leaders, American polls suggested that no Western European state was rated of crucial importance in international affairs. Admittedly Britain (with Canada) was graded a 'close ally', but West Germany was not far behind.[1]

There were significant negative features in Anglo-American relations as well, not all of which were overcome. In 1981 – and indeed at times thereafter – the British Foreign Office doubted if American foreign policy was under much better management than in the time of Jimmy Carter. Lord Carrington's memoirs on his period as British foreign secretary and Nato's secretary-general admittedly include a reference to the magical effect of Reagan's personality at one Nato briefing, and more generally refer to George Shultz (US secretary of state between 1982 and 1989) and Caspar Weinberger (US secretary of defense) as good friends of Britain. Yet the memoirs are perhaps as revealing for what they omit as for what they include. Carrington apparently found no policy-maker of the calibre of Henry Kissinger, and he makes ('perhaps a little unkindly', he adds) the mischievous comment 'that the only times when consultation has failed [with the Reagan administration] have been when the United States' actions have taken the United States themselves somewhat by surprise'. This may be variously interpreted.[2]

Nevertheless, from the inauguration of Ronald Reagan as president in 1981, both the United States and Britain had governments which were making a determined assault on what the radical right described as the consensus politics and policies which – it complained – had dominated and damaged both countries since 1945. The two leaders were equally vehement in their opposition to the USSR and communism. No Western European leader matched Mrs Thatcher's conviction on the two issues of the free market economy and the Cold War. Thus prime minister and president had more in common with each other than with any other allied leader. It would seem that the new president welcomed Mrs Thatcher's greater ability and eagerness to articulate the principles and attitudes which they shared. The Thatcher government was also one of the few in Europe to honour fully the promise to increase defence spending annually by 3 per cent in real terms. Its readiness to deploy American cruise missiles further enhanced British standing in the United States – even if it was the deployment of Pershing 2 missiles in West Germany which most dismayed the Kremlin and contributed to the later readiness to talk.

The Reagan–Thatcher relationship was one of the reasons why the West Coast groups around the president had a less damaging effect on relations with Britain than some had anticipated. But the Thatcher government itself was steadily gaining credit in the United States as a whole for its strong stand against trade union power. For a time, too, there seemed to be convincing evidence of a transformation of parts at least of the British economy. The emphasis on self-help and individual enterprise did much to persuade Americans that their old ally was not in terminal decline. They were impressed not only by Margaret

Thatcher's commitment to the free market but also by her robust approach to every problem. Numerous Americans were delighted by what she said and the way she said it.[3]

There could, however, be problems even in the realm of economics. As Richard Portes argues,[4] 'Trade has never been the warmest area of Anglo-American relations', especially compared with the common interests of the two as suppliers of financial services. The 1980s saw further disputes over trade between the EC and the United States. Fortunately the Reagan administration stood out against most domestic calls for protectionism, though it continued to use a trigger-price mechanism to protect American producers from what was deemed 'unfair' foreign competition. American trade policy remained sufficiently liberal for the British at times to try to act as mediators between Washington and the EC. The British and Europeans were also protected to some extent from transatlantic ire by the greater challenge posed to the American economy by Japan. Yet even this created problems, as American pressure on that country led to increased Japanese efforts to penetrate European markets. Nevertheless, despite much huffing and puffing, threats of a transatlantic trade war were eased or postponed in the 1980s by last-minute compromises or agreements to keep talking.

Indeed, in the mid-1980s the British economy was much assisted by a great American consumer boom – that is until concern began to develop over the soaring American budget and trade deficits, with consequential high interest rates and a volatile dollar. But British lectures to Washington on the dangers of financial improvidence were speedily silenced when Britain herself began to suffer from inflation, a huge trade deficit and crippling interest rates from the end of the decade.[5]

The most notable feature of the Reagan administration in its early years was its strident hostility to the USSR – 'the evil empire'. Its conduct of foreign and defence policies often caused profound unease and even outright hostility in Britain and Western Europe, and whatever its own feelings on East–West relations the British government could hardly have felt entirely happy about American behaviour. Indeed Mrs Thatcher as early as the autumn of 1983 delivered speeches which stressed the common interest of East and West 'in peace and security at a lower level of weapons'. This was some six months before Nato formally committed itself to a renewed search for detente.

If there were some divisions from the outset within the Reagan administration on the conduct of East–West relations,[6] it was the more belligerent remarks which attracted most attention. There was the president's reference to the USSR as 'the focus of evil in the modern world'. He caused even more alarm with his comment, as reported in the *International Herald Tribune* of 21 October 1981, that 'I could see where you could have an exchange of tactical weapons against troops in the field without it bringing either one of the major powers into pushing the button.' Early in the administration the US secretary of defense also frightened the Europeans when – without prior reference to the US State Department or America's allies – he spoke of the possible deployment of neutron warheads by Nato. Anything which suggested the feasibility of a war confined to Europe naturally alarmed America's allies. Indeed Helmut Schmidt later spelt out in his memoirs (*Men and Powers*) the reasons for his fundamental opposition to any strategy of flexible nuclear response: this would involve the destruction of that which Nato had been created to defend. Millions of Germans would die in a few days. There were other examples of acute West German sensitivity on deterrence.[7]

The Reagan administration continued the search, already begun by its predecessors, for a strategy for the selective and controlled use of nuclear weapons to replace that of mutual assured destruction.[8] The US secretary of defense, Caspar Weinberger, denied that the United States was trying to devise a strategy with which to win a nuclear war. At the same time he insisted that the United States required a 'margin of safety' since the credibility of 'extended deterrence' in Europe depended upon America's ability to use nuclear weapons meaningfully, both to end major wars on terms favourable to Nato, and 'in particular to deter escalation in the event of hostilities'.[9] But many Europeans were not happy to see a strategy of deterrence spelt out in terms which they feared might lessen its credibility and, in some degree, suggest that Europe was in a different category from the American homeland. For their part the Americans continued to grumble that the Europeans were not pulling their weight inside Nato. They also argued that the United States should not be expected to police the rest of the world unaided against communist threats.[10] If the sympathies of the British government varied between the Americans and Europeans according to the issue under discussion, it shared the Western European desire for American protection through but not American domination over Nato. Nor was it entirely happy with those in Washington who seemed to regard the Cold War not only as a game in which either side's gain must represent a loss by the other, but also as a game which the United States might be able to win outright.

The vehement Cold War rhetoric of the Reagan administration provided ammunition for the peace movements. Opposition in Britain and Europe was increased in step with the approach of the date when cruise and Pershing missiles were to be deployed in Europe. In Britain by March 1981 polls suggested that just over 30 per cent were opposed to these weapons. Although the British government was unmoved by the protesters, it too showed some unease and embarrassment when Washington emphatically rejected Soviet offers of talks on intermediate-range missiles in 1982. It was relieved when a more flexible tone was later adopted.[11] The same year saw the British prime minister take a particularly strong stand when Washington tried to bully all the Europeans into a policy of comprehensive sanctions as a result of the latest twist to the crisis of communism in Poland.

Unrest under communist rule in Poland had finally – in December 1981 – resulted in the imposition of martial law. Mrs Thatcher, for all her reputation as the 'Iron Lady' in her attitudes to communism, sided emphatically with the Europeans when zealots in Washington pressed for unanimity on sanctions. There were widespread fears that American policy might cause Poland to default on its extensive debts to the West. The situation was exacerbated by concurrent American efforts to obstruct European involvement in the construction of a pipeline from the USSR to supply gas to Western Europe. In February 1982 the prime minister bluntly warned the Americans that a Polish default could have a domino financial effect throughout Eastern Europe, with dire consequences for the banking systems of the West. As for the Siberian pipeline, the Europeans, she declared, would desert the United States rather than abandon that project. American policy might do more injury to the economies of Western Europe than to the intended targets – the USSR and Poland. Thus one British company, John Brown Ltd, had more at stake in its contracts with the USSR than the total American exports to that country in one year. To the American threat of possible legal action against some British firms (arising out of their connections with American companies) Mrs Thatcher retorted that the British government also possessed legal powers (based on its right to protect national interests) which it could invoke to force such firms to fulfil their contracts with Eastern countries.[12] Later, on 29 June 1982, she accused the United States of interfering where its jurisdiction did not run. Relief was soon forthcoming when the Reagan administration undercut its own case by agreeing to a new grain deal with the USSR. A gradual retreat followed as Washington re-evaluated the effect of its actions on Nato, and discovered other flaws in its policies.[13]

THE FALKLANDS AFFAIR

Yet even while these matters were in dispute between London and Washington, the invasion of the Falkland Islands by Argentina on 2 April 1982 was to bring about the most striking demonstration of Anglo-American military co-operation since the Korean War. The ensuing British success strikingly enhanced Margaret Thatcher's standing in the United States. Nevertheless at the start of the crisis American backing could not be taken for granted. The American media showed great interest, but the general mood was one of cool detachment towards Britain. In the US State Department, according to Secretary of State Alexander Haig, 'most of the staff [at first] shared the amusement of the press and public over what was perceived as a Gilbert and Sullivan battle over a sheep pasture between a choleric old John Bull and a comic dictator in a gaudy uniform'.[14] Many relished the comment of Jorge Luis Borges that the affair was 'like two bald men fighting over a comb'. British diplomats – mindful of Suez and of the Latin American dimension in American policy – launched an intensive campaign to win support from the White House, Congress and the public. Fortunately they had one assured ally from the start in Caspar Weinberger. Haig's position was more complicated. He later argued that as long as Britain and Argentina were not engaged in hostilities his most useful role was that of an honest broker.

Haig's problems were compounded by divisions in his own department and the government as a whole. There was a powerful Latin American lobby among the diplomats who feared – or argued – that American interests would suffer if the United States ranged itself against Argentina. Haig himself thought it politically expedient that Argentina should gain something from the crisis.[15] There were also those who doubted Britain's will and capacity to recover the islands. Mrs Thatcher had yet to capture the American imagination. It was not enough, therefore, for the Argentinians to have taken the first aggressive step by invading the Falklands. Much would turn on the presentation of the Argentine and British cases in the United States.

These divisions in Washington meant that there could be no early American 'tilt' in favour of Britain, a move which Laurence Freedman suggests 'might have brought home to the [Argentine] Junta the reality of its diplomatic position', and thereby have defused the crisis. Nevertheless, from the outset the British benefited from their especially close ties with the American defence and intelligence establishments. Naval and intelligence officers in particular began to work with their opposite numbers in Britain long before it became official policy to abandon the role of mediator.[16] Haig himself admits to his surprise at the strength of belligerent feeling when he arrived in London on 8 April. Mrs Thatcher invoked the 1930s as a warning of the danger of weakness, and pointedly showed Haig portraits of Wellington and Nelson. She would have nothing to do with interim solutions or an international presence on the islands. British sovereignty was a fact, while the islanders must have the right to self-determination. Haig, however, persevered as honest broker in the hope that some compromise might emerge, and that the two sides could somehow be persuaded to accept the absurdity of war over so small an issue.[17]

The story of his efforts is too lengthy and complicated to follow here. One American scholar, Douglas Kinney, makes the interesting distinction between American strategic and tactical thinking. Strategically Washington was always closer to the British given the widespread reluctance to see aggression rewarded. Tactically, however, it seemed important to avoid a conflict, even if this led to some concessions to the Argentinians in return for their withdrawal. But the Junta in Buenos Aires was unimpressed by American diplomatic efforts, and accused Washington of increasing bias against Argentina. For their part the British rightly took nothing for granted. Washington had to be persuaded that Britain deserved support. Unhappy memories of Suez were ever present – for Haig as well as the British. Both sides were aware of the need for clear and effective communication, and both were – in the end – well pleased with their efforts.[18] Indeed Haig later contended that any final chance of peace had been destroyed before the controversial sinking of the Argentine cruiser, *General Belgrano*, by a British submarine.[19]

With the virtual breakdown in negotiations at the end of April, Haig announced that the United States would support Britain and would exert economic pressure on Argentina. By 30 April Washington had also accepted (though it was a conclusion disputed by figures such as its ambassador at the UN) that Britain's value as an ally outweighed any possible injury to American interests in Latin America. Unlike the Middle East in 1956, the American administration had decided that it could not tolerate a British defeat or humiliation. Amid all these hard-headed calculations there was, perhaps, some room for pro-British sentiment and the sense of shared values. Certainly the dialogue with the British had been meaningful if not without its problems. With Buenos Aires there was nothing to suggest any meeting of minds.

The scale of American aid was impressive, perhaps indispensable. John Lehman, the US navy secretary from 1981 to 1987, claimed that a British climb-down would have been inevitable if the United States had shut off its assistance. Caspar Weinberger (later given an honorary knighthood by a grateful British government) more modestly described it as 'important' but not 'crucial'. He had approved the despatch of key supplies and intelligence even before the conflict began in earnest, and when important groups in the Pentagon still doubted the possibility of a British victory. The US navy was especially helpful and sympathetic, and years of inter-service co-operation paid off handsomely.[20] But there was also the calculation that if the British were determined to fight, it was of prime importance to the United States that they should not lose. Some diplomats also hoped that through aid to the British they would enhance America's moderating influence in the event of victory.

The assistance took various forms. American Sidewinder missiles enabled British Harrier fighters to attack Argentine bombers head-on. The bombers responded by flying lower with the fortunate result that many of the bombs which struck vulnerable ships failed to explode. The British also gained useful satellite intelligence from the United States, together with information on the operational effectiveness of Argentine forces. The Americans passed on intercepted signals traffic during the diplomatic build-up and the war itself.[21] Lord Whitelaw, a major figure in the British government, later remarked concerning the value of American facilities on Ascension Island.

> If we hadn't had the use of that base, we would not have been able to send the Task Force. The Americans could have said 'No' at any stage if they disapproved of what we were doing.[22]

Ascension Island was still some 4,000 miles distant from the Falklands, but it was near enough and just qualified as a half-way base.

The extent of American assistance was not at first known outside the relevant government departments in Britain, and some offence was taken when the United States understandably moved swiftly after the Argentine defeat to try to placate opinion in Latin America. Within Whitehall the response was more calculated. Washington might not have given the British all they wanted, but it had given enough, and without the United States Britain would have been hard put to recover the islands.

There had been, as we have seen, mixed feelings in Washington about the whole affair. But in the end the Anglo-American relationship obviously benefited from the satisfaction felt by many leading Americans at this display of British patriotism, vigour and professional military skill. At the same time many in the American services commented on the deficiencies in and shortages of British equipment. There had again been abundant evidence of the degree to which the British had been running their armed forces on a shoe-string.

But for the US secretary of state the conflict had assumed much broader significance. If at one level it still seemed 'senseless and avoidable', in the real world of politics it could be regarded as 'the most useful and timely reminder of the true character of the West in many years'. The British were willing to fight for their beliefs. He applauded Mrs Thatcher as 'by far the strongest, the shrewdest, and the most clear-sighted player in the game'. Caspar Weinberger similarly gave most credit to the British prime minister for the recovery of the islands.[23]

MISSILES, BASES AND ARMS CONTROL

A little over a year later the Americans felt poorly compensated for their role in the Falklands War when their intervention in the tiny Caribbean island of Grenada (a member of the Commonwealth) to remove an extreme left-wing government provoked a general outcry in Britain. The president was aware of Mrs Thatcher's objections, but decided to press ahead. Of the subsequent protests a former British ambassador, Lord Harlech, remarked that 'twenty minutes' diplomacy' could have settled the matter. But his complaint that Mrs Thatcher had resorted to 'myopic and fuddy-duddy legalism' bypassed the fact that this was not a matter which could be dealt with simply at the level of 'high politics'. The Opposition was in full cry, with Denis Healey mischievously portraying Mrs Thatcher as Ronald Reagan's 'obedient poodle' who had now to suffer the ignominy of being ignored despite past loyalty. The episode was also exploited by those who opposed the deployment of American cruise missiles in Britain. This was to begin in November 1983. Critics asked if the Americans could be trusted not to fire the missiles without reference to the British government.

In general talk of a crisis in Anglo-American relations was greatly exaggerated, although Latin America did continue to cause friction between the two capitals. London watched with some unease as the Reagan administration set out to destabilize the Marxist regime in Nicaragua. But a new US president in 1989 brought a policy change, and free elections took place in Nicaragua in 1990. Meanwhile the United States was busily repairing broken bridges in Latin America after the Falklands affair. It pointedly reminded the British of the precariousness of the new democracy which was emerging in Argentina, and complained, for instance, in 1988 of the timing of a military exercise designed to test Britain's ability to reinforce the Falklands garrison at short notice. From 1989, however, a new government in Buenos Aires under President Menem seemed intent on rebuilding links with Britain – and the question of the Falklands (or Malvinas) was put to one side.

The renewed tension with the USSR ensured that Nato defence policies continued to be keenly debated. The pessimists called for annual defence spending increases of 4 per cent in real terms by the member states of Nato. Any realistic increase by the British, however, seemed unlikely to do more than relieve existing weaknesses within their forces.[24] Meanwhile the chief cause of popular excitement in Britain remained the deployment of cruise missiles – the concern being increased by distrust of the judgement of Reagan and his advisers. Such was the apparent strength of the opposition to the missiles that Caspar Weinberger himself participated in an Oxford Union debate on the subject in 1984. Among the literature generated at this time was Duncan Campbell's book, *The Unsinkable Aircraft Carrier: American Military Power in Britain*, (1985). Although Lawrence Freedman questioned if it revealed much new information, the book conveniently compressed within its covers details and analyses which were scattered through a host of obscure and abstruse sources. Nor did Freedman's thoughtful counterargument to Campbell's critique of Britain's exposed position as a frontline American base offer much comfort in the atmosphere of the time. He concluded in the British *Times Literary Supplement* of 30 August 1985 that if 'war breaks out in Europe then Britain will be scarred one way or another, however much we try to distance ourselves'. From this it followed, in his view, that 'if war can be prevented then the issue of the degree of our vulnerability in the conflict is less relevant'.

Opinion was further excited by American air strikes against Libya in 1986, some of the attacking aircraft flying from bases in Britain. Washington claimed that it possessed evidence of the Libyan regime's association with international terrorists. Although Mrs Thatcher had earlier described retaliatory action against states on this count as contrary to international law, she agreed to the use of the American bases. Her decision was widely condemned. Some 70 per cent of those questioned in a MORI poll (*The Times* of 17 April 1986) were hostile.

There were renewed claims that the Americans would fire cruise missiles from Britain against the USSR without waiting for the approval of the British government. More suggestions followed that the Western alliance was 'visibly crumbling'. In the United States, however, Margaret Thatcher's assent had been extremely well received. No other European leader had helped, and her reputation rose accordingly.[25]

All this controversy over Britain's relations with the United States in the mid-1980s – though embarrassing to ministers at times – failed to injure the government in either the 1983 or 1987 elections. The administration in Washington did not conceal its alarm at the implications for Nato and American bases in Britain if Labour were to return to power. But the latter's shift to the left led to the departure of four leading figures and the formation of the Social Democratic Party. Support for Labour among the electorate also fell sharply. But under the first-past-the-post voting system major increases in votes for the centre meant that this was not translated into proportionate strength in the Commons. Thus a divided Opposition gave the Tories large majorities with only a little more than two-fifths of the poll in each election. Even so it should be noted that the campaign against the deployment of cruise missiles in Britain enjoyed more support in the opinion polls than unilateralism. The anti-missile demonstrations at the Greenham Common base also attracted great publicity.[26]

One of the most controversial policies of the Reagan administration was the revolutionary Strategic Defence Initiative (SDI or Star Wars). It was hoped that with laser and other new technologies the United States could be effectively shielded against ballistic missile attack. The Europeans feared that if the United States once began to feel secure against a Soviet nuclear assault, it might either lose interest in Europe or be more ready to risk a 'limited' war in that theatre. The prime minister put the European point of view to the president at Camp David at the end of 1984. But the value of the four points which the president apparently conceded remained open to doubt. White House watchers thought it important not to confuse presidential politeness with acquiescence or, like Haig, speculated on the role of 'hard men' behind the scenes in various parts of the administration. Sir Geoffrey Howe reiterated British unease in March 1985. Many in Britain hoped that so speculative a venture would ultimately be restrained by technical difficulties and financial costs. Meanwhile the British gave qualified support in the hope that SDI would remain essentially a 'research' programme which would not create too many difficulties with the USSR or injure the credibility of the Western deterrent. Hopes of lucrative contracts for British firms were fulfilled to only a limited extent.[27]

The strengths and weaknesses of Mrs Thatcher's personal relationship with the president were most graphically demonstrated in 1986. This occurred at a time when the British and their European partners were already seriously troubled by the scale of the American budget and trade deficits, the Reagan administration's activities in Central America, and the Iran–Contra scandal.[28] Mrs Thatcher's personal friendship with Reagan had seemed solid enough at the Tokyo economic summit of May 1986. But in October there occurred a remarkable display of American independence at the Reykjavik Summit when the two superpowers appeared close to a comprehensive agreement on nuclear disarmament without reference to their European allies. Mrs Thatcher was said to have described this episode as 'one of the most shattering things' she had ever experienced.[29]

At Reykjavik the Soviets had surprised the West by taking up an earlier (propagandist) American proposal for the removal of all intermediate-range missiles from Europe (the so-called zero-zero option). Even more alarming from the European point of view, however, was American treatment of the superpower strategic nuclear armoury. It seemed that only the US president's commitment to his controversial SDI programme (Gorbachev insisted that no development or testing should take place outside the laboratory) prevented agreement in principle for the abolition of all strategic nuclear weapons by 1996. While the extent of superpower disarmament would in practice have been restrained at the very least by the existence of other nuclear forces (such as the Chinese), the conduct of Reagan and his closest advisers at Reykjavik was widely and rightly criticized. A former US (Republican) secretary of defense, James Schlesinger, castigated the administration for its 'casual utopianism and indifferent preparation'.[30] To the Europeans it all seemed feckless and amateurish on a scale beyond the worst fears of even the most patronizing of European critics of American foreign policy. They were shocked by the easy disregard of their interests by a president and his colleagues. For the British prime minister comprehensive nuclear deterrence was a *sine qua non*.

Mrs Thatcher again took wing to Washington in search of reassurance on behalf of Britain and her European allies. On this occasion she was certainly supported behind the scenes by powerful friends in Washington, the most radical schemes at Reykjavik never having been discussed seriously with the US Joint Chiefs. Paul Nitze, the experienced arms negotiator, denies that the American delegation was poorly prepared, and suggests that a plea from Shultz for 'bold ideas' had put the thought of total strategic nuclear weapon abolition into circulation (as an idea but not as a recommendation). Nitze, however, hardly addresses the question of Western alliance interests or co-ordination.[31]

Richard Perle, who was present at Reykjavik, seemed to feel that the exchange of proposals with the USSR had been allowed to get out of hand. Certainly in a British television interview he later claimed that – with others – he had been 'rather pleased at the prospect that some of the more intemperate and visionary views of the President might be modified, as indeed they were' by Mrs Thatcher's visit. He praised her for helping to relieve the administration, at least temporarily, from some of the president's more nonsensical ideas.[32] The nuclear triad of bombers, inter-continental missiles, and submarine-launched ballistic missiles had been axiomatic in American defence thinking for a quarter of a century before Reykjavik, annually reaffirmed in the reports of US secretaries of defense, and underlined in the president's acceptance in 1983 of the findings of the Scowcroft Commission. Similarly James Schlesinger could only marvel at the irresponsibility of the president and his team, and he too praised Mrs Thatcher for her intervention: 'Once again, as with the earlier rhetoric of SDI replacing (immoral) deterrence, Mrs Thatcher helped save Americans from their own folly.'[33] Perhaps what she had really done was to spare major figures in Washington the embarrassment of bringing the president to heel themselves.

Nevertheless the accumulated strains in transatlantic relations led Sir Michael Howard (Regius Professor of History at Oxford) to warn a scholarly American readership in 1987 that 'relations between the governments of the United States and its European allies [had reached] a nadir for which it would be difficult to find an equal – the Suez crisis of 1956 excepted – during the whole of the postwar period'. Nor was European confidence in the United States being helped by the Reagan administration's activities in Central America, or by the Iran–Contra scandal (an extraordinary and complex affair in which some government agents were acting in defiance of Congress).[34]

Fortunately Washington responded to pressure from Mrs Thatcher and other sources, and agreed that arms control talks should proceed in the context of long-standing Nato strategy. Thus conventional arms, chemical warfare and the entire range of nuclear weapon systems would not be forgotten even though priority was accorded to the negotiation of major cuts in intermediate-range nuclear missiles (INF) and the halving of strategic weapons. But the shock waves from Reykjavik probably contributed to a renewed display of interest in European military co-operation – at first by the French and West Germans, and later the British. The British also seized the opportunity to underline the importance of their nuclear deterrent. Mrs Thatcher bluntly affirmed in April 1987 that a world without nuclear weapons would be more dangerous for everyone. Meanwhile British critics of Trident had failed to shift the government from its view that a less sophisticated force, or additional conventional units, would prove of comparable value.[35]

Soviet acceptance of the so-called 'zero-zero option' early in 1987, together with other examples of quickfooted and imaginative diplomacy by Moscow, at first led the British foreign secretary in April to warn that the 'apparent swiftness of the Soviet hand could deceive the Western eye'. Mikhail Gorbachev was attracting rather too much attention and popularity in Britain and Europe for comfort, especially compared with the American president. The zero-zero INF option, however, had been proposed by the West some years earlier so that it was difficult to find grounds on which to object when Gorbachev reopened the issue. The British government was also approaching a general election, and ironically Mrs Thatcher was able to draw advantage from the Soviet willingness to single her out for special attention among the Western European leaders. The British were further reassured by the evident desire of the Americans to avoid a second Reykjavik, a development for which London could claim some credit. US secretary of state Shultz was now firmly in control. He provided much needed reassurance, and refused to be rushed into any deal.

Thus in the course of 1987 the removal of Pershing and cruise missiles from Europe began to seem more tolerable to London, given adequate verification and with the assurance that further arms limitation would be carefully related to the overall defence requirements of the West. Furthermore the government in 1987 had reason to believe that the Americans would, if necessary, take the lead in the modernization of the sizeable theatre nuclear armoury in Europe, so that from its point of view the credibility of the Western deterrent would not be seriously damaged. Mrs Thatcher argued that 'we should not disarm further in nuclear arms, at least not until we have a ban on chemical weapons and an approximate balance in conventional weapons'.

The prospect of an INF settlement was a bonus for the British government and the Conservatives in the 1987 election. Soviet concessions could be presented as a vindication of earlier Western firmness, and especially of the determination to deploy cruise missiles in reply to the Soviet SS-20s. Progress towards an INF treaty brought not only hopes of the return of detente but also a greater promise this time of lasting and comprehensive arms limitation and control.

Mrs Thatcher could be portrayed as a world leader at a time when Labour leaders could gain a respectful hearing neither in Washington nor in Moscow. While public confidence in the state of the economy was the key to Tory success in the 1987 election, there was also wide agreement that Labour suffered a further and significant loss of votes as a result of its posture on defence, and from low public confidence in its ability to protect the national interest.[36] In 1987 both Reagan and Gorbachev found it useful in their moves towards the INF agreement to be seen to have Mrs Thatcher's approval. Her record as the 'Iron Lady' made it difficult for critics of the agreement to gain much support. The treaty provided for the elimination of all intermediate-range missiles (a cut of some 5 per cent in the total nuclear stockpiles of the two superpowers).

MIDDLE EASTERN AND WESTERN EUROPEAN QUESTIONS

Meanwhile the British government had been following certain other aspects of American policy with varying degrees of unease and sympathy. Relations in the Middle East during the Reagan era as a whole were mixed. The European Community continued to try to develop a distinctive European approach to the Palestinian question. While its proposals did not go far enough to impress the Arabs, they displeased both the Israelis and the Americans. The British diverged more obviously from Washington in 1981–82 over participation in a multinational observer force to monitor the Israeli–Egyptian treaty in Sinai and to try to bring some order to the chaos which followed the Israeli invasion of the Lebanon in June 1982. The British Foreign Office believed that the Americans should have exploited Israeli unpopularity in the world community after its intervention in Lebanon to wring concessions for the Arabs, or that they should at least have adopted a more even-handed position. But Haig had strong ideas of his own, and was not at all pleased by any show of British independence.[37]

American policy, however, suffered severe setbacks during the next year or two, not least from its intervention in the troubles in Lebanon, where a token British force was also briefly involved in the ill-fated 'peace-keeping' efforts. Meanwhile British and Western European initiatives over the vexed question of the Palestinian Arabs had not produced any obvious dividends. It seemed, in any case, that Mrs Thatcher was more inclined to co-operate where possible with the Americans. The British could also rely on their newly acquired self-sufficiency in oil, and thus enjoyed more freedom of manoeuvre than their European partners.

Already, from the start of 1981, there had been useful talks with the Americans over the politically troubled Persian Gulf and Soviet threats to South-Western Asia. The British Defence White Paper of June 1981 spoke of the need for Nato 'to look to western security interests over a wider field than before . . . Britain's own needs, outlook and interests give her a special role and a special duty in efforts of this kind'.[38] Admittedly it required the Falklands War to reverse projected cuts in precisely those British naval and amphibious capabilities which were needed to help make this sort of claim credible. Mrs Thatcher expressed her approval of the new American 'rapid deployment force' (RDF) – the Middle East was its most likely theatre of operations. As a result of the long-drawn-out Iran–Iraq War which began in 1980 the British effected a partial reversal of their retreat of 1968–71 from the Gulf. The Royal Navy's 'Armilla patrol' was instituted to shepherd British shipping at the mouth of the Gulf and to show the flag near the war zone. This was maintained independently of the United States. Yet the convergence in Anglo-American policy in the Middle East was sufficiently apparent for one scholar to claim that the British government 'lacks the determination to . . . chart a truly independent and assertive course in the region'.[39]

On 20 July 1987, the five permanent members of the United Nations momentarily combined to call upon the two Persian Gulf belligerents, Iran and Iraq, to agree to a cease-fire under threat of an arms embargo. But it was soon evident that American and Soviet priorities differed, while the British government backed Washington's rejection of a Soviet proposal for a multinational naval force to protect neutral shipping in the Gulf. Washington responded to Kuwaiti fears for the safety of their oil exports through the Gulf by agreeing to 'reflag' Kuwaiti tankers with American colours. Almost immediately a ship under American naval escort struck an Iranian mine. The Americans, having no minehunters of their own, appealed to the British for help. The British government at first firmly but politely refused to become involved in a further escalation of the conflict. This was soon partly modified when mines were discovered in waters used by the 'Armilla patrol' and minehunters were promptly ordered to the Straits of Hormuz. While their orders confined them to operations in waters already patrolled by the Royal Navy, these clearly could have been revised had a more serious emergency materialized within the Gulf itself.

The British government continued to give broad diplomatic support to the American position that Iran was mainly to blame for the continuance of the war. But American policy was causing feelings of unease which were not confined to the Labour party. In Britain *The Times* of 18 August 1987 thought it unwise to sidestep the United Nations, while the *Financial Times* on 20 October speculated that a serious escalation of the conflict in the Gulf might occur as a result of the imprecision of American aims. Michael Howard was much disturbed by America's bias towards Israel and its 'visceral' hostility towards Iran. The United States could not undertake 'the role of dispassionate international policeman to which it laid claim and which the situation obviously required'.[40]

Finally in the summer of 1988 the strain of the conflict forced Iran to accept a cease-fire, and the war at last stuttered to a halt. But the critics of American policy were vindicated at least in part by subsequent events when – with the ending of the Iran–Iraq War – Washington apparently failed to recognize the degree to which the balance of power in the Middle East had moved in favour of Iraq. It also failed to read the mind of the Iraqi leader, Saddam Hussein, and possibly missed an opportunity to deter his invasion of Kuwait in 1990. The British continued to distance themselves from the Americans in the Arab–Israeli dispute. With their European partners they reaffirmed the Venice Declaration on 23 February 1987, and again looked for ways to promote a Middle Eastern peace conference. Their criticisms of Israeli conduct intensified when serious disturbances broke out among the Arab population of Israeli-held territory from the summer of 1988.

The conduct of American policy even in the closing years of the Reagan administration continued to excite criticism from many in Britain who were in no way supporters of the hard left and who favoured at least a selective relationship with the United States. The Iran–Contra scandal was damaging in itself and because it revealed the extent to which the responsible departments and organs of state could be circumvented by ultra-patriotic conspirators. Michael Howard, went so far as to argue that in the 1980s Washington had 'acquired the image, not of a second Rome, but of another Byzantium'. He was highly critical of many of its foreign policy objectives and methods, including its treatment of its allies. Most serious of all, in his view, were the American trade and budget deficits. Economic and social stability in the West were the best defence against communism, just as they were also the essential bases for an effective defence policy. But despite his many criticisms of the Reagan administration he remained a supporter of the transatlantic dialogue and links as well as of more positive British policy towards the EC.

Others, however, were less sure of the relevance of the special relationship, and wished to give more weight to Europe. Fears persisted that Britain might once again be failing to take a sufficiently incisive look at national priorities. Lord Carrington commented in his memoirs that Dean Acheson's sombre aphorism of a country in search of a role was 'still applicable to a great many British hearts'. The far left, meanwhile, remained as uncompromising as ever in its anti-American views. Thus Tony Benn protested in March 1988 that Britain was 'occupied by American troops controlled by a President we do not elect and cannot remove'.[41] Such views, however, counted for less and less with the radical revision of Labour policy by Neil Kinnock and his allies after the 1987 election débâcle, the end of both the Cold War and the Reagan administration.

The American deficits reinforced European fears that pressures would intensify in the United States for cuts to American forces in Europe. Sir Geoffrey Howe called for a seminal reappraisal of European defence policy, warning on 16 March 1987 that 'Europe no longer dominates American defence priorities', and that at least in the longer run Europe might find itself less strongly supported by the United States. Zbigniew Brzezinski supplied an American point of view in the US journal *Newsweek* on 7 December 1987:[42]

> Surely, 374 million Europeans with an aggregate economy of $3.5 trillion should not need to depend for their defense as heavily as they do on 241 million Americans with an economy of $4 trillion – against an opponent with 275 million people and a GNP of only $1.9 trillion.

It was clearly time for the Europeans to bestir themselves.

Western European Union (WEU), last seriously heard of in 1954, had already been showing some flickers of life since 1984. In October 1987 talks were held in The Hague which resulted in a high-sounding declaration entitled 'Platform on European Security Interests'. Ongoing ties with the United States were still emphasized – Howe underlined the assertion that European security was made up of a 'single arch with two pillars' – but the need for a larger European role was acknowledged. In addition to a continuing American nuclear umbrella, the importance of the British and French nuclear deterrents was reaffirmed, and there was a token expression of interest in Anglo-French nuclear co-operation.

But the British government, while acknowledging that Europe had to bear more of Western defence costs, continued to cherish its American connections. Admittedly it was not always easy for ministers to agree on the balance to be struck between Europe and the United States. In 1986 these divisions, for instance, came to a head in the Westland helicopter affair. An inter-departmental dispute over the appropriate partner (American or European) for Westland precipitated a major cabinet crisis and led to the resignation of two ministers. In the end the American connection prevailed.

While committed Europeans or Atlanticists confidently argued one way or the other, many found themselves pulled in different directions. It was possible, for instance, to argue that greater European co-operation was imperative in anticipation of a weakening American interest and involvement in Europe. Yet European co-operation might simply be welcomed by Americans as an opportunity to reduce their own commitments. One specific worry by 1989 was the degree to which the easing of the Cold War was encouraging opposition in West Germany to the modernization of Nato's theatre nuclear weapons – weapons which would be used primarily against targets on German soil. The British government looked to the United States both to exert influence in Bonn and to maintain a significant American military presence in Europe so that Nato's guard was not prematurely lowered. Yet there could be other circumstances in which the British might find it appropriate to appear more European-minded.[43]

Much, however, was happening and was about to happen which would weaken Britain's hand in dealings with the United States, with Nato and with the Western Europeans. Not only did Mikhail Gorbachev continue to produce radical new ideas for comprehensive disarmament, but also the time was not far off when (at long last) the ending of the Cold War could begin to appear irreversible as a result of the growing crisis within the USSR itself and with the collapse of communism in much of Eastern Europe in the winter of 1989–90. Reagan's eight years as president also came to an end, and his successor, George Bush, began his term in 1989 with no strong prejudices in favour of Britain or Mrs Thatcher. Finally the prime minister was determined to protect British national sovereignty to a degree which dismayed Washington as well as Brussels, Paris and Bonn. All these developments abruptly weakened the influence and status which Britain had enjoyed in Washington for much of the 1980s. The Indian Summer of the Special Relationship was being followed by much less settled weather as far as the British were concerned.

NOTES AND REFERENCES

1. L. Freedman, ed., *The Troubled Alliance: Atlantic relations in the 1980s*, Heinemann, 1983, pp. 52–5; L. John Martin, *The Annals of the American Academy of Political and Social Science*, March 1984, pp. 150–1.
2. Carrington, pp. 388–9. But note an interesting study by David Mervin, *Ronald Reagan: the American Presidency*, Longman, 1990, which challenges the view that Reagan was merely an 'amiable dunce'.
3. There is a useful analysis of the decline of the Atlanticists by C. McArdle Kelleher in Freedman, *Troubled Alliance*, pp. 61–5. For an overview of Anglo-American relations and particularly the Reagan–Thatcher relationship, see Geoffrey Smith, *Reagan and Thatcher: the extraordinary inside story of the 'Special Relationship'*, Bodley Head, 1990. The British remained loyally silent during the Iran–Contra scandal – about which they had some information by way of intelligence links with the Americans. Note also S. Gill, ed., *Atlantic Relations in the Reagan Era and Beyond*, Brighton: Wheatsheaf, 1988.
4. Louis and Bull, pp. 241–2.
5. From 1985 the United States began to borrow on a massive scale from foreign states (especially Japan) for the first time in seventy years.
6. Garthoff, pp. 1010–12. A. Haig, *Caveat: Realism, Reagan and Foreign Policy*, New York: Macmillan, 1984, pp. 115–16, 141, 145, 150.
7. Park, pp. 140–1.
8. C.W. Kegley and E.R. Wittkopf, *American Foreign Policy: pattern and process*, New York: St Martin's Press, and Macmillan, 1989, pp. 89–95.
9. Park, pp. 99–101, 193, 197. See also Carrington, pp. 387–8, who also thought the Europeans unhelpful outside Europe, though the British were less at fault here.
10. On European and American defence contributions to Nato in 1985 see C.E. Baumann, ed., *Europe in Nato: deterrence, defense and arms control*, New York and London: Praeger, 1987, pp. 116–18.
11. The British were on their guard against any hint of American decoupling from Europe or of any reference to the British deterrent in superpower arms talks. See M. Smith in P. Byrd, *British Foreign Policy under Thatcher*, Oxford: Philip Allan; and St Martin's Press, 1988, p. 17.
12. Ibid, pp. 15–16.
13. A.J. Blinken, *Ally versus Ally: America, Europe and the Siberian Pipeline Crisis*, New York and London: Praeger, 1987, pp. 104–12. An opinion poll at the end of 1982 showed that in Britain 64 per cent favoured the continuance of the American alliance – much the same proportion as in November 1974, and a larger proportion than in West Germany or France. L. John Martin, pp. 150–1.
14. Haig, p. 266.

15. Ibid, pp. 261–93. Caspar Weinberger (*Fighting for Peace: seven critical years at the Pentagon*, Michael Joseph, 1990, pp. 143–52) was unimpressed by the Latin Americanists or those who sought to mediate. He also claims that Reagan always favoured America's oldest ally. For the crisis as a whole see M. Charlton, *The Little Platoon*, Oxford: Basil Blackwell, 1989; L. Freedman, *Britain and the Falklands War*, Oxford: Basil Blackwell, 1988, especially pp. 42–4, 78–80; L. Freedman and V. Gamba-Stonehouse, *Signals of War: the Falklands conflict of 1982*, Faber and Faber, 1990.
16. Charlton, pp. 159–60, 163–4.
17. See Carrington (p. 366) for his account of early exchanges with Haig.
18. Douglas Kinney, *National Interest/National Honor: the diplomacy of the Falklands Crisis*, New York: Praeger, 1989, especially pp. 103–48; *The Economist*, 12 November 1983; Charlton, pp. 179–80, 195–7.
19. Kinney, pp. 103–48; Charlton, pp. 173–9.
20. Dimbleby, pp. 314–15.
21. Freedman, *Britain and the Falklands War*, p. 72.
22. *Observer*, 3 April 1989.
23. Haig, pp. 297–8; Weinberger, pp. 151–2; Charlton, pp. 180–1.
24. Park, pp. 112–15, 175, 179, 189.
25. Around the same time a British poll recorded that 75 per cent believed that the USA would fire missiles in Britain without the permission of the British government. See also John Palmer, *Europe Without America?*, Oxford: Oxford University Press, 1987, pp. 1, 4. Meanwhile the British government was able to help persuade some hesitant European governments to accept cruise missiles (J. Baylis, *British Defence Policy: striking the right balance*, Macmillan, 1989, p. 43).
26. At the time of the general election in 1983, General Bernard Rogers (SACEUR) had made the alarmist claim that the adoption of a unilateralist policy in Britain would unravel the Western alliance and lead to an American withdrawal from Europe. He also warned that despite some strengthening of Nato's conventional forces, a major Soviet attack could not be held by the West for more than a fortnight without nuclear weapons. See Dimbleby, pp. 319–20.
27. Baylis, *British Defence Policy*, pp. 45–7.
28. M. Howard, 'A European Perspective of the Reagan Years', *Foreign Affairs: America and the World 1987–8*, especially p. 479. See also note 3 above.
29. *Financial Times*, 23 June 1987.
30. J. Schlesinger, 'Reykjavik and Revelations: a turn of the tide?' *Foreign Affairs*, 1986, p. 430.
31. Ibid, pp. 430–1. Paul H. Nitze, *From Hiroshima to Glasnost*, Weidenfeld and Nicolson, 1989, pp. 427–37.
32. Dimbleby, p. 328.
33. J. Schlesinger, pp. 430–7.
34. Howard, *Foreign Affairs, 1987–8*, pp. 479–80.

35. Byrd, pp. 159–64; Baylis, *British Defence Policy*, pp. 63–9, 89–90, 122–6; and Malone, pp. 35–9, 94–8, 174–8. West Germany and France, at that time, both favoured British possession of Trident to increase Soviet uncertainties and targeting problems.

36. Baylis, *British Defence Policy*, p. 46. See also D. Butler, *The British General Election of 1987*, Macmillan, 1988, pp. 281, 293. On 27 May 1987 Reagan observed that should Labour come to power, it would be necessary to dissuade it from 'the grievous error of nuclear disarmament'.

37. Carrington, pp. 340–5.

38. Baylis, *Anglo-American Defence Relations*, p. 189.

39. Tareq Y. Ismael, *International Relations of the Contemporary Middle East*, Syracuse University Press, 1986, p. 127.

40. Howard, *Foreign Affairs*, 1987–8, pp. 486–7.

41. Ibid, pp. 484–91. For alternative views see John Palmer, *Europe without America?*, and C. Coker, *Less Important than Opulence*, Institute for European Defence and Strategic Studies, July 1988. See also Carrington, p. 310; *The Times*, 26 March 1988.

42. Ashton, p. 210.

43. *Financial Times*, 12 April 1987. Note also Trevor Taylor, 'Britain's Response to the Strategic Defense Initiative', *International Affairs*, 1986, pp. 221–6. On WEU revival see D. Harvey and D.J. Smith in C. Coker, ed., *Drifting Apart: the Superpowers and their European Allies*, London: Brassey's Defence Publishers, 1989, chapter 8. For contrary European and American pulls on Britain, see Baylis, *British Defence Policy*, pp. 41–2, 47–9, and M. Clarke and R. Hague, eds, *European Defence Co-operation: America, Britain and Nato* (Manchester University Press, 1990). WEU was interestingly described as something which served everyone's purposes without as yet producing any decisive results. For the British WEU was clearly intended to facilitate Nato co-operation; it was not the 'embryo of a revised defence arrangement for Europe' (154).

CHAPTER EIGHT
Into the 1990s

THE RELATIONSHIP IN ECLIPSE, 1989–90

The crisis of communism in Eastern Europe and the official statements that the Cold War was at an end gave rise to hopes of a new era of peace and stability in the world. The early months of 1990, in particular, were a period of great optimism. On the other hand expectations of far-reaching disarmament in the heart of Europe, and of lasting friendly relations with the USSR lessened the importance of the special defence ties which existed between Britain and the United States. Furthermore the dialogue between Moscow and Washington was now so well developed that Mrs Thatcher's services were no longer needed as an intermediary. As the reunification of the two Germanies and the economic transformation of Eastern Europe became the issues of the moment, Bonn (with all the power of the West German economy behind it) was naturally the European capital which attracted most interest in Washington. It was only with the Iraqi invasion of Kuwait in August 1990 that Washington was at least temporarily reminded of the special value of Britain as an ally. No other European state was so active in the American-led coalition which expelled the Iraqi invaders in January–February 1991.

The Bush administration made a quiet start in foreign affairs, as if anxious to distance itself from some of the more turbulent aspects of policy under its predecessor. It also clearly regarded West Germany as more important than Britain with regard to the future of Europe. The British, for their part, feared that American public opinion, excited by 'the end of the Cold War' and the promise of a 'Peace Dividend', might demand excessive and premature arms cuts. There was a worrying drop in American popular interest in Europe, especially among teenagers and students.[1] At least the British could draw some comfort from the Gorbachev–Bush summit in Malta (2–3 December 1989). The president was careful to consult European leaders afterwards, and he promised (despite considerable arms cuts) that some American forces would remain in Europe as long as necessary until a new and peaceful order was firmly established.

At the same time British officials in Washington were privately acknowledging the influence of a small group of advisers in the US State Department (with supporters in the White House), who wanted the United States to establish a special relationship with the EC as a whole, and with West Germany in particular. Closer European integration was imperative to bind West Germany to the West, especially in anticipation of German reunification. The British would most please by becoming fully committed and wholehearted Europeans. Despite some consoling and explanatory messages to London from both the president and secretary of state, the main thrust of American policy seemed disturbingly ambitious. The Americans were running true to form – in British eyes – as a 'mercurial' people, impatient for quick solutions, and confident that they had all the answers.[2]

Matters were proceeding so quickly in Europe following the breaching of the Berlin Wall and the collapse of communist regimes in Eastern Europe that even Mrs Thatcher (on 18 February 1990), if with cautionary qualifications and evident reluctance, acknowledged that the two Germanies would be reunited. The mood in Washington, however, was much more enthusiastic. In London the *Sunday Times* complained on 18 February 1990 that the British were encouraging Washington to treat them 'as marginal to the great developments' which were engulfing Europe. There were also signs in 1990 that even over Nato the British and Americans were not wholly in agreement. Thus the US State Department was beginning to show more interest in the political rather than the military dimensions of Nato. Yet the British could not ignore the growing difficulties that any United States administration was bound to have in persuading fellow Americans to continue to spend $170 billion a year on defending Europe once the Soviet threat had been removed. In the last resort Nato, even if diluted militarily, appeared to be the best organization through which to secure continuing American participation in European affairs. It had often been said in the past that Nato existed to contain Russia to reassure the Germans, and to contain Germany to reassure the Russians.

A major Nato summit in London early in July 1990 announced a significant transformation in Western strategy. Both President Bush

and Mrs Thatcher described this as a turning point in European history. But it was also evident that the two leaders differed over the
emphasis which they placed on sections of the text of the London
Declaration of 6 July. For the Americans the critical advance was the
modification of the strategy of flexible response whereby nuclear arms
were now described as 'truly weapons of last resort'. It was agreed that
as long as the weakening and withdrawal of Soviet forces continued,
Western forces would – in a hypothetical crisis – have much more
time before they would need to consider recourse to nuclear weapons.
Mrs Thatcher, however, still insisted that the 'fundamental Nato strategy of reliance on nuclear weapons and the possibility of using them
remained unchanged'. She had already, in February 1990, pledged that
Britain would retain its independent nuclear deterrent. The British
were also interested in the acquisition of air-launched tactical nuclear
missiles. These were needed to decrease the vulnerability of aircraft
(carrying free-falling bombs) over hostile territory. The revolution in
East–West relations achieved under Gorbachev – they argued – did
not mean that one could assume that new threats would never develop
in the future.

One aspect of the special relationship was revived in 1990. Labour's
abandonment of unilateral nuclear disarmament made it possible to restore the usual links between the American administration and Her
Majesty's Opposition. The British government itself was also continuing to gain some credit in Washington with its resistance to the
more protectionist tendencies within the EC. Sir Geoffrey Howe had
already issued a warning in November 1988 that if a 'fortress' Europe
were to be created the Europeans would find that they had elected to
be its first 'prisoners'. Mrs Thatcher spoke in similar vein of the economic injury that would result from intensified protectionism, especially
if the advanced economies of the world were to split into three great
regional blocs – the EC, the American hemisphere led by the United
States, and a Pacific region led by Japan. The British were particularly
dismayed by the repeated failures of GATT (General Agreement on
Tariffs and Trade) to reach agreement on such matters as the reduction
of various types of agricultural subsidy – and not least the EC subsidies
on farm exports which were a particular cause of resentment in the
United States. If the British stood squarely with their partners at a
particularly sterile and acerbic GATT conference late in 1990, they
also did their best to urge the Europeans and the Americans to find a
compromise.

Meanwhile, despite the notorious divisions in the Conservative
cabinet and party over Europe, public opinion in Britain was at last

beginning to view the Community in a more positive light. Its importance was ranked above that of the Commonwealth or the United States by the end of the 1980s.[3] Both the Labour and Liberal Democrat parties were determined to present themselves as more European-minded than Mrs Thatcher's government. There were also influential business and financial groups which believed that Britain had no choice but to involve herself wholeheartedly in the latest EC moves towards monetary and political union – not least to maximize British influence over the final outcome and to avoid a repetition of the assumed errors of the 1950s when the EEC was created without British participation. Nearly half of British trade was now with the expanded Community.

Divisions in the British government came to a head in the autumn of 1990. Sir Geoffrey Howe, deputy prime minister, resigned in November. Both the content and presentation of British policy on Europe contributed to his decision. Howe argued that Britain must adopt a more positive attitude towards the Community. Mrs Thatcher had survived a number of ministerial crises, but this one coincided with a growing belief among many backbenchers that their chances of re-election under the current prime minister were not good. She was particularly identified with the profoundly unpopular poll tax, and also with the growing unease over the state of the economy. Such was the tension that a challenge to the leadership became unavoidable. Michael Heseltine secured enough support on the first vote for Mrs Thatcher to be persuaded (finally and with great difficulty) that she stand down in the interest of party unity. A seond ballot carried John Major into Number 10 Downing Street on 28 November. But while he set out to try to heal divisions both within the party and with Europe, his first months in office were dominated by the worsening crisis in the Persian Gulf.

THE GULF CRISIS, 1990–91

Iraq's invasion of Kuwait on 2 August fortuitously coincided with a visit by Mrs Thatcher to the United States. While she was but one of many influences acting upon President George Bush, her intervention was so quick and decisive that it must have strengthened those in Washington who favoured action. One of the president's aides described as her 'a big influence'. George Bush himself later remarked,

'Thank God for allies and friends like Margaret Thatcher when the going gets tough.' An official commented that 'Bush was really impressed with her, perhaps for the first time'.[4] At least the Americans were again anxious for British support.

In response to the invasion, Britain and the United States, in company with France, immediately froze Iraqi assets. But it was not until 25 August that the United Nations Security Council agreed that force might be used to back up the trade embargo against Iraq. In general in the early days of the crisis it was from the British that the Americans received most support and encouragement. The crisis was clearly seen by Mrs Thatcher as an opportunity to strengthen Anglo–American relations. Her tone was Atlanticist rather than Western European, although in her speech to the Aspen Institute, Colorado, on 5 August she tried to reassure Americans that Britain had no intention of standing 'on the sidelines' in Europe. Britain's destiny lay in full membership of the Community, but it was a community of 'independent sovereign nations' which she had in mind, and one which would always seek the closest possible partnership with the United States. There were other signals from the British government that America could not be expected to 'police' the world without assistance in a crisis, and echoes, too, of British thinking in the 1950s when Bevin and others had argued that the United States would derive more assistance from a Britain that was not Euro-centred in its policy. At Aspen Mrs Thatcher also took the opportunity to reaffirm her fears of the division of the advanced industrial world into three great closed economic blocs.

Mrs Thatcher and the British had, by their actions, undoubtedly recaptured much American attention. But this was followed by widespread bewilderment in the United States when the crisis in the Conservative party forced the resignation of the prime minister on 22 November 1990. The New York *Wall Street Journal*, in its tribute, ranked her with America's greatest foreign friends, Winston Churchill and Lafayette. It emphasized her support in 'the last dangerous decade of the Cold War, the installation of the Pershing missiles in Europe and now the confrontation in the Gulf'. But despite American consternation at the passing of Mrs Thatcher, John Major, the new prime minister, quickly won the confidence of the Bush administration. His first visit on 21–22 December 1990 took place at an opportune time, the resignation of the highly regarded Soviet foreign minister, Eduard Shevardnadze, stirring fears that hardline communists and anti-Western militarists might be about to regain the upper hand in Moscow. John Major insisted that there would be no alteration in British policy on

Kuwait and Iraq under his leadership. On Europe his greater flexibility (without apparently wishing to distance Britain from Washington) was a further bonus given earlier American worries over the differences between Mrs Thatcher and her EC partners. The old joke resurfaced that there were three centres of power in Washington: the White House, Capitol Hill and the British embassy.

At home the new prime minister enjoyed similar success in retaining the confidence of the great majority of the public during the later stages of the Gulf crisis. No one could meaningfully accuse John Major of jingoism, militancy or triumphalism. Strong as was the national desire to avoid war, polls showed overwhelming support for effective action under the umbrella of the UN to remove Iraq from Kuwait, although peace demonstrations and rallies continued in Britain as well as in the United States. Opinion in Congress was uncertain and fluid until late in the day. The votes of 12 January 1991 in favour of force were hardly overwhelming. In contrast the Commons backed British policy by 534 to 57 on 15 January. American public opinion did, however, move strongly behind George Bush once the fighting began, and by mid-February equalled or surpassed that in Britain (polls suggested averages of 80 per cent and 78 per cent respectively).

The campaign to liberate Kuwait began on the night of 16–17 January 1991. British forces in the Gulf reached a peak of some 43,000 a month later, though a build-up on this scale proved possible only by stripping other units of equipment and key personnel – notably in Germany. RAF Tornados played a major part in the strikes to paralyse the Iraqi air force. Attacks against well-defended airfields were a particularly hazardous operation. The Royal Navy was active in the Gulf, with its sophisticated minehunters doing much to guarantee freedom of movement for the ships of the coalition. In the fast-moving and devastating land offensive which began on 24 February, British armoured forces were prominent in the operations which outflanked the Iraqi lines in southern Kuwait and drove directly against the elite Republican Guard. American B-52 bombers also operated from a base in Britain. The coalition suspended its military operations on 28 February.

Over 30 states contributed in various ways to the campaign. Washington had to pay special attention to a number of other capitals in addition to London. But the closeness of Anglo-American contacts was highlighted, for instance, by the regular exchanges between the US national security adviser, Brent Scowcroft, and Sir Charles Powell, the foreign affairs private secretary in Downing Street.[5]

Uprisings against Saddam Hussein following the war led to massive repression, and the subsequent flight of up to 2 million people towards and into Turkey and Iran in the first weeks of April. Both London and Washington were anxious not to become embroiled in the internal politics of Iraq, but a movement of refugees on this scale – with the accompanying desperate shortage of the basic amenities of life, and the growing numbers of civilian deaths – began to make official action of some kind imperative.

This, however, turned out to be an occasion when the British acted ahead of and independently of Washington.[6] The plan to establish 'safe havens' for Kurdish refugees in northern Iraq was announced by the prime minister at an EC summit in Luxembourg on 8 April. Admittedly it was obvious from the start that the establishment of 'safe havens' in northern Iraq would require a substantial military presence, especially by the United States. It could even lead to renewed military action against Iraq. In public the plan was given a chilly reception in Washington, and even in private some officials complained of the way it had been launched. Yet astute American diplomats might well have seen the value of letting another country make the running. Such officials might have recalled that during the Kuwaiti crisis the United States had been charged with selfishly bidding for greater influence (and even a permanent presence) in the region. It was important not to revive such suspicions in some quarters in Moscow and the Middle East. Whatever the truth, within two days of Mr Major's move the Americans had come round and had begun to issue warnings to Baghdad to cease military action in areas which threatened relief operations. President Bush announced his intentions on 16 April and American forces began to identify potential 'havens' for the Kurds, and to prepare units for their protection. The British (and some other members of Nato) also sent out troops and helicopters. These were withdrawn to covering positions in Turkey in mid-July.

Nevertheless many observers were impressed by the fact that John Major and his colleagues had decided to launch a proposal relating to the Middle East at an EC summit – an improbable eventuality had Mrs Thatcher still been in Number 10. Meanwhile Nato's foreign ministers had discussed the future of the alliance in the middle of December 1990. Agreement on the need for a stronger 'European pillar' was easily reaffirmed: how it was to be erected was of course another matter. American support for such a 'pillar' was qualified by concern lest this should lead to a weakening of Nato and of American influence. Douglas Hurd argued in Berlin in mid-December 1990 that 'European security without the United States simply does not make sense. If we were ever foolish enough to try it, we would soon realise what nonsense it was.' Britain's worries on this score continued to be fuelled by the strength of anti-militarist feeling in Germany and by the independent line of France.

The British foreign secretary returned to the subject on 19 February 1991 when Mr Hurd argued that common European foreign policies should be allowed to evolve and not be artificially created. Britain did, however, agree that the nine-nation Western European Union (a forum for the discussion of the defence and foreign policy issues) should come under the general direction of the Community. In the long term, Hurd also expected the balance of power in Nato to move from the United States to Europe. The corollary, however, was a proportionately greater effort by the Europeans, and he firmly rejected 'the notion that the definition of a good European is someone who finds out what the Americans are doing in order to do something different'.[7] The prime minister was equally careful to describe British policy as the creation of a European identity which sustained 'a long-term American presence'.

A meeting of Nato defence ministers in Brussels at the end of May 1991 produced an agreed statement that Nato would remain 'the essential forum among the allies', but there was perhaps the hint of a warning in the comment from the US secretary of defense that whatever was done 'in the European context should be done in a way that strengthens the alliance'. But uncertainties concerning the future were very much in the mind of the new US ambassador to London (Raymond G.H. Seitz) who, at his confirmation hearing before the Senate in April 1991, remarked that while the relationship with Britain was one that 'could not be recreated with any other nation', some of the very 'basics about security' would have to be rethought.[8] On the other hand there still existed the possibility that joint Anglo-American fears of great protectionist blocs might provide one basis for a continuance of some kind of special relationship.

HOW SPECIAL A RELATIONSHIP?

These latest fluctuations in the importance or otherwise of the special relationship help to put the past fifty years in perspective even as they underline the difficulty of commenting on its future. The relations, as Michael Clarke recently noted,[9] have never been static or easy to define. If defence was always at the heart of the partnership, there were variations even within the defence community itself. Contacts were most comprehensive in all that related to intelligence and surveillance, closely followed by ties between the air forces and the navies. In these areas it was evident that habits of co-operation had become deeply 'ingrained'.

Indeed many of the intelligence facilities were not even part of the Nato framework; they formed a distinct global Anglo-Saxon operation. American as well as some Commonwealth representatives attended at least part of the weekly meetings of the British cabinet's Joint Intelligence Committee. It was reported in June 1991 that Britain was to be the base for the American Joint Intelligence Centre for Europe. On the other hand, with the 'ending of the Cold War' and the American need to cut defence costs, the closure of several American bases in Britain was announced, while others were put in mothballs or their activities reduced. The nuclear submarine base in the Holy Loch was also to be run down. It was still likely, however, that common interests such as the security of the Atlantic would provide lasting links.

Meanwhile the great diversity of British elite attitudes towards the United States was highlighted in a 1989 survey. But there was at least broad agreement that some kind of special relationship did indeed exist.[10] Nevertheless, as the fluctuations in Anglo-American relations between, say, the 1930s and 1991 have demonstrated, the permanence of the partnership was not guaranteed. Thus the seemingly incompatible verdicts on the relationship of Max Beloff and of Dawson and Rosecrance may well in fact be complementary. Beloff contended that British governments put the United States at the top of the list of their allies essentially because they had no choice. Personal connections were of limited importance.[11] Dawson and Rosecrance, however, suggested that from 1949 relations between London and Washington began to defy conventional theories concerning alliances. The British leaders were engaged in a long-term act of faith which was 'difficult to understand in traditional power terms. . . . History, tradition, affinity were crucial to the alliance.'[12] The evidence as set out in this volume suggests that, while the origins and durability of the relationship are to be found in common fears and interests, once in being the alliance could often be distinguished by intimacy, vitality and comprehensiveness well beyond the norm.

NOTES AND REFERENCES

1. *The Times*, 4 December 1989.
2. *The Times*, 13 March 1990.
3. Note MORI poll December 1989 which rated the USA in importance (19 per cent) after the Commonwealth (21 per cent) and Europe (50 per cent). In 1969 the USA and Commonwealth had been level with 34 per cent while Europe trailed at 21 per cent. See Eric Jacobs and Robert Worcester, *We British: Britain under the Moriscope*, Weidenfeld and Nicolson, 1990.
4. *Independent on Sunday*, 3 December 1990. Mrs Thatcher, however, is barely mentioned by Bob Woodward (*The Commanders*, Simon and Schuster, 1991) in his chapters on American planning from August 1990.
5. *The Times*, 20 January 1991.
6. *The Times*, 18 April 1991.
7. *The Times*, 20 February 1991.
8. *The Times*, 22 April 1991.
9. M. Clarke and R. Hague, *European Defence Co-operation: America, Britain and Nato*, Manchester University Press, 1990, p. 29.
10. Clarke and Hague, p. 153. See also pp. 30–3. G. Edwards and D. Sanders, *British Elite Attitudes and the US*, London, RIIA, 1989, pp. 15 ff.
11. M. Beloff, 'The Special Relationship: an Anglo-American Myth', in M. Gilbert, ed., *A Century of Conflict, 1850–1950*, Hamish Hamilton, 1966, pp. 151–71.
12. R. Dawson and R. Rosecrance, 'Theory and Reality in the Anglo-American Alliance', *World Politics*, October 1966, pp. 21–51.

Appendix

LEADING AMERICAN AND BRITISH POLITICIANS AND ADVISERS

Acheson, Dean (1893–1971) American under-secretary of state 1945–47; secretary of state 1949–53

Attlee, Clement R (1883–1967) British (Labour) prime minister 1945–51; leader of the opposition, 1951–55

Bevan, Aneurin (1897–1960) British minister of health 1945–51; minister of labour 1951; opposition spokesman for foreign affairs, 1956–60

Bevin, Ernest (1881–1951) British foreign secretary 1945–51

Brzezinski, Zbigniew (1928–) American assistant to the president for national security affairs 1977–81

Bush, George (1924–) American vice-president 1981–89; president (Republican) 1989–

Byrnes, James (1879–1972) American secretary of state 1945–47

Callaghan, James (1912–) British chancellor of the exchequer 1964–67; home secretary 1967–70; foreign secretary 1974–76; prime minister (Labour) 1976–79

Carrington, Lord (1919–) British secretary of state for defence 1970–74; foreign secretary 1979–82; Nato secretary-general 1984–88

Carter, Jimmy (1924–) American president (Democrat) 1977–81

Churchill, Sir Winston (1874–1965) British prime minister (wartime coalition) 1940–45 and (Conservative) 1945 and 1951–55

Cripps, Sir Stafford (1889–1952) British chancellor of the exchequer 1947–50

Dalton, Hugh (1887–1962) British chancellor of the exchequer 1945–47

Douglas-Home, Sir Alec (1903–) British foreign secretary 1960–63 and 1970–74; prime minister (Conservative) 1963–64

Dulles, John Foster (1888–1959) American secretary of state 1953–59

Eden, Sir Anthony (1897–1977) British foreign secretary 1940–45 and 1951–55; prime minister (Conservative) 1955–56

Eisenhower, Dwight D. (1890–1969) American general and supreme allied commander in Northern Europe 1944–45; supreme allied commander in Europe 1950–52; president (Republican) 1953–61

Ford, Gerald (1913–) American president (Republican) 1974–77

Forrestal, James (1892–1949) American secretary of defense 1947–49

Gaitskell, Hugh (1906–63) British chancellor of the exchequer 1950–51; leader of the Labour party 1955–63

Haig, Alexander (1924–) American secretary of state 1981–82

Healey, Denis (1917–) British secretary of state for defense 1964–70; chancellor of the exchequer 1974–79; opposition spokesman for foreign affairs 1980–87

Heath, Edward (1916–) British leader of the Conservative party 1965–75; prime minister 1970–74

Hopkins, Harry (1890–1946) American presidential adviser 1941–45

Howe, Sir Geoffrey (1926–) British foreign secretary 1983–89; deputy prime minister 1989–90

Hull, Cordell (1871–1955) American secretary of state 1933–44

Humphrey, George M (1890–1970) American secretary of the treasury 1953–57

Hurd Douglas (1930–) British foreign secretary 1989–

Jenkins, Roy (1920–) British chancellor of the exchequer 1967–70

Johnson, Lyndon (1908–73) American president (Democrat) 1963–69

Kennedy, John F (1917–1963) American president 1961–63

Keynes, Lord (1883–1946) British adviser to the Treasury 1940–46

Kissinger, Henry (1923–) American special assistant to the president for national security affairs 1969–73; secretary of state 1973–77

Macmillan, Harold (1894–1986) British foreign secretary (1955); chancellor of the exchequer 1955–57; prime minister (Conservative) 1957–63

McNamara, Robert (1916–) American secretary of defense 1961–68

Major, John (1943–) British chancellor of the exchequer 1989–90; prime minister (Conservative) 1990–

Marshall, George (1891–1967) American general and chief of staff of the army 1939–45; secretary of state 1947–49; secretary of defense 1950–51

Morgenthau, Henry (1891–1967) American secretary of the treasury 1934–45

Nixon, Richard (1913–) American vice-president 1953–61; president (Republican) 1969–74

Reagan, Ronald (1911–) American president (Republican) 1981–89

Roosevelt, Franklin (1882–1945) American president (Democrat) 1933–45

Rusk, Dean (1909–) American secretary of state 1961–69

Sandys Duncan (1908–88) British minister of defence 1957–59

Shultz, George (1920–) American secretary of state 1982–89

Stewart, Michael (1906–) British foreign secretary 1965–66 and 1968–70

Stimson, Henry (1867–1950) American secretary of war 1940–45

Thatcher, Margaret (1925–) British prime minister (Conservative) 1979–90

Truman, Harry S. (1894–1972) American president (Democrat) 1945–53

Vance, Cyrus (1917–) American secretary of state 1977–80

Weinberger, Casper (1917–) American secretary of defense 1981–87

Wilson, Charles E. (1890–1961) American secretary of defense 1953–57

Wilson, Harold (1916–) British prime minister (Labour) 1964–70, 1974–76

Bibliographical Essay

ANGLO-AMERICAN RELATIONS IN THE TWENTIETH CENTURY

For an overall guide see David A. Lincove and Gary R. Treadway, *The Anglo-American Relationship: an annotated bibliography of scholarship, 1945–85*, New York: Greenwood Press, 1988.

Overall studies of Anglo-American relations include H.C. Allen, *Great Britain and the United States*, Odhams Press, 1954; H.G. Nicholas, *The United States and Britain*, University of Chicago Press, 1975; and D. Dimbleby and D. Reynolds, *An Ocean Apart: the relationship between Britain and America in the twentieth century*, Hodder and Stoughton, 1988. D.C. Watt's, *Succeeding John Bull: America in Britain's Place, 1900–75*, Cambridge University Press, 1975, is an important and stimulating work, but it is not for the beginner. C. Hitchens, *Blood, Class and Nostalgia: Anglo-American Ironies*, Chatto, *1990*, tackles social and cultural as well as political relationships. One reviewer described it as 'combative', 'opinionated', and 'wonderfully readable'.

Major works which relate to the period since 1945 include W.R. Louis and H. Bull, editors, *The Special Relationship: Anglo-American Relations since 1945*, Oxford: Clarendon Press, 1986; J. Baylis, *Anglo-American Defence Relations, 1945–84*, Macmillan, 1984; A.P. Dobson, *The Politics of the Anglo-American Economic Special Relationship, 1940–87*, Brighton: Wheatsheaf, and St Martin's Press, 1988. Note also M. Dockrill and J.W. Young, editors, *British Foreign Policy, 1945–56*, Macmillan, 1989.

FROM WORLD WAR TO COLD WAR (1941–47)

For the relationship in the transition period from the war against the Axis to the Cold War, see F.S. Harbutt, *The Iron Curtain: Churchill, America and the origins of the Cold War*, Oxford University Press, 1986; T.H. Anderson, *The United States, Great Britain, and the Cold War, 1944–47*, Columbia and London: University of Missouri Press, 1981; R.M. Hathaway, *Ambiguous Partnership: Britain and America, 1944–47*, New York: Columbia University Press, 1981; R. Edmonds, *Setting the Mould: the United States and Britain, 1945–50*, Oxford University Press, 1987; R. Ovendale, *The English-Speaking Alliance: Britain, the United States, the Dominions and the Cold War, 1945–51*, Allen and Unwin, 1985. An indispensable study on the British side is A. Bullock's *Ernest Bevin: foreign secretary, 1945–51*, Heinemann, 1983.

FROM NATO TO SUEZ (1948-56)

The respective roles of Britain and the United States in the origins of Nato are explained by R.A. Best, *'Cooperation with like-minded Peoples': British influences on American security policy, 1945–49*, New York: Greenwood Press, 1986; T.P. Ireland, *Creating the Entangling Alliance*, London: Aldwych Press, 1981; and L.S. Kaplan, *The United States and Nato: the formative years*, University Press of Kentucky, 1984.

On Britain and the United States in the Middle East in the late 1940s and early 1950s see especially W.R. Louis, *The British Empire in the Middle East, 1945–51*, Oxford: Clarendon Press, 1984; and G. McGhee, *Envoy to the Middle World*, New York: Harper and Row, 1969, who provides interesting personal insights from the American point of view. For many aspects of American policy, however, there is no substitute for the relevant volumes of the *Foreign Relations of the United States* (Washington DC).

A start to the detailed study of defence issues can be made with J. Lewis, *Changing Direction: British military planning for postwar strategic defence, 1942–47*, London: Sherwood Press, 1988, and M.S. Sherry, *Preparing for the Next War: American plans for postwar defense, 1942–47*, Yale University Press, 1977. M. Gowing, *Independence and Deterrence: Britain and Atomic Energy, 1945–52*, Macmillan, 1974, is still the classic study of the origins of Britain as a nuclear power. R.A. Best, *'Cooperation with like-minded Peoples': British influences on American security policy,*

1945–49, New York: Greenwood Press, 1986; Simon Duke, *United States Bases in the United Kingdom*, Macmillan, 1987; I.S. Clark and N.J. Wheeler, *The British Origins of Nuclear Strategy, 1945–55*, Oxford: Clarendon Press, 1989; G. Rumble, *The Politics of Nuclear Deterrence*, Cambridge University Press, 1985; and P. Malone, *The British Nuclear Deterrent*, Croom Helm, and St Martin's Press, 1984, all make important contributions on the nuclear question. In addition to Baylis's *Anglo-American Defence Relations, 1945–84*, see his latest thoughts in *British Defence Policy: Striking the Right Balance*, Macmillan, 1989.

The start of the ups and downs in the relationship between 1951 and 1956 can be followed in M.L. Dockrill and J.W. Young, editors, *British Foreign Policy, 1945–56*, Macmillan, 1989; and J.W. Young, editor, *The Foreign Policy of Churchill's Peacetime Administration, 1951–55*, Leicester University Press, 1988.

Suez has attracted many writers. Among recent accounts note D. Carlton, *Britain and the Suez Crisis*, Oxford: Basil Blackwell, 1988; W.R. Louis and R. Owen, editors, *Suez 1956*, Oxford: Clarendon Press, 1989; and A. Horne, *Macmillan, 1894–1956*, Macmillan, 1988. To understand the thinking in Washington it is essential to consult S. Ambrose, *Eisenhower the President*, Allen and Unwin, 1984, and D. Neff, *Warriors at Suez*, New York: Linden Press, and Simon and Schuster, 1981.

REVIVAL AND DECAY OF THE SPECIAL RELATIONSHIP (1957–80)

American interest in the rebuilding of the relationship with Britain after Suez is still best studied in the *Foreign Relations of the United States, 1955–57*, vol. iv (see above chapter 4, notes 33 ff.). For British policy in general after Suez see especially A. Horne, *Macmillan, 1957–86*, Macmillan, 1989; Louis and Bull, *The Special Relationship*; and A.L. Gorst, W. Scott-Lucas and L. Johnman, *Post-War Britain, 1945–64*, Pinter Books, 1989, chapter 12; and J.P.G. Freeman, *British Nuclear Arms Control Policy in the context of Anglo-American Relations, 1957–68*, Macmillan, 1986. British influence in Washington over the test-ban talks is discussed by Glenn T. Seaborg in *Kennedy, Khrushchev and the Test-Ban*, Berkeley: University of California Press, 1981. Some points of interest on defence policy and relations with the United States are to be found in Lord Carrington's *Reflect on Things Past*, Collins, 1988.

On the Labour government in the 1960s, C. Ponting, *Breach of Promise: Labour in Power, 1964–70*, Hamish Hamilton, 1989, is critical both of the Wilson government and the United States. He is more revealing than Harold Wilson in his own book, *The Labour Government, 1964–70*, Weidenfeld and Nicolson, and Michael Joseph, 1971. There are some gems buried in Richard Crossman, *The Diaries of a Cabinet Minister, 1964–70*, Hamish Hamilton, and Jonathan Cape, 1975–77, and much of interest in B. Reed and G. Williams, *Denis Healey and the Policies of Power*, Sidgwick and Jackson, 1971. Note also P. Buteux, *The Politics of Nuclear Consultation in Nato, 1965–80*, Cambridge: Polity Press, 1983; and W. Park, *Defending the West: a history of Nato*, Brighton: Wheatsheaf, 1986.

For the 1970s Henry Kissinger, *The White House Years*, Weidenfeld and Nicolson, 1979, and *The Years of Upheaval*, Weidenfeld and Nicolson, 1982, make many useful and revealing references to Britain. See also A.G. Adrianopoulos, *Western Europe in Kissinger's Global Strategy*, New York: St Martin's Press, 1988. Unfortunately Z. Brzezinski in his *Power and Principle: memoirs of the National Security Advisor, 1977–81*, Weidenfeld and Nicolson, 1983, had less reason to be interested in Britain. Defence should be followed in Rumble, Buteux and Park (see above).

R. Garthoff, *Detente and Confrontation: American–Soviet relations from Nixon to Reagan*, Washington DC, 1985, provides a detailed and analytical survey of the period, while the British dimension is conveniently summarized in the last chapters of David Sanders, *Losing an Empire, Finding a Role*, Macmillan, 1990, and in other general works already mentioned.

ANGLO-AMERICAN RELATIONS SINCE 1981

More specifically on the 1980s, the Falklands War of 1982, the personal friendship of Mrs Thatcher and President Reagan and rapid changes in the world scene have generated some interesting literature. Note L. Freedman, editor, *The Troubled Alliance: Atlantic relations in the 1980s*, Heinemann, 1983; S. Gill, editor, *Atlantic Relations in the Reagan Era and Beyond*, Brighton: Wheatsheaf, 1988; P. Byrd, editor, *British Foreign Policy under Thatcher*, Oxford: Philip Allan, and St Martin's Press, 1988; Geoffrey Smith, *Reagan and Thatcher*, Bodley Head, 1990;

P. Cosgrave, *Carrington: a life and a policy*, J.M. Dent, 1985; and Carrington's own memoirs.

On individual issues see C.E. Baumann, editor, *Europe in Nato*, New York and London: Praeger, 1987; J. Baylis, *British Defence Policy: striking the right balance*, Macmillan, 1989; A.J. Blinken, *Ally versus Ally: America, Europe and the Siberian Pipeline crisis*, New York and London: Praeger, 1987; L. Freedman, *Britain and the Falklands War*, Oxford: Basil Blackwell, 1988; L. Freedman and V. Gamba-Stonehouse, *Signals of War: the Falklands Conflict of 1982*, Faber and Faber, 1990; M. Charlton, *The Little Platoon*, Oxford: Basil Blackwell, 1989; and Douglas Kinney, *National Interest/National Honour: the diplomacy of the Falklands crisis*, New York: Praeger, 1989.

Also of interest are C. Coker, editor, *Drifting Apart? The superpowers and their European allies*, London: Brassey's Defence Publishers, 1989; John Palmer, *Europe without America*, Oxford: Oxford University Press, 1987; and C. Tugendhat and W. Wallace, *Options for British Foreign Policy in the 1990s*, RIIA, Routledge and Kegan Paul, 1988. America's problems are interestingly explored by S. Ungar, *Estrangement: America and the World*, New York and Oxford: Oxford University Press, 1985.

Index